Lieve Joris, who was born in Belgium, is one of Europe's foremost travel writers. In addition to an award-winning book on Hungary, she has published widely acclaimed accounts of her journeys to the Middle East and Africa. Lieve Joris lives in Amsterdam; *The Gates of Damascus* is her fifth book.

THE GATES OF DAMASCUS

LIEVE JORIS

Translated by Sam Garrett

LONELY PLANET PUBLICATIONS
Melbourne • Oakland • London • Paris

The Gates of Damascus

Published by Lonely Planet Publications
    Head Office: PO Box 617, Hawthorn, Vic 3122, Australia
    Branches: 155 Filbert St, Suite 251, Oakland, CA 94607, USA
                10 Barley Mow Passage, Chiswick, London W4 4PH, UK
                71 bis rue du Cardinal Lemoine, 75005 Paris, France

Published 1996

Printed by SNP Printing Pte Ltd, Singapore

Author photograph by Chris van Houts; map by Trudi Canavan

First published as *De poorten van Damascus* (J.M. Meulenhoff bv, Amsterdam, 1993).

This edition was produced with the support of the Administration for Art of the Flemish Community.

National Library of Australia Cataloguing in Publication Data

Joris, Lieve, 1953-
[Poorten van Damascus. English]
The Gates of Damascus

ISBN 0 86442 368 3.

1. Joris, Lieve, 1953- – Journeys – Syria, Damascus.
2. Syria – Description and travel. 3. Damascus (Syria) – Description and travel.
4. Syria – Politics and government. 5. Syria – Social conditions.
I. Garrett, Sam. II. Title. III. Title: Poorten van Damascus. English.
(Series: Lonely Planet Journeys).

956.91042

Text © Lieve Joris and J.M. Meulenhoff bv 1993
English-language translation © Sam Garrett 1996
Map © Lonely Planet 1996

THE GATES OF DAMASCUS

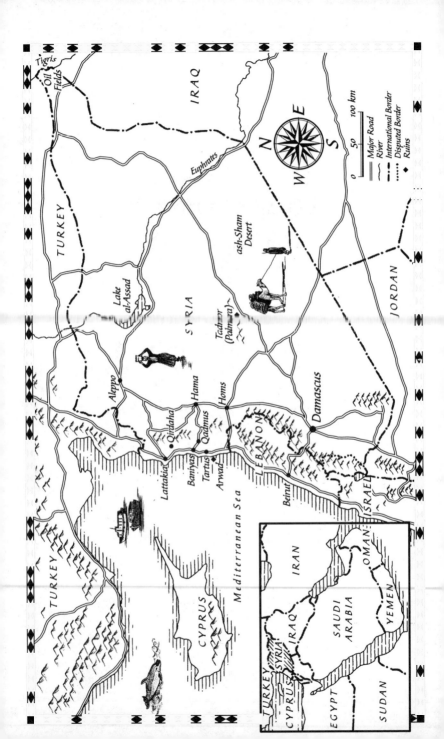

CHAPTER 1

HALA HAS put on weight and bleaches her hair in the local fashion, but her way of looking at things is pleasantly familiar. She nudges me and, with a meaningful nod, points out the mustachioed conductor of the military band in the park – he's practically swimming in his jacket with its heavy epaulets. What pompous gestures! And the musicians are so involved with their instruments that they don't pay him the slightest attention.

"Why aren't there any violins, Mama?"

Hala runs her hand through Asma's hair. "Because it's marching music. Can you imagine going to war with violins? You need trumpets at least!"

This is our first walk through Damascus, and I feel almost blind beside her; she leads me to familiar places, and slowly the memories come back. Above the entrance to the *souq* hangs a panoramic painting of a laughing President Assad, with Damascus as miniature city in the background. The president glances out of the corner of his eye, which gives him a shifty look – not very flattering. The city is filled with such pictures. Young, old, with and without glasses – since my arrival he has appeared to me in many forms. This morning I even saw a Mercedes tear by with his image on its visors.

"I don't remember his being so ubiquitous."

"He brought the idea back from North Korea," Hala says with a knowing smile. "Since his visit there he's had the whole country pasted up. As if we didn't know what he looks like!"

Near the Omayyad Mosque, part of the *souq* has been torn down, ostensibly so the president can be driven there to pray on holy days, but everyone knows the real reason: if there is an uprising in Damascus, tanks must be able to reach the old city.

Hala drags me to the spice bazaar, with its aroma of coffee, cinnamon and nutmeg. Light falls through holes in the corrugated-iron roof, mottling the cobblestones. We pause in front of a shop selling herbs and medicinal remedies; on one of the wooden shelves is a glass bowl of dried sea horses. The shopkeeper has labelled it in English: 'Animal from the sea to make the man strong at night in the bed'.

We laugh and wander further through the narrow streets of the old town. Hala looks at the death announcements pasted to lampposts and walls, and studies the photos of the deceased, figuring out how old they were. She says it's a strange quirk of hers, something she did even as a child.

Excited voices waft into the street from open windows. Asma pricks up her ears. "Her favorite radio program," Hala whispers. Every week they broadcast a dramatization of a famous murder.

"What's it about this time?"

Hala listens. It's about a case which caused quite a stir around ten years ago: a female student was murdered at the University of Damascus, and to quell the panic that broke out, a young man was arrested at random and hanged. "It's difficult to uncover the truth about a crime in this country," she sighs. Years ago, a town in the north of the country was in an uproar after a series of young girls were raped. The man who was arrested confessed to fifteen rapes, but most of the girls were ashamed to admit what had happened. It was a closed city, and the parents of a girl who has been raped may murder her because she is no longer a virgin. No one dared to write about it, out of fear of stirring up unrest.

We have walked on as we talked, but now Asma tugs impatiently on Hala's arm. "Where are we going, Mama?"

"Nowhere special, we're just walking around."

"But where to?" Asma doesn't understand. It is the middle of summer, the sun is beating down on us mercilessly, and she wants to go home. When we finally consent, she does a little dance of delight.

Hala and Asma live in a neighborhood where the streets have no names, the houses no numbers. Their house is separated from the street by a wall, but the woman who lives on the third floor across the street from them can look right into their front room. She sits at the window all day, a white scarf around her head; when she's not there, her son takes over. They see who goes down the street, who enters the grocery store, when someone leaves the house, who comes home when. They see Asma playing soccer with her friends and later pounding on the iron gate, a bag of *bizr*, salted sunflower seeds, in her hand. I fail to understand why we don't sit in the courtyard, in the pleasant shade of the fig tree – until I hang up the laundry one afternoon. The neighbors at the back stare out of their window too. They don't even move when I look up.

Hala had written to me about her house: that it was larger than her old one, that there was enough room for me. My expectations had been high, and I felt somewhat disappointed as I lugged my bags over the threshold. A narrow hallway, a sitting room with a checkered sofa, a bedroom, a small kitchen with a granite counter. High on top of the wardrobe in the bedroom, a plastic flower arrangement, wrapped in cellophane. The large clock in the hall had stopped.

But Hala, I soon discover, is happy here. She has always dreamed of having three things: a bathroom, a telephone and a washing machine. She had to fight hard, but now she has all three. If she moved, she would have to pay ten times as much for a house like this.

Later, I notice how carefully she has furnished the rooms. The blue of the sofa complements the flowered curtains, and everywhere I find traces of her struggle against the lack of space. The wedding presents that were kept under her bed in the old house are now on top of the wardrobe. The folding table in the hall travels throughout the house – from the little kitchen, where we have lunch, to the front room, where we eat when the TV is on. It is Hala's writing table, Asma's play-and-homework table.

The moment we are inside, Hala flings her clothes on the bed and disappears into the bathroom. The bare room with its boiler, tap and plastic basin turns into a Turkish bath full of steam and foam. Sitting on a low stool, she lathers her skin and then pours water over herself. She washes off the heat of our walk, the dust of the streets. Wrapped in a bath towel she comes out, laughing, content, the steam rolling out behind her like a cloud. "On the first day, God created the earth," she says. "On the second day, he created the bath." She slips into a nightgown, a habit that surprises me at first but which I will soon adopt.

Asma is lying on the sofa in the front room watching cartoons, the bag of *bizr* on her lap. Lounging on the large bed in the bedroom, we listen to the latest tape by the Lebanese singer Fayruz. From the courtyard comes the occasional soft thud of a fig falling from the tree, the sound of children crying next door.

Forty years ago this neighborhood lay on the outskirts of Damascus, but since then it has curled up comfortably against the city. It's a village really, though the inhabitants come from all over and have little in common. Last year a propane tank exploded in a house a few blocks away. It happened in the middle of the night; women ran outside in their housecoats. Five dead. The house has since been repaired, but no one walks by without thinking about that night. Through such calamities the neighborhood acquires a history in spite of itself. That afternoon Hala tells me about another incident that the neighbors will not easily forget.

❖

She was heavily pregnant when they moved here. Her aunt, a former nurse, offered to help her with the delivery, but the birth was so difficult that Hala was afraid she wouldn't make it. Halfway through, her aunt gasped: "Shall I call the hospital? Wouldn't you rather go there?" As though that were still possible! Hala's sister Zahra yanked clumsily on her legs – the soreness lasted for days.

Hala had asked Ahmed to stay with her, but he found it such a gruesome spectacle that he fled to the front room and finally left the house altogether. It was an uneasy period in their relationship. That was Ahmed for you, always brimming over with revolutionary ideas but at a loss with that little creature around. He wanted to have her sleep between them at night. Such a small body, such tiny fingers – Hala was afraid he would crush her in his sleep.

When Asma was only a week old he wanted to take her along to the market. She's much too little for that, Hala protested, but he wrapped Asma in a blanket and left. He brought her back an hour later: it was no fun, he complained, the baby hadn't even looked around, she slept the whole time!

But there were better moments as well. Hala had heard that if you put a newborn baby in water it could swim right away. Maybe they should try it – it was an exciting idea. They placed a tub of water under the fig tree and let Asma glide down into it. It was touching to see the little tyke flounder in the tub, but if they hadn't pulled her out she would surely have drowned.

Asma was one month old when the doorbell rang one afternoon. Hala had not yet recovered from the delivery; she was feverish and fatigued. She was just preparing a pan of mutton shanks, Ahmed's favorite dish. She opened the gate and stood facing a swarm of men with rifles at the ready. "Where's your husband?" They pushed her aside and stormed in; there were at least thirty of them. Soon they were all over the house, and began turning the place upside down. Hala moved frantically from room to room. What were they looking for? "We're not Muslim Brothers," she said. She knew that the *mukhabarat*, the Syrian security police, had been rounding up members of the Brotherhood for a few weeks now.

"That's not why we're here," the men snarled at her. "You people are Marxists." They jammed all the papers, letters and newspapers they could find into bags, and then most of them left. Six agents stayed behind: they would wait for Ahmed, they announced grimly.

The smell of mutton shanks filled the house. Ahmed could come home any minute. How could she warn him? She only hoped he had heard something. Or that he would notice the unusual commotion in the street, where agents were bustling about with their walkie-talkies.

The baby began to cry. Hala picked her up and tried to soothe her, and then started crying herself. The doorbell rang. It was a friend of Ahmed's – she caught a glimpse of his bewildered face before they grabbed him and led him away. Everyone who rang the bell that day was arrested.

But Ahmed didn't show up. When the agents made preparations to spend the night in the front room, she retreated to the bedroom. She had cried for hours and her cheeks were burning with fever. In the semidarkness she saw the checkered pajamas that Ahmed had carelessly thrown over the bars of Asma's crib that morning. The door opened, and someone crept into the room. He went to the crib and picked up the pajamas. Her heart pounded wildly: Ahmed had come! "You must go!" she whispered. "The house is full of *mukhabarat* – they're looking for you!"

But when she awoke she was alone in bed and the house was filled with the crackling of walkie-talkies and men's voices. Ahmed had been caught the day before as he entered their street. Later she would learn that he had been horribly tortured that first night – and while he was being tortured, his spirit had come to her in a feverish dream.

The men stayed: they were apparently expecting more visitors. The first to come was her mother; the neighbors had called to tell her something strange was going on at Hala's house. The agents forced her to stay. She slept on a bench in the courtyard, cooked for the *mukhabarat* and sent them out on shopping errands. Asma cried every night and spat out her pacifier a hundred times in a row.

One evening a drunken friend rang the bell. When he came face to face with the *mukhabarat*, he began shrieking; he tore his shirt and shouted that he was one of them. They dragged him

13

inside and called their chief. As it turned out, he did work for the *mukhabarat*, but that didn't keep them from arresting him.

Gradually things quietened down. Hala suspected that the roundup had spread through the city, but by now everyone had probably gone into hiding or been arrested. It turned out that the agents were waiting for one of the key figures in the communist splinter group Ahmed belonged to, but he never arrived. After fourteen days the agents went slinking off.

❖

Evening has fallen, the muezzin at the nearby mosque has just called out the *'Allahu akbar'*, and all the TVs in the neighborhood seem to be tuned to the same channel. How long have we been lying on this bed? Hala goes on and on, she says she hasn't talked like this in years. Everyone here has the same problems, so what's the sense of bothering each other with them? But now that she's started, there's no stopping her.

The cartoons have been over for a long time. Asma has taken all her dolls out of the cupboard and given them an injection of water, and we're still lying on the bed. She stands before us, defiant: "Mama, I haven't said a thing all day! If you talk to *her* all the time, who am *I* supposed to talk to?"

Hala puts her in between us. The first night the three of us slept in this big bed, but Asma thrashed around so wildly in her sleep that they moved to the front room. They always sleep there in the summer, Hala assures me, it's cooler. In the evening I hear them in that other room, laughing and whispering like lovers.

My arrival has turned Asma's life upside down. She was hiding behind Hala when they met me at the airport, a shy little girl with glistening dark eyes. At home she showed me all her possessions: the Atari game, the telescope, her Madonna and George Michael tapes, the American drinking cup that plays a Christmas tune, the Rambo and Batman stickers, her family of dolls. She takes good care of her things: she still has the bear I sent her seven years ago, and the red shoulder bag. She has put away the presents I brought her this time in the drawer next to the bed. Every once in a while she displays them on the card table.

But after these rites of introduction we have fallen irrevocably silent. My Arabic isn't good enough for us to really talk; they teach her French at school, but I haven't heard her speak a word of it yet. She has lived alone with her mother for eleven years. I have invaded her territory, I'm taking something away from her. And what do I give in return? I have never heard of the singer Sandra, I don't play Atari, I cannot play cards, I can't do anything! The hesitancy of the first few days has disappeared completely; she has become resistance incarnate.

"She'll get used to it," Hala soothes. She goes out for grilled chicken and runs into the milkman on the way back. His hoarse voice sounds nearby: "*Halib! Haliiib!*" The bags he has slung across his horse's back hold two metal jugs. "Fresh from the horse," Hala laughs as she scurries to the kitchen. It used to be that a man would come by with his herd of sheep, and he would milk them for you right on the spot.

It's become cooler outside, and the jasmine tree in front of the house begins giving off a sweet odor – the ideal moment to go out. The shops are still open, their windows lit. Young men grouped together on the corner whisper: "Marlboro, Winston, Lucky Strike." Contraband, Hala says, from Lebanon.

People are walking past the shop windows, the men with little fingers linked. They buy little bowls of *foul* (beans), which they eat standing up. The evening breathes life into the streets, smooths away the hard edges. The characterless blocks of new housing fade in the darkness, the light-green minaret of the mosque glows fairylike in the distance. The ugly raincoats many Muslim women wear these days suddenly seem less drab – from under their scarves the women chatter as excitedly as everyone else. Even the photo of Assad taped to the *foul*-seller's bicycle looks cheerful in this light.

For the first time since my arrival, I have the exciting feeling of entering this city's intimacy. This was how Hala and I once walked through the *souq* in Baghdad, where my eye was caught by a tiny barbershop, not much wider than its own door. Red light, glittering decorations on the walls – the frivolity of a brothel – and in the midst of it all, reflected in a broken mirror, a man's face being generously lathered. To judge by the way his lips moved, the barber was telling a story; the two men waiting in worn-out armchairs laughed heartily. All the violence of the Gulf War has not been able to obliterate that scene from my memory. During the day, the banners with hollow slogans, the huge portraits of President al-Bakr and his right-hand man, Saddam Hussein, and in the evening those four men, united in a ritual so private that I turned my head away shyly when they noticed me.

Hala smiles. She recently read a book by a Damascene barber who had a shop two centuries ago in the heart of the *souq*. It was called *Daily Events in Damascus between 1741 and 1762*. The barber wrote about the dreaded Pacha al-Azem, the governor who ruled Damascus in the name of the Turkish sultan, about the murders in the old city, the soldiers who chased girls, the rising prices, the bribes that had to be paid. "When you read that, you realize nothing has changed. Back then it was the pacha whose spies peered into every nook and cranny; now it's the president and his men."

Asma disappears into a shop and comes back with a sack of the local version of M&Ms, in fluorescent colors. She may hang onto her mother at home, but in public she is more independent than other girls her age. More of a tomboy, too: she wears jeans, and a T-shirt on which Hala has ironed the number of her favorite soccer player; she refuses to wear a skirt. In a few years her behavior will become a real problem. Hala already gets comments: does she let Asma play outside, just like that? With boys? What if something happens?

It's the neighborhood, she says. All these people who come from all over, they're so conservative because they've already lost so much. Real Damascenes are much more liberal. She herself grew up in a better neighborhood, and she always played with boys when she was little.

We've walked quite a way. Damascus lies in a valley, and now we see Mount Qassioun rising up, crisscrossed with lights. Up there are the open-air cafés, with beautiful views of the city. We used to go up there sometimes to smoke the *nargileh* – the water pipe. But Hala's thoughts are elsewhere. "There are tanks on all the hills. If there were ever an uprising here, the city would immediately be under siege from all sides." Her voice is sad. "Sometimes I feel so locked up, as though Damascus is one big prison."

❖

I'd left the Arab world behind, or so I'd thought. The conspiracy theories about Israel and its Western henchmen who were out to destroy the Arabs had started getting on my nerves. In 1982 I had been to Israel: it had not been an easy visit, nor a pleasant one – I was too familiar with the Arab grievances for that – but it was difficult to return to the rhetoric of my Arab friends. Exhibitions of Palestinian children's drawings showing the aggression of the Israeli enemy . . . I no longer believed in them.

And then came the Gulf War. At first I felt quite uninvolved. They should teach that Saddam Hussein a lesson. I had been to both Kuwait and Iraq: if forced to choose, I would have chosen the regime of Emir al-Sabah above that of Saddam Hussein.

But I couldn't go along with the campaign of hatred that accompanied the war. During a visit to my parents' house I discovered that my father had been glued to the TV for weeks. He referred to Saddam Hussein as 'Hitler'; the Americans were the great heroes. He remembered how the Allies had freed us during the Second World War: without their help, he said, we would have been a lot worse off. We got into a furious argument.

"You haven't bothered to find out what the Arabs themselves think about this war," I accused him.

"The Saudis seem happy enough with the American intervention!" he shouted.

"The Saudis!" I spat the words. "They've got something to defend, all right! The biggest gamblers and whoremongers in the world, and back home they cut off hands and lock up their wives. The Americans sure know how to pick their friends!"

I was amazed at myself. What on earth was I doing? I was defending my Arab friends. I didn't have to talk to them, I knew their arguments without asking. Back in Amsterdam I tried to look at the war from my father's point of view, and I could imagine how, from the seclusion of his home, he had instinctively backed the side closest to him.

But at a friend's party I heard the same arguments. I was

18

surprised – these people had access to so much more information. When I hesitatingly tried to break through the cordon of consensus, someone snapped at me: "And you actually have the nerve to defend those demagogues and religious fanatics!"

By this time my Arab friends had taken on names and faces again, and I was no longer indifferent to the desperation they must be facing. I regularly called Joseph, a Lebanese friend in Paris. And how would Kamal be holding up under it? He lived in Washington D.C. – the heart of General Schwarzkopf country.

It must have been during those days that I began thinking about Hala again. I had met her twelve years earlier at a conference in Baghdad; we had been drawn to each other like magnets through the hustle and bustle. Before long we had fled the vaulted rooms of the conference hall to wander through the *souq* and talk feverishly on the banks of the Tigris. When she left for Damascus, I followed her on a whim. And there the magic continued: to everything I saw, she gave meaning.

She bought a statuette for me that has stood on my mantel in Amsterdam ever since: unglazed ceramic, not particularly pretty to look at, but I loved the story she told about it. The ugly god Zeus was so infatuated with Leda that he changed himself into a swan to please her. And Leda loved him: with a tender gesture she holds the swan's neck to her naked body.

Greek mythology in the streets of Damascus! But that was how it was with so many of the stories Hala told: they made me feel that although I was far from home, in a country that had a reputation for being so isolated, I had found a kindred spirit.

I carefully saved the snapshot a photographer took of us next to the fountain at the Takiyyeh Mosque. Time had laid a green film across the photo, but when I looked at it I felt the warmth and freedom of those days all over again. Twenty-five years old, still just girls, full of confidence in the things to come. She was small and slight, with delicate features, long black hair and expressive eyes. Compared to her I was big, almost clumsy.

She had just married Ahmed, who had lived in Jordan until 1970 and had come back to Syria full of fighting spirit. They both worked in the sociology department at the university and belonged to a group of friends who met every evening, put together improvised meals and talked endlessly.

In Baghdad we had eaten grilled fish beside the Tigris; in Damascus we ate in outdoor restaurants on the banks of the Barada. The love affair between Iraq and Syria was still in full bloom. The loudspeakers broadcast songs about how the Tigris and the Barada would mingle to form one mighty stream – an impossibility, according to my mental cartography. A few months later, love had grown cold and the borders between the two countries were closed for good.

At home Hala and Ahmed talked freely, but when we were out they glanced around suspiciously. Everyone was afraid of the *mukhabarat*. They urged me not to put a word on paper during my stay: a relative had once read Hala's diary and threatened to turn in a report about her. When I wanted to visit a Dutchman who lived up on embassy row, Hala walked me to the corner of his street. She didn't dare go any further – she didn't want trouble. At that moment I sensed that her world was perhaps more confined than I could imagine.

I listened with interest to the conspiracy theories traded across the table each evening – they were all the talk in Amsterdam as well. I still believed in the power of the world's oppressed, and that someday everything would be different. But when Hala and I were alone we talked about different things. She spoke of Ahmed as she would of an impetuous child. He thought he could solve everything with rifles; she didn't believe in that.

He was not the first man in her life. When she went to college at eighteen, she regarded her virginity as something to be rid of as soon as possible. She selected her first lover with care, and casually set him aside later on. She told the men she met afterwards that she was no longer a virgin. One of them wanted to marry her. She asked him whether she should undergo a minor operation to restore her hymen, so as not to dishonor him on their wedding night. He nodded. She broke off the relationship on the spot; she didn't want a hypocrite like that. Things were different with Ahmed: he had such an aversion to petit bourgeois morality that she never even needed to bring up the subject.

And so, in that landscape of big words and all-embracing discussions, she incited her own little revolution. I liked the way she fought; that was why it was so hard for me to accept what happened to her later. She had planned to travel, just like me. How often our paths could have crossed. But our paths did not cross again, and whenever I travelled I realized that she was staying at home.

Sometimes I wondered what would have become of me if I had been in her shoes. How many years had it taken me to choke down my bitterness about the Arabs' fate, how many countries visited, how many sides of the story seen? And what had happened to her in the meantime? Since the Assad regime had intervened in her private life, all roads had been closed to her. And now that same regime had sided with the Americans in the Gulf War – what would she think of that?

I wrote her a letter: did her invitation still stand? No reply – she wasn't a faithful letter writer. Then I called. I was welcome, she said; if I waited until Asma's school vacation, we could travel together through Syria.

"The Arab world!" a colleague sighed wearily when he heard my plans. "Why don't you go back to Eastern Europe? That's so much closer to us; that's going to be *the* subject for the next few years."

"We can't just write off the Arabs," I said, "we'll have to live with them, won't we?"

He laughed pityingly: "You've got it all wrong. *We* don't have to live with *them*; *they* have to live with *us*."

"Syria!" a friend objected. "At least go to Iraq!"

But I was already packing. "I'm not going to Syria," I said. "I'm going to Hala."

Now that I'm finally here, I'm afraid of offending her with the questions that race through my mind. She has her reservations too; I can tell from the cautious way she's spoken of the war until now. In the park this afternoon she said that the wind blowing through the streets of Damascus isn't normal. People are calling it the 'Gulf War' wind: the burning oil fields in Kuwait have blown the sky to pieces and thrown everything up there into disarray. "Before you know it, soot will be blowing into the city."

I looked at the corncob I was holding, the one the vendor had just fished from a tub of steaming water. "Do you really think so?"

But she laughed. "That's what they say." Then, hesitatingly, she added: "They also say it's not over yet; another war is coming."

"Another war against Iraq?"

"No, no, between Israel and Syria."

For a moment I felt the repulsion of the last few months coming over me again. Another war! Oh please, as if there hadn't been enough war already; as if the outcome wasn't clear from

the start! And what about the Middle East peace talks they had
announced just before I left home? Hadn't Syria promised to
participate? But I kept these fractious thoughts to myself. I only
asked: "War between Israel and Syria? Who says that?"

"Everyone."

"But why?"

"Do you really think Israel will let Syria stay in Lebanon?" It
was a rhetorical question. It's like the story about the Gulf War
wind: the people who spread such rumors need no evidence to
back them up. And why should they? So many inexplicable
things happen in this part of the world.

❖

Hala's mother is peeved. Why didn't we tell her we were going
to the *souq*? She needed saffron! "Mama, you can buy saffron
around here too."

"But not like in the *souq*!"

Hala tosses me a weary glance. Her mother rarely goes out –
she always sends Hala to do this kind of shopping. With a bit of
luck it might save her fifteen Syrian pounds – fifty cents – but
of course she doesn't count the twenty-five pounds Hala spends
on the taxi. Every week Hala has to buy meat for her from a
special butcher on the other side of town. It has to be meat from
a ram; absolutely no ewe's meat, that's too tough. Her mother
thinks Hala takes the bus. The bus! As if she actually had time
for that.

I have to laugh at their quibbling. Grandmother used to send
me to all the shops in the village too: cookies from the Nera,
cheese and meat from Theunis, licorice at Mia Wuytjens' – I
wouldn't have dreamed of coming home with anything else. But

that only lasted until I was eighteen, when I left the village and its shops behind.

But after Ahmed was arrested, Hala had no one to turn to but her family. She had a 'burned face': anyone who came in contact with her was immediately interrogated by the *mukhabarat*. Why had they visited her? What was their connection with Ahmed? Her family were the only people they couldn't question. After a while she moved back in with her parents: it was impossible to work and take care of Asma at the same time in the neighborhood where she lived. They didn't move back into their own house until Asma was older.

It's broad daylight outside, but Hala's mother is sitting cross-legged in semidarkness, watching an American nature film with Arabic subtitles, a cigarette in her mouth, a cup of arabica coffee within arm's reach. She has put aside the thick book of Koranic verses that was on her lap and peers at me through her spectacles. "You see what my daughter's like? And they're all the same. They don't care about their poor mother." She learned French somewhere in the distant past; she blows a thick layer of dust off the words to lend force to her lament. "It's a good thing I have my house in Wadi al-Nakhleh. Once it's finished, they won't see me around here anymore.

"*Ya rabb!* – Oh, God!" she sighs, then stretches her stiff legs and goes into her kitchen to make lunch. She's no taller than Hala, but twice as heavy.

Hala says I came here last time too, but I've forgotten. I can't remember her family playing any part in her life; she and Ahmed seemed like people without families.

All the rooms in this house open onto the living room, which is furnished with long couches and coffee tables that travel back and forth, just like Hala's little folding table. The garden has a fountain and a citrus tree heavy with fruit. Asma hugged 'Tété', as she calls her grandmother, and went straight outside: now she's circling the house on her bicycle.

When Shirin and Zahra come home from work, panting from the heat, Tété sticks her head out the kitchen door. "Did you get what I asked you to, Shirin?" Hala winks at me. "See how she terrorizes her daughters?" Her mother keeps a record of all her expenses in a black book almost as thick as the one with the Koranic verses. No pound goes unaccounted.

One of the side rooms is lit by a neon lamp. In the middle of the room, surrounded by cupboards filled with jars of marmalade and preserved vegetables, is a table on which Tété sets a steaming platter of rice and meat. Everyone sits down quickly, and begins eating just as quickly; Shirin and Zahra have already put on their nightgowns. Hala eats standing up – she can't find a chair. Tété says she's not hungry, but after some coaxing she takes the smallest plate and proceeds to eat more than anyone else.

When the phone rings, Hala goes to the living room, talks to the person on the other end and calls Tété. Then Shirin rushes to the phone with her mouth full. Within ten minutes I'm surrounded by so much chaos that I can't eat another bite. I'm back in the house where I grew up, where eleven of us sat at the table every Sunday – a situation that sometimes got so out of hand that I would take my plate and flee to Grandmother's house across the street. Hala nods to me encouragingly: "Have some more, you've hardly eaten a thing."

An enormous mirror stands against the wall. I look at myself in it, and at the fat little people around me who carelessly, almost wearily, knock back plate after plate of food. Suddenly, without my asking, Shirin dishes me up a heaped spoonful, then another.

"I don't want any more!" It pops out before I know it, and I see Shirin stiffen.

"You don't have to eat it," Hala soothes. "If you don't want to, you don't have to."

"But you need to put on some weight," Shirin says sternly, "twenty pounds at least – you're much too skinny."

"That's my business!" My face in the mirror is flushed with exasperation.

"Shirin was only joking," Hala says. They're all laughing now, but I can tell Shirin was shocked by my outburst. Once the table is cleared and everyone is sitting in the big room, they start telling stories about an aunt who is so fat that she has to be hoisted out of her chair, and about another who can only walk through the door sideways. They waddle across the room and act three times as fat, so convincingly that I begin to feel like a beanpole and everyone around me seems slim as a reed. Tears of laughter run down my cheeks. I put my arm around Shirin and offer my apologies. She lends me a yellow nightgown and a little later Hala and I are lying in the twin beds in Tété's room, where a pink plastic fan blows cool air in our direction. After all the laughter, the quiet of the siesta has descended on the house – even Asma has fallen asleep on the couch in the living room.

The bedroom smells of the jasmine blossoms Tété puts between the sheets and blankets. Hala lies on her back, arms folded behind her head, suddenly younger in this childlike decor of light-blue cabinets and bedspreads. "I'm sorry about what happened with Shirin," I say, "I'm not used to Arab hospitality anymore." But Hala doesn't even know what I'm talking about. "We go from one crisis to the next around here. Don't worry about it."

Then I ask her a question that's been on the tip of my tongue:

"How did you survive in this house all those years?"

Hala smiles. "My father was still around then." His picture hangs in the living room, next to the barometer. A handsome man with mild features. "He loved Asma, he was like a father to her." Since his death, the house has been like a battleship roaming the seas, with no one at the helm. Her only brother works in the Gulf; all the family cares have settled on her shoulders. "Did you hear my mother going on about her house at Wadi al-Nakhleh? It's all she talks about these days." The house is about fifty kilometers outside Damascus, and after five years of work, it still isn't finished. Every trip there is an expedition for which the entire family is drummed up. "I've never seen my mother go there once without taking all of us with her!" Meanwhile, the name Wadi al-Nakhleh has assumed mythical proportions. Hala and Asma had an argument a while ago: it was eleven o'clock at night, and Asma had burst into her grandmother's bedroom crying, "Tété, give me the keys. I'm going to Wadi al-Nakhleh!"

We must have fallen asleep while talking, because when I wake up, the house is full of sounds again and I hear someone shuffling through the room. It's Tété. I sit up in bed, but she doesn't seem to see me. She rolls a rug out on the floor, places a white cloth over her head and shoulders, kneels down facing Mecca, bows to the ground and begins to pray.

❖

Our taxi driver almost runs over a woman. It frightens me, but Hala just laughs. "Wait, you haven't seen anything yet!" Large signs bearing edifying messages have been posted in the city center: 'If you see someone commit a traffic violation, give him an angry look. These are the words of our leader, Hafez al-

Assad'. But according to Hala, it's his own soldiers who cause the most accidents. Like the president, many of them come from the mountains in the north; they're not city people. A soldier here once ran over a two-year-old boy. It was the talk of the town, but none of the newspapers dared to write about it.

My amazement at everything I see amuses Hala. Only now does she realize that she's become used to the strangest things. "You have to meet Ahmed's family," she says. "My family's nothing by comparison! Before I met him I didn't even know such households existed in Damascus."

"What's so different about them?"

"I can't explain it, you'd have to see them to believe it."

As we're walking through the old town one afternoon, Hala stops in front of a door with a little copper hand on it. She uses it to knock on the door. We hear excited female voices and then someone asking: "Who's there?"

Ahmed's mother opens the door. The women, who had fled in all directions like frightened birds, reappear laughing. They are Ahmed's sisters, sisters-in-law and their children. While we sit in the whitewashed courtyard, new faces keep appearing at innumerable doors in the upper galleries. After a while I lose count completely.

"How many people actually live here?" I whisper to Hala.

"I wouldn't know, it's a surprise to me every time I come by." One of Ahmed's sisters is visiting from Amman; she's brought her mother-in-law with her, and a little niece Hala has never seen before.

The men are nowhere to be seen: they work during the day in the lumberyard owned by Ahmed's father; or they're asleep, for some of them work at night. The women look at me inquisitively. One of them breast-feeds her baby; giggling, she asks whether women do that in my country as well.

Do I have a husband? And children? These are questions I'd rather avoid; the answers are so disappointing. If I tell them I'm married, they'll wonder why my husband allows me to travel alone. That there are women who choose not to have children is something they can't understand at all. But Ahmed's mother looks at me so expectantly that I say to Hala: "Tell her my husband and I are unable to have children."

Her look is full of compassion. "Is it because of her or her husband?" she wants to know. I regret my lie immediately.

Why did Hala take me to the *souq*? Ahmed's sisters sputter; she should have shown me the modern shopping streets of Damascus! But Hala says they wouldn't know their way around there themselves, because the men do all the shopping in this household. When the women do go out, Ahmed's mother always chaperones.

We drink coffee and Asma disappears into the house with her cousins. Everything here is in constant motion: children are taken out of bed, others are put in, and Hala and I quickly become part of the ever-changing decor – no one seems to mind that we're speaking a different language.

Time doesn't exist in this family, Hala says; they never look at the clock. They live according to a rhythm barely influenced by the outside world. How often they've invited her to a lunch that wasn't served until six in the evening! The girls are raised very differently from Asma: they only go to school until they turn twelve and they can barely read or write, but they know many more female secrets than Asma – nothing is kept from them.

Sometimes a group of women leave the house to visit relatives. These outings are a real exodus: when one of Ahmed's

29

sisters-in-law visits her family, she not only takes her children, but also her mother-in-law and a couple of Ahmed's sisters. If dinner is served late, they can't go home – they don't travel after dark – so they have to spend the night.

When she met Ahmed at the university, Hala thought he was alone in Damascus. He had a Jordanian accent and didn't talk about his family – she assumed that they had stayed behind in Amman. In fact, he never talked about himself at all. Politics, that was his subject, and when Hala suggested spending a weekend with friends he just kept talking politics and never even tried to touch her.

One afternoon during a second weekend she simply pulled him into the woods. He was clumsy – she could tell he had never been with a woman before. That evening he began discussing politics again, wiping the sweat from his forehead with a hand-kerchief and glancing at her in confusion.

Her father was disappointed that she wanted to marry Ahmed. A family of woodcutters, what would they have to talk about! She was still young, she had all the time in the world – what was her hurry?

"Yes, what was the hurry?"

"I wanted respect," she says. "I couldn't go on living an independent life, I had to think of my reputation. People here don't know the difference between freedom and prostitution."

"Were you in love with him?"

"No, not really." She laughs. "It wasn't very romantic. I thought I could live with him, that's all."

Another knock on the door causes the women in the courtyard to flee in all directions, but they breathe easier when they hear the voice of Rashid, Ahmed's younger brother. He's a slim young man with his hair slicked back – he looks like Ahmed. We were just getting ready to leave, but that's out of the question now. Rashid invites us to come into the house and sends one of his little nephews out to buy local ice cream with pistachio nuts.

Hala says no one ever sits in the parlor, but Rashid is bent on showing it to me. Heavy Damascene furniture, cabinets inlaid with mother-of-pearl and high-backed chairs – objects that require a lot of space, but here they're all crammed together. A clock with a picture of the Ka'aba shrine in Mecca is ticking away on the wall.

In the living room a tinted photograph of Ahmed hangs in a gilded frame above the TV. At home Hala has a small black-and-white print of the same photo; I'd recognized it as Ahmed immediately. When I was last in Damascus, he had offered to stay with a friend. I liked him for that, for not feeling threatened by Hala's friendship with this stranger she had met in Baghdad.

In these surroundings I suddenly see him in another light. He's not an exceptionally handsome man, but his eyes radiate masculine pride and self-confidence. Rashid has the same look. It has to do with the natural authority he holds over the women in this house, the outside world he represents to them. It confuses me to think of Ahmed's pride in connection with such things – it doesn't fit the image I had of him until now.

Hala had told me that Rashid raises pigeons. "He sits up on the roof with his friends for hours," she said. "You have no idea of the kinds of things they do up there." "Feed the pigeons," I ventured, but she said there was more to it. She was so secretive about it that I became curious. Rashid laughs shyly when I ask to see his pigeons. The roof is men's territory: women never go up there; they're not even allowed to hang up the laundry on the upper floors when there are no men in the house. But you can't refuse a foreign woman a request like that.

31

We climb the stairs to the top floor, a group of children in our wake. As soon as we step onto the narrow wooden ladder leading to the rooftop terrace, feathers begin swirling down around us. The light on the terrace is blinding, and we stand there blinking at the sea of roofs, domes and minarets spread out before us. Rashid disappears into one of the pigeon coops and proudly shows me a couple of new female pigeons. "They're very expensive," Hala says, "you wouldn't believe what he'll pay for one of those birds."

Rashid releases about thirty males. They fly in tight formation above our heads, in ever-widening circles. "The neighbors have pigeons too," Hala says. "When they let them go at the same time they sometimes get caught in each other's flight." That's the sport, as it turns out, the neighbors waylay each other's pigeons.

Hala was right: this has nothing to do with the pigeon racing I remember from my youth, with the old men who met in cafés smelling of tobacco and flat beer. This sport belongs to the closed ranks of the old Arab city. The *kashash al-hamam* (pigeon racers) usually don't have a good reputation: people say they're mama's boys who can't make it out on the street, but who play the hero up on the roof; they say they take drugs and can't be counted on to keep their word.

"But what do they do with each other's pigeons?"

"That depends," Hala says. "A while ago, Rashid caught a beautiful pigeon that belonged to one of the neighbors. He wrung its neck and left it on their doorstep. Now it's war. Sometimes the arguments become so heated that they actually start fighting. Every once in a while you hear that someone in the old city has been stabbed over a pigeon."

The birds continue to circle, but there's no sign of the neighbors. I think of Ahmed. How was he able to reconcile his revolutionary ideas with these family practices? Hala is leaning over the balustrade; she signals to me to come over. Far below us is the street, and the doors with their hand-shaped knockers.

"I'd get tired of this real fast," I say.

"But not Rashid and his friends!" Hala whispers. "Maybe one of them has a pair of binoculars so they can look into the neighbors' houses. Who knows, maybe a woman throws them a secretive glance; maybe they can watch her dress." She laughs at my amazement. "A closed society looks for windows facing out. That's why the men of this house keep their women on such a short leash: they know the dangers that are out there. Rashid doesn't even let his friends know his wife's name. If he wants coffee or food up here on the roof, he whistles down and she puts a tray on the stairs. When one of his friends is leaving, Rashid bends over the railing and yells: '*Yallah!*' Then all the women rush into the house."

Hala was here once when a group of Rashid's friends came by. "All the women had to go inside, but I peeked through the kitchen window. I saw about eight men go up the stairs, their heads wrapped in black-and-white checkered shawls. One of them stood out: he walked differently and his face was completely hidden by the shawl." She gives me a conspiratorial look. "You'll never guess; it was a woman!" Later on she noticed that the men hadn't gone up to the roof, but were leaning over the railing of the third floor: they took turns going into the little room where the woman must have been.

"Do the women here know that these things go on?"

"I think so. Rashid's wife complains about it sometimes. Every once in a while he sends her off to her family for a few days, and when she comes back she can tell that someone has been sleeping in her bed, even wearing her clothes."

"And she puts up with that!"

"She doesn't know any better. She's better off than she was before! Her father wouldn't even let her watch TV, and when he comes to visit she just sits in a corner, quiet as a mouse. Rashid's mother chose her for her strict upbringing."

It makes me think of Abdelgawad, the family patriarch depicted by the Egyptian writer Naguib Mahfouz in his *Trilogy*: he spends every evening in a brothel, but beats his wife when she dares to go to the mosque on her own.

"What if his wife had an affair, what would Rashid do then?"

"Kill her," Hala says without hesitation, "don't doubt it for a moment." Not so long ago, one of Ahmed's married sisters had such an argument with her husband that he left her alone in their home for days on end. Ahmed's father was worried: what would happen if she was hanging up the laundry and a man whistled at her? And what if someone saw that happen and told everyone about it? Then, he wailed, he would have to cut her throat to preserve his honor.

Rashid holds a new female pigeon in the air and makes cooing sounds to lure the males back to their coop. They react immediately. In one fluid motion they land on the roof and meekly let themselves be locked up. Rashid laughs. "Did you see that?" He lets us go down the narrow ladder first, to where the ice cream awaits.

"You should marry a man like Rashid and have a bunch of children," Hala says on our way home later that afternoon. "After ten years of that, you could definitely write a book about Syria."

The very idea! "You don't think I'd have enough energy after ten years to even put one word on paper?"

"Why not?"

I can't believe she's serious. During the last few days she herself has kept trying to work out some research data for the university. She never gets far: Asma, Tété, Shirin, they all seem to be standing in line to pull her away from her writing table. The long sheets of paper on which she writes are always getting lost in the shuffle between Asma's drawings and soccer coupons. She thinks I'm extremely disciplined, even though I do nothing but keep up my diary. "Tell me the truth: you don't really believe that, do you?"

Hala laughs mysteriously: "I only got to know this country's problems once I was married. You could always try it, couldn't you?"

All three of us are glad to be home again. Asma is just in time for 'Captain Majed', her favorite cartoon, about a little soccer player who has been trying to score a goal for the last three days. All the children in the neighborhood are watching, and shouts of encouragement echo up and down the street. Asma hangs groaning in her chair and is so wound up by the time it's over that she ricochets through the room, bouncing off imaginary objects. Then she has to go outside, along with all the other children in the street. They scream in little cartoon voices: "Majeeed! Captain Majeeed!", their soccer ball pounding against the walls. When Asma comes home she has a poster of the Dutch national soccer team with her, and a photograph of Marco van Basten which she tapes to the dresser in the bedroom, next to an unsightly Captain Majed sticker.

Hala is cleaning the house. I'm not allowed to help: she'll take care of it, she'll be done in a flash, she assures me. Bent over at the waist, she sweeps a wet rag back and forth across the floor. I can't stand to watch. "Why don't you use a squeegee?"

She wipes the sweat from her forehead. "Don't worry about it, I'm used to doing it like this."

She sprays the courtyard clean with a garden hose and sweeps the fallen leaves and splattered figs into a pile. "This is nothing compared to my parents' house," she says. "I don't know how many times I scrubbed that place!" When she occasionally had to go out in the evening for her work, her mother would shout: "How dare you leave your daughter alone! Have you forgotten that you're a married woman?" Then Hala would snap: "What do you mean married? So where's my husband?" But she didn't dare to leave until she had scrubbed the whole house.

She looks fondly at the washing machine in which our clothes turn round and round. Her floor was always covered with water when she still did her washing by hand. "I have a lot of respect for this machine," she says, "she's courageous, and she works for me without complaining. I love her more than my own mother, you know that? My mother wouldn't do anything for me without asking me to return the favor a hundred times over."

She climbs the stairs on the outside of the house and spreads a sheet on the flat roof. Her mother has asked her to dry some *mulukhieh* (a kind of spinach). She arranges the fresh leaves carefully on the sheet; during the next few days she will turn them continually until they are completely dry. "It's good to know that my mother will eat this when winter comes," she says kneeling, "good to know there will be a winter."

When all the work is done and the bottle of vodka has been taken from the freezer, she tells me that Ahmed's mother has announced a visit soon. "I hope she forgets about it. Can you imagine that whole flock of women in my house?" They travel in a convoy of taxis. Once they're in the house, they're every-where: the living room, the bedroom, the kitchen. The place where they take off their shoes is transformed into a shoe bazaar. There are never enough cups for everyone, and while Hala trots back and forth with the coffee, food and sweets, the children climb up on the beds with their shoes on, pee in the corner and knock everything over. Their mothers pull Hala's clothes from the closet, put on make-up in front of the mirror, inspect every new object they find and ask where she bought it. Once they've finally left, the doorbell rings again: someone has walked out with Hala's slippers, or they realize that they've left one of the children behind.

Worst of all is when they announce their visit, but somewhere along the way drop in to check on a family with a marriageable daughter for one of their nephews, leaving Hala waiting in her shiny house with all the pots and pans she's borrowed from friends for the occasion and more food than she and Asma could finish in a week. Sometimes they call up later on to tell her that they had decided to come by the next day anyway, and had been terribly disappointed not to find Hala at home.

❖

Hala gets up earlier than usual; she shuffles through the bedroom in the semidarkness, rummages through the closet and puts the clothes she ironed the night before in a big bag. "Sorry, I didn't mean to wake you," she whispers. But I already have my bathrobe on.

"Can I do anything?"

"No, no." In the kitchen she spoons sugar into a plastic bag. "He needs two kilos a month. They share it. Some of them never get visitors."

"Do they cook for themselves?"

"Yes, but don't ask me how. Do you know what they eat? Eggs with yogurt!" The very thought makes her shiver.

The books he asked for are lying in the living room. Hala shakes Asma. "Get up, we're going to visit Papa." Asma is a dawdler. She arranges the little pillows she slept on in a row – they all have names, from Suleyman to Simsim – and stands in front of the closet for ages, trying to decide what to wear. "Time means nothing to her," Hala sighs, "just like Ahmed's family." Asma dreads these visits. An hour in the bus, then the wait at the iron gate until the *mukhabarat* call their name. There's nowhere to get out of the burning sun in summer; in wintertime, the snow blows in their faces.

"Shall I come along?"

Hala laughs. "If you put on beige nylons and wear a black *abaya*, they'll think you're one of Ahmed's sisters." It's an absurd thought, and tempting to toy with, but what if someone tried to talk to me?

They go out the door, weighed down with baggage, past the poultryman whose shop is so small that he always stands in the doorway, past the old man pushing a cart full of pastries, past the greengrocer who is just setting up his wares at this hour. I follow them in my thoughts; this is the first time I'm not allowed to go along.

Unfamiliar clothes are hanging on the line that afternoon. Pajamas, tracksuit pants, underpants, plaid shirts. "I'm a married woman," Hala says, "but the only physical contact I have with my husband is washing his clothes."

She had told him about my visit. "I can tell it's doing you good," he said, "you look better than usual." A new prisoner had been put in his block a few weeks back, a Jordanian spy who had seen a great deal of the world. They would talk for hours on end – that had done him a lot of good too, he admitted.

"Ahmed says you should write something about the struggle for freedom in this country." The struggle for freedom – apparently he still has the same abstract ideas about how the problems of the world should be solved.

Asma is playing absentmindedly with the little balls her father gave her. She turns them over and over in her hand, and tests their resilience on the floor. They're balls of dough that Ahmed has painted red and yellow. That same evening they're placed behind the glass doors of the cupboard, along with the beaded vases, necklaces and palm-resin boxes Ahmed has made over the years. The miniature house made of varnished matchsticks is the most touching of all: its roof is made of olive pits, the lawn is grains of rice painted green.

Hala was gone for four hours. I'd expected her to have a lot to talk about, but she's quiet and withdrawn. The closely written letter Ahmed smuggled through the mesh barrier remains in her shoulder bag, unread.

"Did something happen?"

"No, I'm just tired." Her voice sounds flat. "I'm always like this after I've been to the prison. It takes me at least a day to get back to normal." She laughs. "At first it was much worse: then it took me a whole week!"

She was barely allowed to see Ahmed during the months after his arrest, but finally she was given visiting rights. Damascus for her became a city marked by the buildings of the *mukhabarat*: there was the hospital where Ahmed lay in intensive care after they had tortured him; there was the office where she had to ask permission to visit him; there was the tower where he was being held. The electric shocks he received during his first days of imprisonment were so severe that he was barely able to walk for six months.

They had fought just before he was arrested. She wanted to arrange things in their marriage, but he was behaving like an irresponsible student. Before they were married he had said he wanted to learn to cook – afterwards he never mentioned it again. His own teaching style was unwieldy, but he tried to give her advice about how to deal with her students.

She had more experience with men than he did with women; he camouflaged his uncertainty by being secretive, by staying out for nights on end, never saying when he would come home. One evening, as they were sitting across from each other reading, he put down his book, looked at her and said: "You're stupid: you think men want to be friends with you because they like you, but all they're interested in is going to bed with you!" A year after their wedding he suddenly started crying because she hadn't been a virgin when they married.

She thought she had married only him, but before long she found herself confronting his whole family. The more threatened she made him feel, the more he called in their help. He didn't even hesitate to bring Tété into play. "Did you know your daughter drinks?" he asked her. Tété acted shocked – of course she knew Hala drank.

They grew further and further apart during the pregnancy. Sometimes he packed his belongings and disappeared to his parents' house for a few days. She suspected he had a girlfriend, and she heard he had asked Rashid for ten thousand pounds – the amount he would have to pay her for a divorce settlement.

But she forgot all these conflicts when he was arrested: now it was between them and the *mukhabarat*. She imagined that he would only be in prison for a year or two, and considered herself fortunate to be allowed to visit, fortunate that he hadn't been sent to the notorious Tadmor prison in the desert, where no visitors were allowed and the prisoners had almost no food or clothing.

He asked her to knit him a sweater. Whenever he wore it he would know she had thought of him. She didn't have the faintest idea how to go about it, but she got hold of a pattern and spent whole evenings working on it. She took pictures to the prison each month, of Asma and of their house she was furnishing; they'd had almost no furniture when he was arrested.

For the first few years of his imprisonment she felt numbed: she had no desires, and it was as though everything inside her were dead. Sometimes she envied him: after all, didn't he have it easier in prison than she did outside? He was taken care of, she had to struggle to stay alive.

At the university, everything had changed. She had gone to a conference in Morocco when she was heavily pregnant with Asma; now other colleagues went instead. But did she really even want to go anymore? Wasn't it bad enough that Asma was growing up without a father? Her frustration sought an outlet: when Asma cried, she struck her hard, just like the mothers in the *souq* who pulled their children along by the hand and kept yelling: "*Bess! Bess!* Stop it! Stop it!"

She was spanking Asma one day, beside herself with rage, when her father said: "Stop hitting that child." She came to her senses with a start. "Leave her alone; I always let you have your own way." She knew he was right, and she never hit Asma again.

At first Ahmed was in a prison tower in the center of Damascus. Sometimes Hala took Asma with her when she visited him. They had to climb stairs that looked down onto the inner courtyard; they saw a man being beaten there one day, beaten so hard he screamed as though he were being flayed alive. His cries echoed in the stairwell and spiraled up along with them. Asma had just turned three; she climbed the steps in front of Hala on

41

her little legs, looking down over the railing but saying nothing, not even after they got home.

One time she thought Ahmed was going to be released. The city was buzzing with rumors, so she bought new clothes, scrubbed the house, borrowed big pans and waited. But he didn't come; it took her a year to get over her disappointment. She stuffed the clothes she'd bought into the closet. "They're too small for me by now," she laughs wanly.

The years ran like sand through her fingers. When it started to get cold, she would unpack Ahmed's warm clothes from the suitcase on top of the dresser, take them to the prison and bring his summer clothes back home. When he asked for a new sweater she got someone else to knit it on the sly. The third sweater came from a store.

"He'd rather have me spend each evening with my mother, waiting for him," she says, "but I can't take it anymore." Today he asked her to bake a cake for him. "I'll buy one," she suggested. "No," he insisted, "I want you to think of me while you're working in the kitchen." Hala looks at me wearily. "His brothers are exactly the same: hard, but sentimental. You should see them cry when they visit him!"

That evening her mother calls to ask why she hasn't come by. She wants to go to Wadi al-Nakhleh; the kitchen is finished, and she's anxious to see it. Hala's brother Salim calls from Qatar to announce that he's coming to visit. Hala hangs up with a sigh. "Imagine that! Mr Big suddenly wants to get married and asks me to start looking for a girl. As if I didn't have enough to think about already!"

She can't help feeling guilty about her callousness towards Ahmed. "Everyone's after me all the time, and what do I do? I take it out on the most defenseless one of all." But she's not going to bake that cake, that much is clear to me by now. And I even seem to be more curious than she is about Ahmed's letter – at bedtime, she still hasn't read it.

❖

By the time the shopkeeper has put a liter of yogurt and a loaf of bread on the counter, he can contain his curiosity no longer. "Bulghari?" he asks, and then, when I shake my head: "Ruski?" Hala doesn't chat with shopkeepers – it's better not to for a woman alone, she says. I have resolved to do the same, but when I go out to explore the neighborhood for the first time, I discover that it's not so easy. They're used to Eastern European women married to Syrians here, but a 'Beljikiyyeh' – that's a new one!

The pharmacist studied in Germany, and he warns me that the Syrian toothpaste he sells will be a real letdown. When I ask the grocer about the quality of the local jam, he opens a jar and lets me have a taste: just stick your finger in it, sure, why not? He advises me not to buy paper handkerchiefs – a box of tissues is a much better deal. Back home, Hala laughs: "They never give me that kind of advice!"

The cigarette sellers, their evenings filled with whispering, are standing on the street corner, feet wide apart, not saying a thing. The young man in the middle, the one with the handsome face and leather jacket, is obviously their leader. His friends look the other way nervously when I walk by, but he boldly tosses back my furtive glance.

There's Asma. At home she keeps me at arm's length, but now she leaves her little friends in the lurch and bounces along happily, pointing out the stores where Hala usually shops and helping me look for *labneh* (strained yogurt).

"It's time we had a key made for you," Hala decides that afternoon. The shoemaker-cum-locksmith runs his business from a sooty hole in the wall. He takes our order without a word; he's wearing Coke-bottle-thick glasses, and his unbuttoned dust coat is black with polish.

"His son used to help him," Hala says as we walk on, "but something terrible happened to him." A few years ago, a car driven by two Muslim Brothers was being chased through this neighborhood by the *mukhabarat*. The Muslim Brothers jumped out of their car at a traffic light and were shot dead while trying to escape. The *mukhabarat* thought that the Brothers must have had a hideout in that street. Suspicion fell on a house used by merchants from Homs for storing the songbirds they sold at the market.

One evening the *mukhabarat* decided to search the house, but they couldn't get in. "Is there a locksmith around here?" they asked the neighbors. They pointed out the old man's shop, which was already closed for the day. "Where does he live?" They showed them his house across the street. The old shoemaker answered the door; he had just taken a bath and already had on his *jellaba*. "I'll go with them," his son offered.

He used a skeleton key to get in. The ground floor was full of empty birdcages so they went upstairs, where they came across a locked door. The boy used his skeleton key again. When he pushed the door open, he was cut down by a hail of bullets. The *mukhabarat* dragged the boy's body from the doorway and pulled it outside. A few minutes later, the house blew up.

Hala looks around nervously. "If you want to, I'll show you where it happened, but we have to walk by without stopping."

A chunk is missing from the row of houses. Between the blind, whitewashed walls a little square has been furnished with tiles, and planters full of red flowers. At any other time I would have walked by without giving it a second thought, but now that I'm paying attention I see that everything is newer and cleaner than in the rest of the street: history has been scrubbed away here with a certain briskness. "Apparently, the cellar was full of weapons," Hala says.

Asma has stopped to buy chewing gum, so we stand across from that vacant spot, those white walls, those red flowers, a bit longer than we'd planned. Somewhere a door opens; a man comes out and stares at us. "Let's get out of here," Hala warns.

I walk on with a leaden feeling in my legs. The shoppers who bump up against us in the throng, the locksmith, the man in the doorway – what secrets they share.

"What does Asma know about all this?"

"I don't know," Hala says pensively. "She realizes that there are ordinary people, and *mukhabarat*."

Asma tugs angrily on her arm and hisses something in her ear. Hala tries to hush her, but Asma keeps pulling at her, annoyed.

"What's wrong?"

"She says we shouldn't talk about things like this out on the street; that even she knows what we're talking about, and she doesn't even speak French – think how it must be for other people!"

We walk on in silence. After a while Hala says softly: "The shoemaker has never been the same. It was his firstborn son. They paid him compensation, fifty thousand pounds, I think, and gave him a medal, because his child had died in the war against the Muslim Brothers."

"Does he know that your husband's in prison?"

"No, he doesn't. He's had enough sorrow in his life. Besides, everyone has a family member who's been killed or put in

45

prison." Since the Ba'ath Party came to power in 1963, a state of siege has been in force – a military court can sentence someone to death within twenty-four hours. "Remember that friend I told you about, the one who came to our door drunk after Ahmed had been arrested, and shouted that he worked for the *mukhabarat*? Do you know how much time he served? Eighteen months! They want you to feel that you're not in control of your own life, that everything's up to them."

I think of the Muslim Brothers in that birdhouse, hearing the *mukhabarat* come upstairs, hearing the key turn in the door of their hideout and knowing what they had to do. I'm amazed, actually, that they're still active. In 1982, a revolt by Muslim Brothers in Hama was brutally crushed by special units of the Syrian army – ten thousand dead and a city destroyed. I didn't think they had survived that defeat.

But they are very much alive, Hala says. A policeman who had killed a lot of people in Hama was recently murdered in bed by two intruders. "It's usually young people who do those kinds of things. Seventeen, eighteen – they're not afraid to die."

The way she talks about these boys – I can barely imagine her sympathizing with their ideas, yet I hear fondness in her voice. Some of them are in prison with Ahmed, and sometimes she delivers messages for them. In 1980, more than a thousand Muslim Brothers were shot and killed in the prison at Tadmor by soldiers working for Assad's brother Rifa'at. Since then, most of the Brothers are no longer allowed visitors: the authorities are afraid they will reveal who was killed. One of the Muslim Brothers Ahmed knows in prison does have contact with his family, but he doesn't dare tell them that his brother was murdered at Tadmor.

"Supporting the Muslim Brothers is a way to say 'no' to the

government," Hala says circumspectly. "Assad is an Alawite; the Muslim Brothers consider him an infidel."

She herself is none too impressed by the religious virtue of the Alawites. Like seventy per cent of all Syrians, she is a Sunni Muslim; the Alawites belong to a sect which split off from Shi'ite Islam. To escape persecution they withdrew to the mountains around the coastal city of Lattakia, where they lived in isolation for centuries.

'Moon worshipers' is another name the Sunnis call the Alawites. The story goes that the Alawites were outraged when Armstrong landed on the moon: they thought he had driven God away. During the first half of the century they still had a prophet, Suleyman al-Murshid, who was hanged in 1946. Some Alawites believe that Assad is his successor.

"It would be better if the country were ruled by a Sunni," Hala says.

I'm truly amazed. "What do you care about the president's religion?"

"*I* may not care, but it would definitely make a difference to other people. We need a charismatic leader, one who's supported by the majority of Syrians." She sighs. "It's a complicated issue. I don't know whether I can explain it to you."

When she was about fourteen, she went through a very religious period herself. She prayed regularly and observed Ramadan. She had a female mathematics teacher who talked very enthusiastically about Islam; the class was so enthralled by her that all the girls began wearing headscarves. But one morning, Hala saw herself in the mirror and decided she looked silly.

Before long she began reading Sartre and Camus, and when she was eighteen she said to herself: religion doesn't help. At university she became acquainted with the work of Pascal and Descartes. How excited she was to read the words of these philosophers! Far away, in a world that didn't look at all like hers, they had written things which seemed so familiar to her, things she could easily project onto her own surroundings. A professor who had studied in Paris gave them Epicurus to read and urged them to form their own opinion about everything.

Those were eventful years. She began doing her first field research, into the experiences of rural doctors. One of them told her mockingly that, in this society, the hymen was a more important membrane than the eardrum. Then he told her about Marx. Her ears were ringing when she came home; she was so impressed by what she had heard about Marx that she immediately went looking for his writings.

When she was twenty-three she went to Paris with a cousin. "We left our luggage at the hotel and you know where we went first? To Pigalle!" But as she walked around, peeping obliquely at the red-lit windows, she was amazed: in front of her she heard a Hama accent, behind her walked a group of men from Aleppo; it was like being back in Syria! And everywhere she saw little restaurants selling felafel and other Arab food.

She spent the next few days wandering through Paris. Whenever she stopped to look at her map, someone tried to pick her up. "Can I help you with something?" They were always Arabs, although some of them said they were Portuguese. One man followed her so doggedly that she fled into a phone booth. He opened the door and whispered: "How would you like to do it Portuguese style?" "No, thank you very much. I've already done that twice today," Hala said. Only then did he go away.

She had wanted to continue her studies at the Sorbonne, but after a few weeks in Paris she began to have second thoughts.

Couldn't she spend her time more wisely in Syria? How little she knew about life outside Damascus; there was so much she still had to learn. After two months she left Paris and never returned.

Back in Syria, she continued her research in the countryside. Marx had taught her how much economics determines people's lives, and during the time we spent together in Baghdad she often talked about the poverty of Syrian farmers; she still believed she could change that by writing about it.

The French books she read in those days sit in the wardrobe in the bedroom, all in a row. Sartre, Camus, Pascal, Descartes – she talks about them as though nothing has been written since, as though with them the outside world stopped transmitting signals. The books belong to a period in her life which came to an abrupt end when the *mukhabarat* raided her house.

During her time at university, religion was not important; she would never have asked if someone was a Muslim or a Christian, she felt linked to the other students by international ideas. But since then, people have retreated to their own positions and view each other with suspicion.

"People go to the mosque because they're not allowed to get together and talk about anything but religion," she says. "It's the only gathering that isn't illegal. If ten people meet at any given spot, they're already suspected of forming a political movement."

❖

Hala's mother wants to take the bus to Wadi al-Nakhleh, but Hala has her heart set on taking a taxi; it's hard to imagine, however, that the battered Ford Galaxy we end up in is any more comfortable than the bus. At first there are three men in the front seat,

49

but at the last moment an acquaintance slides in on the driver's left. They talk and laugh, and when the driver lights a cigarette, his friend holds the wheel, making it unclear for a moment exactly who's steering this wreck.

The driver yells "*Ahlan!* – Hello!" to someone he knows at a traffic light and, in all the commotion, almost runs into a white Peugeot. We tear away, but a little later the Peugeot passes us, almost scraping our door. The two men in the car signal for us to stop; they climb out and approach threateningly. They're big bruisers, much stronger than our driver, who wilts under their gaze and suddenly seems in much less of a festive mood. The men shout and yank on the door, but the driver refuses to get out. Tété tries to mediate, but Hala pushes her aside, sticks her head out the window and yells: "You should be ashamed of yourselves, there's a foreigner in the car!"

One of the men looks at us – three panicky women in the back seat of a dilapidated car – hisses something to his friend and drags him off. They slowly walk back to the Peugeot.

"*Mukhabarat*," Hala whispers as we drive on, "those were *mukhabarat*."

"How do you know that?"

"I could tell by their car. Black curtains in the back window – that's not officially allowed. And did you hear them go wild? They're not afraid of anything, they know they'll always get their way."

Now that the danger has passed, the mood in the car improves considerably. The driver lights up again and sticks a tape in the cassette recorder. A wave of sound crashes over us. I look at Tété, aghast, but she's sitting there with her bag on her lap and doesn't even flinch. Soon Salim will be coming back from Qatar – her mind is brimming over. Where will she find a suitable girl for him, where can she buy the ingredients for the dishes she's planning to make? It's been three years since he last saw Wadi al-Nakhleh, he'll be amazed at how lovely it's become. They'll rent a car, they'll be able to go there whenever they like. Hala winks at me – according to her, Salim is not at all interested in Wadi al-Nakhleh, and the main reason he needs the car is to get away from his mother.

Ever since we left Damascus, a blistering wind has been blasting through the open windows. We're surrounded by hills with almost no vegetation, but I expect to see an idyllic oasis any moment now; a stream must run through Wadi al-Nakhleh. In the distance the landscape seems to take on more variety: outdoor cafés, a few trees, a merry-go-round, roadside stands selling toys. The taxi driver pulls into a parking lot in the midst of all the carnival hubbub and Tété starts climbing out. "Here we are," Hala says, "my mother's dream, her children's nightmare."

Tété's legs are swollen, making it difficult for her to walk, but now she hurries along in front of us, across a little bridge between two outdoor cafés and towards an unfinished apartment building that leans up against a mountain. Resolutely, she begins climbing the stairs. I follow hesitantly past mounds of sand, cement mixers and scrap iron.

Five flights to the top; Tété holds on to the railing and stops to rest at every floor. Five times an empty elevator shaft gapes. The stairwell smells of decay and of fires lit by intruders, but Tété doesn't bat an eye. She stops before the whitewood door on the top floor and pulls a key from her handbag.

Inside the rooms are bare, except for a bed and a couple of chairs. Tété heads for the kitchen, where blue tiles swerve crookedly across the walls; she takes it all in with great satisfaction, opens the cupboard doors, turns on the tap and puts water on for coffee.

Hala shows me around. The rooms are spacious, but when I look out of the window I feel claustrophobic: the apartment is at the back of the building, hemmed in by identical blocks on both sides. Jagged rock formations loom just outside the bedroom windows.

It takes the two of us to force open the balcony doors. The mountain is close enough for me to reach out and touch it; if I climbed over the edge I could scramble right up its face. The balcony was Tété's idea; it floats partly in thin air, resting one corner on a jutting rock. The crack between the mountain and the building is full of garbage: dried-out loaves of Arab bread, empty oil cans, cardboard boxes.

"Wadi al-Nakhleh," I say, "doesn't that mean Valley of Palms? So where are the trees? I don't see anything but rocks!" Hala is sitting on the balustrade, her legs dangling, grinning. "Trees? Well, now that you mention it, there aren't any here."

Tété arrives with the coffee. She sinks down onto a stool and says worriedly: "There's something wrong with the refrigerator – it's not working properly."

"Oh, God," Hala sighs, "she'll be talking about that for the next week." It's because the electrical current in the countryside is so weak, especially in the summer when the lakes and rivers are low. But her mother refuses to understand; she thinks it's the refrigerator.

"Lieve is disappointed; she had a slightly different picture of Wadi al-Nakhleh," Hala says maliciously. "She thinks the name should be changed to Wadi al-Sahreh – Valley of *Stones*."

Tété doesn't think that's funny. Haven't I noticed how quiet it is? Have I heard a single sound? That's why she comes here: to escape the noise of Damascus. When the house is finished, she's going to have a sheep butchered, she muses.

Hala is getting fidgety, but Tété seems glued to her seat. "Shall we spend the night?" She looks at us hopefully.

Hala sighs. "Come on, Mama – what about Asma?"

"She's with Shirin and Zahra, isn't she? They'll be fine!" Evening has come, and the warm red glow which had the mountain in its grip just a while ago is weakening. I'm glad that Hala is sticking to her guns: the idea of spending the night in this empty apartment doesn't appeal to me either. We make our way down the dark stairwell by sense of touch.

The cafés are festively lit. Little fountains spout green and red water, and through the ornamental shrubbery I can see families and romantic couples sitting at the tables. Suddenly I feel glum, cut off from the intimacy and light-heartedness on the terrace. How long has it been since I laughed freely? It's as though I have taken on some of the suffering that weighs Hala down. "Shall we drink something?" I suggest hesitantly. But Tété is not at all interested, and Hala wants to get home too.

On the way back little pairs of lights pop up here and there in the dark landscape of hills. Jackals, Hala tells me. We sit close together, talking. I look at her and see her, years ago, sitting beside me in the bus from Baghdad as we travelled to the holy city of Kerbala, gesturing with her hands, so wrapped up in what she was saying that she forgot everything around her. And while she was talking, the mosque of Kerbala rose up out of the shimmering desert heat, glistening like a jewel in the sun. The fever of those days, I think regretfully, will never come back again.

"Why don't the two of us go to Beirut?" I whisper. We've made wild plans before.

"Everything is possible," Hala says. "We just have to wait until Salim arrives."

"What are you two talking about?" Tété sounds disgruntled. "You never talk to me as much as you do to her."

Hala laughs: "Mama, you sound like Asma! She gets jealous whenever I talk to Lieve too."

That night Hala dreams that her mother is dead. Shirin walks like a ghost through the house in a long white dress, and she herself cries inconsolably, thinking about the things she denied her mother through the years, things she can never make up for now. I have a strange dream as well. I'm carrying a child around, swaddled in translucent plastic. He's still a baby, he's only just been born, but he can already talk and he looks at me with knowing eyes. What are you supposed to feed a child like this, I ask myself. Does it still need baby food once it can already talk?

❖

"Sorry, Mama, but do you have a plate for this bread?" Salim looks at me apologetically. "I'm used to Qatar," he says, "you never just put bread on the table there." The table is loaded with food: *foul*, deep-fried cauliflower, kidneys. Hala has bought mutton with the balls still on the carcass, so there's no way her mother can say it wasn't a ram. In front of me is a dish of accordion-shaped intestines. Do animals really have stuff like this inside them, and can you eat it? Hala says it's a delicacy.

Zahra and Shirin have cleaned the whole house, and Tété has been busy for days too: scooping out zucchini, cleaning intestines – always with a cigarette smouldering away in the ashtray. "What do you cook when there's a feast?" she asked me. I was ashamed, because I didn't know what to tell her. Feasts, what kind of feasts? I couldn't come up with anything but cream of tomato soup, green beans and roast beef – but those are dishes my mother made, not things I would readily prepare myself.

The table is in its usual state of disorder: Asma refuses to eat, Shirin has a towel wrapped around her wet hair and Hala is standing again, making everyone feel uncomfortable. Tété is sitting with her arms crossed, watching to make sure Salim eats enough. Now that he's here she no longer walks around the house in her nightgown, but wears a dress. Her zipper, I see in the mirror, isn't done up all the way.

Ever since Salim discovered that I've been to Doha, the capital of Qatar, he hasn't talked about anything else. Do I remember the Doha Club, and what about the coffee shop at the Sheraton Hotel? I feel awkward about our English dinner conversation – shouldn't he be talking to his mother and sisters? But Salim clings to me almost desperately. A European and a Syrian who lives in Doha: as far as he's concerned, we're perfect conversation partners. His mother looks at us with tears in her eyes and sighs poignantly at her boy's apparently fluent English. He's changed so much, he's suddenly become such a gentleman. Hala tosses me one of her glances – she says the only thing different about Salim is that he's lost more of his hair.

"But when you're standing at the entrance to the *souq*, the fort of Doha is behind you, right?" Salim is a hydraulic engineer and, by the sound of it, uses his English only for technical discussions. He has a woolly, wearisome way of talking. It makes me wonder how he hopes to find a bride within such a short time. He'll be here for one month – before he leaves, Hala says, it should be in the bag.

That morning his mother sent him to the bank where an old classmate of Shirin's works. One of her colleagues is unmarried – could be something for Salim. I know nothing about all of this, supposedly, and when Tété alludes to his trip to the bank, Salim explains to me that he had to change money. The money here seems grimy to him; whenever he touches it he feels like washing his hands.

I try to imagine his life in Doha: he shares an apartment with a colleague, and at night they probably sit in front of the TV or take a walk on the beach. There isn't much else to do in Doha, especially not for someone like Salim, who's saving money. When he lived in Syria he earned three thousand pounds a month – seventy-five dollars; in Qatar he earns twenty times that much, so he has put together a nice little nest egg by now. That's why he wants to get married.

He left Damascus three years ago, but he looks around with the amazement of someone who has been gone much longer. "This morning I was in a taxi and another passenger just climbed in beside me!" The way they barked at him at the office where he went to arrange his exit visa rubbed him the wrong way too. And it's so dirty here! I can imagine that it seems strange to him – in Qatar everything is always being scrubbed clean by Asian laborers.

"Damascus is being overrun by villagers," he says peevishly. "You know, farmers who were working in the mountains on the coast only a little while ago." He's referring to the Alawites, who have been coming to the capital in increasing numbers since Assad came to power in 1971. "Most of them are uneducated; they may find a job on a road crew or working for the sanitation department, but they usually don't last long – they're not used to that kind of work. A simple job with the *mukhabarat* is often the only thing they're not too stupid to do."

After dinner, Salim retreats to the room Tété has fixed up for him. Standing at the door, she looks in at him tenderly. "He's asleep," she whispers.

"You see how enthralled she is by her beloved?" Shirin mocks.

"He was breast-fed for two whole years," Hala calls out, "we got two months, maximum!"

Tété laughs, ready to forgive all. Since Salim's arrival, it's been hard to ruin her mood, but Hala predicts that the honeymoon will soon be over: Salim still puts up with all the attention he's getting, but he's guaranteed to find it oppressive before long; then they will start fighting.

And indeed, during the next few days, Salim becomes increasingly less of a homebody. Sometimes he doesn't even show up for lunch, after Tété has gone to all that trouble. When he does come home, he's usually tired and sweaty. Nothing is working out for him: every car in Damascus has been rented out to tourists from the Gulf states, and it looks like his exit visa could take longer than expected. The self-confidence with which he returned from Doha is already beginning to wear thin.

Tété feeds him – his clothes are getting too tight, he complains – and converses with him in a whisper about finding a suitable marriage partner. Yesterday evening they went to visit one of Tété's cousins who has two daughters; Salim took a fancy to the younger one. Hala keeps me informed with a mixture of jokes and disgust. An arranged marriage in her family, in this day and age! "But I don't know how he would find a wife otherwise," she sighs. "He's never been interested in worldly matters."

Salim's arrival has turned Tété's whole house upside-down. Relatives who seldom visit are suddenly standing at her door, and aren't put off for a moment by the announcement that Salim isn't home. We find people in her living room at all hours of the day. Tété sits pontifically still on the velvet sofa, her legs pulled up under her, a cigarette between her lips. Her daughters serve coffee; she entertains the guests. In the kitchen her stories elicit sighs and groans from Hala. They're always about when her mother worked at the bank – she knows them by heart. "And pretty soon the others will know them by heart too, because once she gets to the end she just starts all over again!"

One afternoon, while I'm reading in the garden, Hala and Shirin tiptoe up to me. "Come and look at the rabbit who's visiting us," Hala whispers.

"Don't be so mean," Shirin hisses.

"Right, he's here to visit you, we all know that!"

The visitor turns out to be an uncle whose eye has fallen on Shirin. He's about fifty and has lived alone with his two little boys ever since his wife died. "He sits on the sofa for hours without opening his mouth – he doesn't say a word: 'How are you, Uncle Yassim?' 'Fine, thank you.' " Hala twists her mouth into a saccharine smile. "Nothing else, not a word. What a rabbit! His children have picked it up from him; they're already just as rabbity as he is!"

"And what about you, do you like him?"

Shirin's face clouds over. "Uncle Yassim? Oh, no, I don't even want to think about it." Shirin has been unlucky in love. She had a secret affair for years until it suddenly ended, and now she's over thirty: the only men still interested in her are over-aged uncles. But recently she met someone she's being secretive about.

Evening comes and the mosquitoes drive us inside, where Uncle Yassim is still sitting on the sofa, flanked by his young sons. The three of them stare blankly at the TV.

"How are you, Uncle Yassim?" Hala enquires, with a wink in my direction.

"Fine, thank you," he says, with such a perfect imitation of the stupid little grin that Hala treated us to in the garden that I have to run into the kitchen to keep from bursting out laughing.

Sitting opposite Uncle Yassim is a robust, unattractive woman wearing a headscarf and a baggy raincoat. "That's Noura, an old school friend of mine who works at the post office," Hala says. "We disagree on everything, but we've always stayed friends."

Could she be one of the girls the mathematics teacher had once moved to prayer? But Noura's conversion, it seems, is more recent than that: she has fallen in love with an Iranian sheikh who used to preach in a mosque outside Damascus. Recently, to her great chagrin, he was transferred to Algeria. "The sheikh is gone," Hala says, "but the headcloth still remains."

Noura wouldn't turn down a proposal from Uncle Yassim, and Hala and Tété occasionally make hints in that direction, but he feigns innocence. "He's a money-grubber," Hala says, "he's got his eye on the cash Shirin will inherit when my mother sells this house."

We've started spending a lot more time at Tété's, and I begin to understand what it must have been like when Hala still lived here. After the siesta, the whole family sits bickering in the living room while the hours tick by and darkness falls. I sometimes feel annoyed: at them, at Asma – who hangs around in front of the blaring TV, eating M&Ms, potato chips and *bizr* all at the same time – but also at myself, for just sitting here while a whole city I barely know awaits me outside the door.

Sometimes Hala disappears to the university. The summer term is quiet, but she has to show up every once in a while. While she's gone I try to read, but Tété's disapproving glances ruin my concentration. Stuffing grape leaves, that's her idea of doing something worthwhile.

I feel an old, forgotten lethargy come over me. Why do I do this to myself? What am I looking for? One night I dream of Holland. A story I've written has been hopelessly mangled by my editor. I try to save the situation, but only end up getting deeper and deeper in trouble. When I wake up I feel awful. I recognize the atmosphere of the dream: it's part of the uncertainty of my first few years in Holland, the difficulties of finding my way in new surroundings, the loneliness, the failures. Hala brings those fears back to life.

For me those years marked the beginning of a time full of discoveries; for her it was a period in which she became entangled in problems. She was forced back to this house, where every desire for independence was crushed. But was she really willing to struggle for a different kind of life? Why hadn't she stayed on in France? Was she afraid of the loneliness to which her compatriots seemed to have fallen prey, afraid to spread her wings? Is that why she came back? We don't talk about these things – I wouldn't know when to start, for the next household incident has already arisen.

"Zahra, where are the scissors, you've hidden them!"

"No I haven't!"

"Yes you have! Come on, where did you hide the scissors!"

At home Zahra always wears a black *abaya* over her night-gown, and during my first visits she veiled herself in such sphinxlike silence that I barely noticed her. But now that I've been here for a while I notice that she is the center of a never-ending conflict: she has the tendency to hide anything that's lying around the room. She filches the most ridiculous things: Asma's schoolbooks, Hala's pens, Tété's medicine. Under her mattress are cigars that belonged to her father, empty notebooks she once bought on sale, old back issues of *Reader's Digest*.

Zahra works in a state-run store, a vestige from when everything was still scarce in Syria. My heart broke when I saw her standing behind the counter there one afternoon. *Our* Zahra: small, troubled, wearing a too-tight, homemade sweater that pressed her heavy breasts flat, surrounded by so much socialist drabness that she seemed extremely vulnerable. The shop was empty, and nothing indicated that it had ever been otherwise. I felt so awful that I bought a little pot of hand lotion. I had to walk back and forth twice with the sales slip between Zahra and the cashier before I was allowed to take it home.

Zahra is a bit slow, Hala says. She flunked the same class six times in elementary school; she just never passed. Men never interested her at all. At school she was all aflame for the Italian nun who taught their class; later she idolized the Holy Virgin Mary, and after that it was the female singer Fayruz. She hung up posters of her and talked about her all the time. She reminds me of my mongoloid sister, Hildeke, who falls in love with game-show hosts and the men on 'Dallas' and 'Dynasty' – so in love that she follows the series on Belgian, Dutch and German TV, all at the same time.

Zahra washes the dishes with a Walkman on, so she won't have to listen to Tété's grumbling, Zahra scrubs the floor on her knees, Zahra walks through the living room in a bath towel, Zahra pinches cigarettes from Tété's pack. No one ever pays any attention to her – except, of course, when she's hidden something.

"Zahra, give those scissors back." Hala is angry and impatient.

"I don't have them!"

"If you find them, I'll give you a pack of cigarettes."

And suddenly the scissors appear. Zahra waits until Tété isn't looking, then stuffs the cigarettes into her bra. I throw her a knowing glance, but she gives me a grumpy look in return – and that reminds me of Hildeke too.

❖

One Friday afternoon after lunch, Zahra and Shirin disappear into the bedroom to get dressed, while Asma takes off her slippers and puts on some shoes. "We're going to the movies," Hala announces.

It's so quiet on this day off that the five of us walk down the middle of the street undisturbed. The sickly sweet perfume, Amour, which Zahra has sprayed all over us, travels with us like a cloud. The sun is shining and I feel like I did when my sisters and I would go to the Tijl Theater. On the way there we'd go past Mia Wuytjens' sweet shop, which was open on Sunday; outside was a sign showing a boy eating a water ice. A water ice cost two francs. There was no one on the street except for us, or at most a lone cyclist. An entire village held together by the doldrums.

"Hala tells me you've been to Africa," Shirin butts into my thoughts. She giggles. "They eat white people there, don't they? Weren't you afraid they would have you for lunch?"

"What a bunch of nonsense," I say gruffly. "Did you know that the Africans are just as afraid of Arabs as you are of them?"

"What do you mean?" she asks in amazement. She wasn't expecting me to pursue her story – she only wanted to make small talk during our walk to the movies.

"Haven't you ever heard about the Arab slave traders in Africa? The Africans certainly remember them. When African mothers want to frighten their children, they tell them the Arabs will come and get them." It was one of the first things I'd learned when, after years of travelling through the Arab countries, I had arrived in Africa: the Arabs had definitely left their mark there. My Arab friends had never told me about that; they only talked about the injustices they had suffered down through the centuries.

I feel like shocking Shirin, like punishing her ignorance of those black pages from Arab history. But a little later I regret it. What does she know about the unspoken blame I lay on my Arab friends, what does she have to do with it? She only nods, she has no idea what I'm talking about. Fortunately, Hala hasn't heard my outburst – she's too busy with Asma. I walk on, disgruntled. Why do I have to be so harsh and unreasonable?

"Hala, what's the name of this movie we're going to?"

"*Cinema Paradiso*." It's an Italian movie; she's seen it before.

"Who's the director?"

Hala has come over to walk beside me. "I can't remember." She sighs. "It's the people in that house. My whole cultural life has gone down the drain." She feels the same way I do, I realize; she's full of defiance too.

The director's name is Giuseppe Tornatore, the poster says. The theater is almost empty; it smells of sweepings and sawdust. Hala wants to go up to the balcony because there's a group of boys sitting downstairs who could be a real pain when they see a row occupied by no less than five women.

A little later we're sitting in a movie theater in a village in Sicily – a dusty dive just like this one – where an inquisitive little boy dreams himself away from the nasty world around him. Totó's father has been killed in the war, and his mother is poor. His best friend is old Alfredo, the projectionist at the Cinema Paradiso, who protects him from his mother's merciless blows. When the movie theater catches fire one day, Totó drags the unconscious Alfredo down the stairs all by himself.

Acting on Alfredo's advice, the boy goes to Rome where he becomes a famous film director. The old man had made him promise to leave the village for good, but when Alfredo dies Totó decides to go to the funeral. During his visit the ghosts of the past return to life. The Cinema Paradiso is blown up, and the sorrow he feels over a lost childhood love comes back in full force.

"What's wrong, Mama?" Asma brushes her hands worriedly over Hala's eyes. "Why are you crying?" She calms down only when Hala takes a handkerchief, blows her nose and smiles through her tears.

"I don't understand why *The Last Emperor* won so many more prizes than this movie," Hala says as we walk home. "*Cinema Paradiso* is so much more intimate, it summons up so much more emotion."

"They're two completely different films," I say indecisively, "you can't really compare them." But how could she know that? They're the only two films of any significance that have played in Damascus during the last few months. Hala only started going to the movies again a few months ago. The man who used to be in charge of buying films was a complete idiot. "He'd been a butcher, so you can imagine what he brought in: nothing but kung-fu films!"

Tété isn't home when we get back. "She's gone with Salim to visit his new fiancée," Hala guesses. In the dining room we attack the leftovers from lunch. My gaze falls on a photograph that must have been hanging on the wall the whole time. "Is that you?" Hala nods. A girl of about five, eyes shining in a touchingly pretty face; the man with his hand laid protectively on her shoulder is her father. There's so much intimacy in the way he touches her, and she in turn exudes such calm – a child who knows she's loved.

It's almost painful to look at the photo. Those shining eyes – I still see them sometimes, but usually Hala has a dull, worn-out look. She is constantly taking care of everyone, she totes plastic bags from one house to the other, fries chicken for Asma, takes Zahra to the dentist and even tries to involve me in her urge for self-effacement. "What do you want to eat tomorrow?" As if I cared! "You really don't want anything special? I'll fix it for you, it's no trouble!" She even cares for me in her sleep. Last night she dreamed that I was sick, that she had to keep everyone away from me. Sometimes, during all her running around, she suddenly emits a heartfelt "Ufff!" – like a kettle blowing off steam.

"Do you have any more old pictures?"

"Sure, if I can find them."

We plunder Tété's bedroom cupboard and spend hours lying there, flipping through photo albums. Here is Hala being held by her grandfather, a man with glasses and a red fez. He lived in a house in the old town. Everything in it was ordered: no lamp was hung in the wrong place, no object was placed at random. The ceiling was framed in golden arabesques, and the light which danced in through the tinted windows threw a soft glow over the wooden furniture. That house was full of laughter. When there was a party, her grandfather would play the sitar, his sons the lute and drum, and her grandmother would dance through the room with all the grace her heavy body would allow.

The 1950s: it's a time which many Damascenes think back on fondly. The French had left in 1946, and the euphoria of independence still hung in the air. One coup followed the other so quickly that the merchants in the *souq*, who hung up a portrait of the new president after every change of power, could barely keep up with it all.

"What happened to your grandfather's house?"

"It's a complete ruin," Hala says regretfully. When her grandfather died, the house was sold along with the furnishings. The only thing she has left from those days is an engraved copper lamp that stands on the buffet in her living room and which she occasionally reads by. The lamp gives off a diffuse light, too weak to really be practical, but Hala likes the mood it creates. It's just like Grandmother's tall wooden bed I sleep in back in Amsterdam – unwieldy and narrow as it is, it represents so many things gone by that I wouldn't dream of getting rid of it.

Here we have Hala riding her tricycle in the courtyard behind her parents' house. I recognize the fountain, the citrus tree. Before long her mother would get a job at the bank, and Hala would be taking care of Salim, Shirin and Zahra.

One day she fell through a glass door and cut her arm. Her father took her to the doctor, and while they were walking home around dusk they saw that a crowd had gathered in front of the palace where important state guests usually stayed. She forgot her bandaged arm, she wanted to know what was happening. Her father put her on his shoulders; an impressive man was giving a speech from the balustrade, his arms stretched out to the crowd. That was the president of Egypt, her father told her; he was proclaiming the union between Egypt and Syria. Her mother was peeved when she heard why they had been gone so long. She didn't like that Nasser with his socialist ideas – he could only mean trouble.

Her father was an officer and liked to take her with him when he travelled on duty. She was a bright little girl, and he was proud of her. Here they are together in Hama. Hala is wearing a winter coat and matching plus fours, and her father once again has his arm around her. The great waterwheels from the time of Alexander the Great are turning in the background.

During that trip he left her alone for a while in the office of an Egyptian colleague. It was at the time of the union with Egypt, when the foundations were laid for the extensive network of intelligence services. Hala was sitting on the table, looking around inquisitively. "So," the officer asked, pointing to the photos of Nasser and his right-hand man, Field Marshall Amer, "who do you love best?" Seven-year-old Hala looked from Nasser to Amer and said: "Neither of them."

"Why not?" the man asked in amazement.

"My mother says they're both bad."

The man raised a finger in warning: "Take care, the walls have ears around here!" Later on he whispered to her father that he should be careful: if the *mukhabarat* knew what his daughter had said about her mother, it could mean trouble. From that time on Hala understood that she was not to talk about what she heard at home.

She often thought back on that incident when Asma was learning to talk. How often she embarrassed her with impertinent questions! "Mama, why is this called the Assad Bridge? Does that mean it belongs to him?" They were in a taxi – Hala felt the other passengers freeze. In offices filled with portraits of Assad, Asma would ask: "Mama, does this building belong to Assad too?" But in the course of time Asma too would learn what was not to be said in public, and now she's the one who places a hand over Hala's mouth in the taxi when she accidentally mentions the word '*mukhabarat*' or 'Alawite'.

Hala's father may not have gone to college, but he read a great deal and was interested in everything. He had become a soldier at seventeen, when the French were still in Syria; he was one of the old guard. In the 1950s, the struggle for political power in Syria was being fought out between various factions of the Sunni elite in the cities; the army grew in power with every coup, however, and the elite was pushed further and further to the sidelines. The coup by the socialist Ba'ath Party in 1963 was a heavy blow for the Sunnis, but it was only when Assad put an end to the political squabbles in 1971 that the Damascenes would realize what they had lost during the euphoria of freedom. The privileged urban intellectuals were all replaced by country people who ruled with the barrel of a gun.

Her father had not belonged to the Damascene bourgeoisie, he had become a soldier because his father drank and he needed to earn money to support his family. The woman he loved didn't want to marry him because he was too poor, upon which – to the amazement of all – he chose Tété, a niece who was anything but pretty. But as far as the new regime was concerned, everyone from Damascus automatically belonged to the odious bourgeoisie. A few years after Assad came to power, Hala's father was put out to pasture. He spent the last fifteen years of his life at home. The books he read are in the room where Salim sleeps – many standard works on scientific subjects, the kinds of books you find in countries far from the hub of scientific research. Zahra has a few hidden under her mattress.

"My father led his own life," Hala says quietly, "he was free. He was like Meursault, the main character in *The Outsider* by Camus: a born skeptic. He never went to the mosque, not even when someone had died." The brief religious period she went through at fourteen amazed and bothered him, but he would never have opposed it; he felt she had to find her own way.

When she began to travel during her studies, her mother was upset: a woman travelling alone, that was the same as a prostitute! But her father gave his implicit consent, and when his friends accused him of throwing his daughter to the wolves, he defended her. "Around here, your father's support is much more important than your mother's," Hala says, "because his honor is tied up with that of his daughters. If he's prepared to defend you, you can do anything."

Asma comes into the room; the Egyptian TV show she has been watching is over. She says she's been invited to a friend's birthday party tomorrow. How's she going to get there? What should she give him?

"I can feel her starting to lead her own life," Hala says once Asma has gone back into the living room. "She's like me: she's open, she talks to everyone, she'd rather play with boys. I want to allow her her freedom, but I'm also afraid, because I don't know how to protect her. Who will stand up for her if she makes decisions that aren't socially acceptable? There's no man around to defend her the way my father defended me."

We hear someone bumping around in the living room, Tété and Salim have come home. We scramble to put the photo albums back in the cupboard. Tété turns out to be in an excellent mood; Salim is watching TV – his expression, as usual, reveals nothing.

"It's all arranged," chuckles Hala once we're in the taxi home. Before long, Salim and Tété will ask for the girl's hand; Hala will go with them.

"Why you?"

"Do you think the two of them could pull off a successful marriage proposal? Salim is capable of being so woolly that it would sound like he wasn't interested at all! And my mother –

you know what could happen with her."

"What?"

"She might spend the whole evening talking about Wadi al-Nakhleh!"

❖

I've prepared myself for this for days. I've been revolving around Hala in ever-widening circles, looking for landmarks. This morning I severed the thin cord which bound me to her since my arrival. I'm ill at ease. In one fell swoop the streets of Damascus have lost their intimacy; I'm in a strange city again, and I'm not sure where Hala fits into it.

This morning I waited for a taxi at the corner of our little street. I could feel the appraising glances of the cigarette sellers; I wanted to get away from them so badly that I climbed pell-mell into a white car that turned out not to be a taxi. Taxis are yellow, I knew that, didn't I? I remembered Hala's stories about crime in Damascus – a taxi driver murdered by two villagers for two hundred pounds – but the boys in the white car were nice. They were just cruising around, I think, and they brought me right to the entrance to the *souq*.

I walk under the panoramic painting of Assad, heading resolutely for the herb *souq* to look for saffron for Tété. "Welcome, madam, welcome!" I wave aside the merchant who stands at the door of his shop, trying to draw me in. Then I see the Bedouin dress dangling above his head; a trapdoor opens in my mind and I tumble back to my very first visit to Damascus. Kamal bought me a dress like that. We had taken a taxi from Beirut, a two-and-a-half-hour drive. It was 1974 – the civil war in Lebanon had not yet begun. After Beirut with its French cafés and seaside restaurants, Damascus was a closed city full of Eastern secrecy. At the Grand Hotel we had to sleep on different floors. Corridors like in a cloister and, at the beginning of each passageway, guards to keep us from going to each other's rooms. That puritanism in a hotel – yet out on the street the men pinched my bottom.

Grand Hotel! Kamal and I laughed about it for years. In Beirut we lived together in an apartment; here they treated us like naughty children. The hotel must be close by. That's Merjeh Square. There, on the corner, could that be . . .? It's called the New Omayyad Hotel now and it's been renovated in Eastern style, with little wooden balconies and a spacious entrance.

All the hotels around the square have posters of Khomeini hanging on their facades: since relations between Syria and Iraq have been broken off, the love for Iraq's archenemy, Iran, has blossomed. The city is full of Iranian visitors: women in black *chadors* and pious men in spotless gowns. They move around in groups, go shopping in the *souq* and visit the Shi'ite mosques and monuments in and around Damascus.

But besides Iranian pilgrims, I also see a lot of Gulf Arabs on the square – the men responsible for the fact that Salim still hasn't been able to rent a car. Some of them have Syrian guides, who look particularly small and meek in their company. Everyone knows what the little Syrian fellow is for: he takes them to the bars, back rooms and whorehouses of Damascus.

Later on, in the palace of Pacha al-Azem, which is now a museum, I come across the Gulf Arabs who have brought their families. They walk around as though at home, completely at ease in robes through which knee-length Bermuda shorts can be seen, a ribbon of veiled women and children trailing along behind. They adjust their headscarves in the pacha's mirrors, while their wives crowd into the bridal suites. The familiar

71

scent of sandalwood wafts in my direction.

At a bookshop in the modern part of town, I buy a copy of *Le Monde*. The bookseller is sitting behind the cash register, reading a book by Jorge Amado. Hala has warned me to be careful with strangers, but we quickly become caught up in an animated conversation. One of the bookseller's friends comes in and joins in our conversation, and by the time I walk out the door I've been invited to the weekly gathering of a group of writers and poets at the Café Havana.

I walk in the direction of Tété's house, in good spirits. In Cairo I sometimes attended the literary salon of Naguib Mahfouz. So those things are going on here too! Why didn't Hala tell me about this? "There will probably only be men there," I said doubtfully when the bookseller's friend invited me. But he assured me that women were welcome too. Maybe I can take Hala.

Tété is pleasantly surprised when I open my bag and take out the saffron I bought in the *souq*. She clutches the brown cornet to her breast. How sweet of me to think of her!

Hala has already gone home. I'm secretly thankful to her: I have to learn how to explain to a taxi driver where I live. It's just getting dark when I climb out of the taxi. The cigarette sellers stand like a roadblock at the entrance to our street. The handsome boy with the leather jacket is there too. His friends nudge him when they see me coming, and I rush by, shyly. He calls out something to me – in French, not in Arabic. The whole street must have heard it. Trembling, I stick my key in the door.

The hall smells of soap. The bathroom door is open. Asma is lying in a plastic tub, talking to a whole family of bottles. It's one of her favorite games: every bottle has a name, just like her pillows. Hala is sitting on the couch in her nightgown. I put the day's trophies down on the table. When I tell her about the invitation to the Café Havana, Hala knits her brow: the Havana used to be a meeting place for Ba'ath Party ideologists. "I wouldn't go. It's crawling with *mukhabarat*, everyone would wonder who you were and what you're doing here."

"You think so?"

"Of course." And what about Hamid, the bookseller, I could trust him, couldn't I? "You never know. People with jobs like that often work for the *mukhabarat*."

A shadow passes over the last few hours. Was I careless? Did I tell Hamid things it would have been better to keep to myself?

"In other words, you can't trust anyone here," I say defiantly. "So how do you make friends, how do you meet new people?"

"The only people I trust are my family and the friends I've known since school," Hala says, "almost no one else has been added to that list."

I have to believe her, yet something gnaws at me. Isn't she being too fatalistic? Isn't she ruling out a lot of opportunities? The festive feeling I came home with is gone completely. I take the copy of *Le Monde* out of my bag and thumb through it, right to page six, which the index says contains the prospects for the Arab-Israeli peace talks in Madrid. But page six is gone, ripped out, sloppily. I knew the papers here were censored, but I'm still shocked. Who do they think they are? I want my money back! "Look at this!" But Hala only laughs: "The president does all our thinking for us," she says resignedly, "we've become used to that."

CHAPTER 2

"SHALL WE take a cruise ship to Egypt?" I got all wound up when Hala came home with the plan, and Asma was thrilled too. Via Turkey and Cyprus, and then on to Egypt – Asma immediately fetched the atlas. "How long does that take, Mama?"

"About ten days."

"And are we going to Cairo too?"

"No, no, the boat only stops at Alexandria."

"But I want to go to Cairo!" Cairo – that's where you can see the actors from the TV programs Asma watches every evening, just walking down the street.

"Why not? We'll jump ship and take the bus to Cairo." To Cairo with Hala, visiting the Hussein Mosque, walking together along the Nile, sitting at Café Fishawi . . .

"Have you ever been to Cairo?"

"No, never, but I've always wanted to go."

"Is there a swimming pool on the boat, Mama?" A swimming pool – Asma saw that one on 'Loveboat'.

"Tomorrow I'll go to the travel agency and ask for some more information, okay?"

The next day Asma maps it all out for me: we'll take a Transtour bus to Lattakia, because that's where the boat leaves from. Transtour is the best, she tells me, suddenly helpfulness itself: they give you a lunch packet and they even have TV. But when Hala comes home she doesn't say a word about our cruise. She's been with Salim and Tété to ask for the hand of his second cousin. She's spun the girl and her mother a whole line about Salim: what a serious young man he is, always caught up in his work and not in emotions – which was probably a reaction to his father, who he thought was a loafer. They wanted time to think about it.

"How much does that cruise cost?" I sound her out. "Do you think it's too expensive?"

Hala looks at me, smiling. "It's one of my projects. Maybe we'll do it sometime, but not right away."

"But Asma's all enthusiastic about it!"

Now Hala really has to laugh. "Asma's used to that. We're always making plans. Next week I'll say we're going to Beirut, then she can dream about that."

I should have known: with a bunch of dreamers like this, you never get anywhere. Hala is on vacation. "Maybe I'll write a novel," she says. A novel – come on! What about that big file full of unfinished stories she'd shown me a while ago? She'd flipped through the pile, sighing: long sheets of paper, feverishly filled on lonely mornings or evenings, but never completely worked out.

As we're lying on the bed that afternoon, it occurs to me that all our travels will probably take place within this room, amid these objects I've come to know by heart: the shelf of French books, the wardrobe with wedding presents and Ahmed's winter clothes. I even know the story behind the plastic bouquet on top

75

of the wardrobe: Hala got it from a Muslim Brother, one of Ahmed's fellow prisoners, who was released four years ago. She doesn't like plastic flowers, that's why she's never taken off the translucent foil, but she hasn't dared throw them away, either. Four years! "I bet Ahmed's mother would like them. I'll give them to her," she says. But I doubt that she ever will.

The next day Hala announces that we're going to the coastal town of Baniyas, and this time it looks like it will really happen. Sahar, a friend whose husband is also in prison, has gone on ahead with her daughter; she's going to rent a chalet for us.

Anyone seeing us walk down the street that morning would think we were going on a long trip. Hala and I are loaded down with suitcases and bags, we've brought our own sheets and towels because Hala says the ones in the chalets won't be clean. Asma is dragging a little blue suitcase on wheels; her soccer ball is hanging in a net over her shoulder.

We couldn't get tickets for the Transtour luxury bus; in summer, they're sold out days in advance. The station where the standard buses leave is a rush of activity, and long lines of people shuffle up to the tattered counters. Hala, small and nimble, cuts in line and returns triumphantly with tickets for the front seats in the *hob-hob* to Baniyas.

Once all the baggage has been loaded onto the roof of the gaily painted bus, the driver yanks on a tassel – just like the ones on old carousels at the fairground – producing the sound of a steam whistle. *Hoooot, hoooot!*

The driver has a towel wrapped around his neck and uses four different horns to chase cars out of our way. His honking is answered vehemently; we whiz onto the highway through a tunnel of echoing sound. The noise on the roads used to be so bad, Hala tells me, that it was forbidden to honk after four in the afternoon. "You should have seen the drivers! They used to blow whistles, flash their lights and pound sticks against their doors."

All the windows are open, and the wind rushes in. Ash from the smokers in the aisle blows all around us. "I'm always promising myself never to take the *hob-hob* again," Hala says, "but before I know it, here I am." A popular Egyptian tune booms through the bus. Asma, sitting at the window reading an Arab pop magazine, sings along mindlessly: "*Azz, azz, caboria, azz azz caboria.*" Hala can't explain what the song is about. '*Caboria*' is some kind of crab, she shudders. "If they'd just sing about something clean – but a crab, what a dirty animal!"

We've both brought along copies of *Seven Pillars of Wisdom* by T. E. Lawrence. Hala's is in Arabic and mine is in English, but we won't be doing much reading on this bus, I soon realize. This is a place for talking, laughing and sleeping.

"Look to the right," Hala whispers. An untidy village of shabby houses, children in torn clothes playing in the sand. "No, back there." High walls, light masts like the ones in a soccer stadium. "That's where Ahmed is." Just like on our walk past the blown-up birdhouse, I don't dare to look too obviously – the passengers have heard us speaking French, and no movement escapes their attention. I steal a glance at Asma. She's engrossed in an article about Madonna; we pass the prison without her looking up or around.

Behind the prison begins the vast desert that Hala, as a sociologist, came to know like the back of her hand. "The people there live like the first people on earth," she says. "They have nothing to say; they sit by the road and stare into space without moving. Twelve kilometers, that's how far a Bedouin woman sometimes has to walk with a jug on her head to reach the nearest well. When she gives birth, she squats above a hole she's dug in the sand. She takes the umbilical cord, severs it with a rock, puts the child on her back and walks on. I once asked a woman when she had last taken a bath. She didn't know what I was talking about – she didn't know the word 'bath'! When I kept asking, she told me she hadn't washed herself since her youngest son was born. And he was thirteen."

I tried to imagine Hala out there, a city girl with city fears – to think that she couldn't take a bath at night! – but with eyes that took in everything. "The wind blows through the desert," she says pensively. "It's all empty, as far as the eye can see. Except for pictures of Assad, of course."

"Do you think we'll ever go there together?"

"Why not? Not now, there are sandstorms – you couldn't see your hand in front of your face. We'd have to take a car, and a man to go along with us. If you stay long enough, we'll go for sure." But what's long? The experiences of the last few weeks have taught me that our sense of time differs considerably.

We're sitting right behind the driver, the seat of honor according to Hala; when she used to go into the hinterland, they always gave her this seat. Next to the driver, with his back to the windshield, sits the ticket-taker; against him leans an old man, his head wrapped in a thick woollen scarf, his long scruffy robe full of cigarette ash. Above him dangle the most improbable paraphernalia: little bells, plastic grapes and cherries, small pink teapots, verses from the Koran, photos of Assad, but also of the driver and his friends.

This is the first time we've left the family behind, and as soon as we arrived at the bus station I saw a change come over Hala. The way she got her hands on our tickets, the ease with which she talks and laughs with the bus driver in the rearview mirror –

she's obviously used to travelling. Just like at Tété's house, she's setting things aright here too: she scolds the driver for refusing to stop for two boys who are hitchhiking, flies to the rescue when a child chokes on its sandwich, gives a young man a rollicking for not standing up for an old woman. She calls him a Merjeh Square man, a dandy with no feeling for honor, someone who isn't worthy of carrying a weapon and fighting for his country. I'm rather amazed to hear that bit about the weapon and the country coming from her, but Hala assures me that she has touched him deeply and, indeed, it makes him stand up.

She seems to take all the world's suffering on her shoulders. Is this what happens to you when you're the oldest, when you've had to take care of your little brothers and sisters from the age of five? I was a middle child, I ducked out of such responsibilities. When there was a conflict, I sought shelter at Grandmother's. That was my salvation, I know – it made it easier for me to break free later on.

There is a lull in the conversation between Hala and the driver, and now he is thoughtfully rubbing a finger over his moustache and casting inquisitive looks in the rearview mirror. Two passengers have been leering at us in that same mirror all the way from Damascus. I recognize this masculine coquetry from Egyptian TV series, but in this setting it seems almost hilarious. With that towel around his neck, the driver looks like a boxer between rounds, and the two characters behind us in their dusty robes aren't exactly what you'd call attractive either.

Hala nudges me secretively. "Can you imagine what it was like when I travelled on my own?" Whenever she got off the bus with her suitcase in some remote part of the country, the people couldn't believe their eyes: a woman alone – this could only be a prostitute. She once took a late-night *hob-hob* back to Damascus. Christmas lights glowed among the tinkling chimes and bells, enveloping the inside of the bus in a veil of red. The driver had been on the road all day, so Hala began talking to him to keep him from nodding off. But the people around her misunderstood: the men began making lewd remarks, the driver threw her come-hither looks in the mirror and before long she was cast in the role of loose woman. The ticket-taker made tea for her and then took a kitten down from a compartment above the windshield. It had been in there for hours! He tried to give it to her, but she was upset and refused, so he held it on his own lap. He petted the little animal slowly, never taking his eyes off her.

"I was always pleased when my colleague, Zuhair, came along. Then we could take his car and I didn't have to worry about being harassed." But she had other problems with him. Zuhair would try to wangle something out of every plant manager or government official they met: a few yards of fabric, a load of wood. Things became even worse when Fathi, the photographer for the university paper, went along. He wasn't a real photographer – he got his job through connections. Every time he took a snapshot of someone, he stuck his finger in the air to indicate where his subject should look – it was a ridiculous sight, and it didn't make the pictures any better. Once, after they had travelled two hundred kilometers, he discovered that he'd forgotten his camera.

One day the three of them had to go to the official opening of the Assad Dam, in a part of the country where she and Zuhair had been doing their research. "This is your chance to finally take a good picture," Hala told Fathi. She was thinking of a picture of Assad with the dam in the background, but by the time Assad arrived, Fathi had vanished. When they went down into the machine hall, he was still nowhere to be seen. Suddenly he popped out from behind a turbine – an extremely dangerous move, as the grounds were crawling with *mukhabarat* – stuck his finger in the air and took a close-up of the president! Hala laughs. "You see how I'm surrounded by idiots?"

During the reception afterwards, Zuhair was able to worm his way up to the president. The *mukhabarat* collared him right away, but Assad gestured to them to let him go and said: "He who arrives at the house of Abu Soufian is saved." Abu Soufian was the ruler of the most important tribe at the time of the Prophet.

"What can I do for you, my son?" Assad asked once they were alone.

Zuhair complained that he lived above a brothel, and that customers often rang the bell when his wife was home alone. That same evening he received a check for the down payment on another house.

After he had moved into his new house, Zuhair travelled to his hometown, Aleppo, requested an appointment with the mayor and informed him of his plans to become a member of parliament. The mayor laughed enigmatically. "You have to find the key first," he said. Zuhair didn't know what he was talking about. Key, what key? A friend who worked for the *mukhabarat* laughed in his face. "Jackass, he means you need at least a hundred and fifty thousand pounds to pay the bribes." Zuhair didn't have that much money, but he did have the presence of mind to go back to the mayor and tell him that he lived above a brothel in Damascus, and that his wife . . . Before long he had a house in Aleppo as well.

Zuhair once accompanied Hala on a trip to the oil fields in the north-eastern corner of Syria, close to the Iraqi border. Six thousand men worked there – not a single woman. The university didn't want to let her go at first, and her mother said she shouldn't bother coming home afterwards, but Hala persevered. She was twenty-three, she remembers it exactly. They put her up in an abandoned villa where Russian delegations usually stayed, far from the workers' camp and three hundred meters from the house where Zuhair was sleeping.

She wasn't used to being alone at night – at home she shared a room with Shirin and Zahra – but this haunted house straight out of Hitchcock beat everything. It was in the middle of a wood with grotesquely shaped trees, the corridors echoed and when she walked to her room on the second floor that night she saw that the bathroom window of frosted glass, still in one piece that afternoon, now lay shattered on the ground. She sat down on the bed, her heart pounding. What should she do? She could expect no help from Zuhair – he had drunk so much *araq* that they'd had to carry him to bed.

It was May; a storm was blowing and the branches outside rattled against the window panes. Wasn't that a door opening downstairs? Footsteps in the hall, on the stairs. A chair being shoved up to the bathroom window. Then all was quiet, deathly quiet. A little later the footsteps retreated.

Should she inform Abu Talib, the old caretaker? But he would definitely report the incident to the university, and she would never be allowed to travel to the east again. A little later she heard more footsteps in the hall. Again it sounded as if someone were climbing up onto a chair. She sat on the bed, shaking with fear. Once the footsteps had died away, she resolutely pulled on her red jacket and hood and walked outside, heading for Abu Talib's house.

Meanwhile a thunderstorm had begun. Rain whipped across

her face and low-hanging branches lashed her cheeks. Somewhere in the distance a faint light was burning – that was where she had to go. She heard a rustling behind her. A flash of lightning revealed the outline of a man pressed convulsively up against a tree. "Abu Talib?" The old caretaker came out of hiding, shamefaced, caught red-handed, every bit as soaked as she. They walked together in silence, towards his house. But what was there left for her to do there? The only sensible thing was to walk on to the supervisor's house. But what would happen to Abu Talib then? That afternoon she had heard that he had recently become a widower, and that he took care of his children alone. Acting on impulse, she turned around, mumbled 'Good night' and went back to the villa.

That night she slept with her clothes on, but the footsteps never came back. She saw Abu Talib again at breakfast. She felt sorry for him. He was sixty – an old man who had hoped to assuage his loneliness by peeking at a naked woman taking a bath. If she told anyone what had happened, he would be fired on the spot.

A year later she went back to the oil fields. Abu Talib was still there, and this time he cared for her like a father. In every gesture, every look, she could feel how grateful he was that she had not betrayed him.

Hala has been telling her story nonstop. Now she looks at me. "You prod my memory," she says, "I had forgotten all about that." In the distance, a monumental building with a broad drive rises up from the monotonous landscape. The village behind radiates an uncommon prosperity. Across the road, on top of a bare peak, stands a gigantic statue of Assad. His hand is raised in a papal gesture – as if he were wishing us a safe trip.

"What's that?"

"That's Deir Attieh, the birthplace of Abu Salim, Assad's private secretary," Hala says. He handles the business contacts with America; some people whisper that he is selling Syria to the Americans. The soil in Deir Attieh is barren and there is no local industry, but the village has blossomed thanks to Abu Salim's rising star. All the sons of Deir Attieh have studied abroad, and government subsidies flow in this direction. As an expression of thanks, Abu Salim erected a statue to Assad. "It's guarded at night," Hala says. "They're afraid someone will try to destroy it."

This is just like Africa, I muse. Zaïre's President Mobutu had an international airport built in his mother's hometown of Gbadolite; Houphouët-Boigny, the president of the Côte d'Ivoire, had a life-sized replica of St Peter's Cathedral built in Yamoussoukro, the village where he was born. But even African businessmen or professors who live in the city feel obliged to share their riches with the members of their tribe who stayed behind. In large parts of Africa, the idea of being a nation is still so fragile that people are quick to fall back on their own tribe.

And isn't that exactly how it is here? *Seven Pillars of Wisdom*, T. E. Lawrence's account of how he fought along with the Arabs against the Turkish oppressors during the First World War, teems with tribal conflict. As soon as the British looked the other way, the Arabs forgot about their common foe and locked horns. Without the help of the British, they would never have succeeded in driving out the Turks. Yet I've never heard this from a single Arab. They only talk about the treachery that followed: about the secret Sykes-Picot Agreement, by which the British and the French divided the Middle East among themselves, rather than giving the Arabs the independence they'd been promised; about the Balfour Declaration, by which the Jewish people were given a national home in what would later become Israel.

It's difficult to talk about these things with Hala. She still clings to the dream of Arab unity, even though that ideal has become badly tarnished. She can tell delightful stories about the childish behavior of Arab leaders: Saddam Hussein never travels without his own chair, and Assad always sends his own car out ahead of him; the two men had a final falling out, she says, after Hussein had Assad's baggage searched at Baghdad airport. Emir al-Sabah of Kuwait became so enraged during a dinner of the Arab League in Cairo that he began throwing crockery and seriously wounded someone.

During our first walk through Damascus we passed the defunct offices of Iraqi Airways; the steel shutters had been sloppily lowered, and the electric sign with its green emblem hung crookedly on its hinges. The way that building stood there dying – it immediately reminded me of Africa, of wrecked airplanes in the *brousse*, of trees struck by lightning. Hala followed my gaze. "We need economic contacts that can stand up to our leaders' bickering," she sighed.

But when it comes right down to it, she never situates the enemy in the Arab camp. America, Israel – those are the evildoers out to liquidate the Arab world. And yet the stories she tells show that the enemy is much closer than that, that the problems are also to be found within this society itself. The way President Assad granted a favor to her colleague Zuhair – that feudalism wasn't imposed by America, was it? And doesn't she depend on the same kinds of favors? At a reception, she once saw the Minister of Education – the minister of the tribe of scientists, her minister! – surrounded by a swarm of people. Her mind raced feverishly: what could she ask of him? She quickly scribbled a request for a telephone on a piece of paper and asked him to sign it.

"It still took six years for me to get the phone," she confided, "but that was because I didn't have any other *wasta*." A *wasta* is the clout every Syrian needs to get ahead. Hala even needed a *wasta* to buy a propane tank for Tété's apartment in Wadi al-Nakhleh.

❖

In Homs, Syria's crossroad where all buses stop, I'm about to buy a soft drink, a milky white substance billed as Bitter Lemon, when Hala stops me in horror. "Not that stuff! You'll get typhoid!" She goes off looking for cans of Canada Dry – that's safer.

"You wouldn't believe how often I got sick in the country-side," she says. Once, when she was out with a farmer in his field in the burning sun and said she was thirsty, the man scooped up a cup of water from the nearest ditch. "What was I supposed to say? That I wasn't thirsty after all?" Or the time she was invited to dinner and saw how the woman of the house washed her cucumbers and tomatoes in a creek where sheep were standing. But when the same woman was getting ready to peel an onion, her husband yelled indignantly: "Put away those onions, quick! Damascenes don't eat that!"

Asma and I succumb to temptation and buy ice-cream cones in flashy pink wrappers. After the first bite we look at each other in disgust. The cones are stale, the ice cream tastes burned. We both head off straight to the trash can.

An hour later we've reached the Mediterranean. Green-houses, olive trees and cornfields surround little houses with rooftop terraces shaded by grape arbors. I recognize this landscape from Lebanon, just a few kilometers to the south. Small boys stand along the road, making rolling gestures – they're selling car tires that come from Lebanon. A lot of smugglers live in this area; donkeys loaded with illegal cargo trot back and forth through the mountains at night. Throughout the years, many lives have been lost in the fighting between rival gangs.

But the real smuggling began only after the start of the Lebanese civil war in 1975. When one of President Assad's cousins zips along from Beirut to Lattakia with a caravan of eight Mercedes with heavily tinted windows, he's not supposed to encounter any difficulties at the border. Top military officials sometimes 'buy' the border crossing for a few hours: they pay the customs officials a hefty sum of money to clear the way for army trucks full of contraband coming from Lebanon.

Cars, foreign cigarettes, alcohol, car parts and electrical equipment – until recently these were virtually impossible to buy in a Syria built according to the socialist model, and they are therefore in great demand. It's an open-and-shut system: the regime creates shortages and then sees to it that its loyal supporters can smuggle the missing products into the country. Yet this very system came close to costing the regime its head – the weapons the Muslim Brothers used during the uprising in Hama probably entered the country in the same way.

Hala went to Lebanon one time, with a group of sociologists. Her colleagues bought TV sets, stereo equipment, video recorders and pornographic movies; they were amazed that Hala didn't want anything. When they came to the border, everyone got the jitters, but the customs officials saw the sign saying 'University of Damascus' and just waved them on through. "A little while after that, when the *mukhabarat* called me in to their offices again, my colleagues panicked," Hala says. "They thought I was going to turn them in!"

❖

Sahar and her twelve-year-old daughter Aisha are waiting for us on the main street of Baniyas. Sahar has bad news: there are no chalets for rent here. She has, however, discovered a campground with tents just outside Baniyas. She's been out there, and it didn't look too bad. A campground on the beach, in this blistering heat – I don't even want to think about it. In dismay, I plop down on our baggage, next to Asma. "Bedu, like Bedouins," I sigh.

"*Khaymah* – tent," she laughs. She's obviously more enthusiastic than I am.

Hala hesitates. "What do you think? Shall we give it a try?" I look at her dejectedly. "Isn't there a hotel here or something?" I'd been looking forward to a cool space where we could safely store our things. I feel ridiculous standing here with my Samsonite suitcase on this dusty sidewalk. Have I reached the age of thirty-eight just to end up like a tourist at a Syrian campground? And we didn't even bring camping gear!

It's a busy street, and we're blocking the sidewalk with our dawdling. "Let's take a taxi. If we don't like it we'll come back," Hala suggests. She sees my disgruntled expression and laughs: "Come on, this is an adventure! What are you going to do in a hotel room!" I'm amazed – during the past weeks she was the one who usually tried to talk me out of doing things. "I'm glad we brought sheets and towels," she says cheerfully. Somewhat reassured by her optimism, I shuffle along behind her. If there's no shower, she won't want to stay either.

But it all turns out just fine. The campground is built on a hillside with five terraces. Our tents are on the fourth terrace; we have a beautiful view of the swimming pool far below, the bay and the fishing boats bobbing in the distance. Music echoes up to us from the valley. The lives of at least twenty families unfold before us on the lower terraces: everywhere I see bossy Tétés, everywhere Zahras are busy doing dishes. A car is parked next to every tent, and the TVs have already been turned on.

Showers, toilets – Hala inspects everything. Then she starts organizing. Sahar and Aisha in one tent, the three of us in the other. Between the two tents is a canvas lean-to which she christens 'our cafeteria'. She calls in the campground supervisor and uses her position at the university to get us a groundsheet, tables and chairs. She sees my look, and laughs apologetically. "What do you expect, it's the only *wasta* I have!" In the past, when she would arrive somewhere and couldn't find a hotel room, she would phone the mayor and call him 'comrade'.

We're the only customers in the open-air restaurant on top of the hill. We eat grilled chicken with *mezze* – side dishes, dips and salads. They don't serve wine. Five women sitting at a long table loaded with food – this isn't the first time I've missed the company of men. Asma, who has been spending a lot of time with Hala's brother Salim, immediately makes friends with the restaurant owner. He takes her into the kitchen and shows her around. Hala watches from the corner of her eye. "I'm afraid Asma will fall in love with an older man later on," she says.

Once Aisha has finished eating, she goes into the kitchen too, leaving the three of us at the table. I had already met Sahar in Damascus. An unobtrusive woman in her early forties who teaches French at the university. She wears yellow beads around her neck, made in prison by her husband; Aisha is carrying a crocheted purse that I also recognize as prison handiwork.

Hala used to spend a lot of time with Sahar, but she confessed to me that it became boring. Sahar and her husband lived together for no more than three months before his arrest, but she spends all her free time with the wives of prisoners. She knows what her husband eats on New Year's Eve, when he's throwing a party and whether the *araq* he distills has turned out well. The first time I met her she had just started baking cookies for him. Two hundred of them, no less; Aisha had passed her exams and the event would be celebrated in the prison. I thought of the cake Ahmed had asked for, the one Hala refused to bake. The same yellow beads Sahar wears rather proudly are in a box in the cupboard at Hala's, along with the earrings, rings and bracelets Ahmed has given her. Only Asma sometimes carries in her pocket the palm-resin key ring, in which Ahmed has inlaid a lute of copper wire.

As the sun goes down and the first cool breeze of the day blows in, Sahar tells us about an ex-prisoner who visited her some time ago. He'd spent twelve years behind bars, and she was shocked when she saw him. He had once held an important position in his party, but now his movements were so shaky that he had to reach for his glass three times before he finally got ahold of it. "He couldn't get enough of the brightly lit streets, the well-stocked shops – he felt like he'd just arrived in Honolulu!" Most people only think about themselves when they're released, she says; they feel they've suffered enough. Some of them want to leave the country as soon as possible. France, England – it doesn't matter.

Hala is listening with one ear: she's peering off into the distance to where Asma and Aisha are talking to the restaurant owner in squeaky little voices. "Do you actually know what

Ahmed's prison looks like inside?" I ask her.

"More or less. He tells me about it sometimes." She picks up a piece of bread from the table and breaks it in two. "They sleep in bunks," she says. "Sometimes one of the men who sleeps on the bottom hangs a blanket in front of his bed, so it looks like he has a room of his own." A smile plays across her lips. "One of Ahmed's cellmates is a good cook. During Ramadan, he invites someone over to eat every evening. On the last day of Ramadan, they all put on their best clothes. 'I'd like to invite you to come by,' one of them will suggest, 'in, let's say, an hour.' And these are men who all live together in the same room! When they're invited for dinner they sit on each other's beds and carry on a conversation." She stares absently into space. "You can tell from their behavior that people need rituals. It's as though they're putting on little plays."

But they can also be hard on each other, she tells me. For four years, Ahmed slept in a bunk next to a man whose politics he didn't agree with; they never spoke a word. During the Gulf War, Ahmed argued with a friend; they've refused to talk to each other ever since.

"What did Ahmed think about the war? Whose side was he on?"

"His own side," Hala says brusquely. "Saddam Hussein was his absolute hero. Ahmed thought he would see to it that the oil fields were returned to Arab hands, rather than to the Americans, and then he would march into Syria and overthrow Assad." She laughs tiredly. "They're all a bunch of little Assads. If Ahmed's faction had come to power, who knows what things would be like – maybe a lot worse than they are now."

At first, some of them were members of the communist party led by Khaled Bakdash, who later joined the government coalition. When Bakdash began installing more and more family members in important posts, he lost some of his supporters. But dissension quickly rose within the splinter group as well; Sahar's husband and Ahmed belonged to competing factions. According to Hala, the conflicts were officially about Marxism-Leninism or Trotskyism, but that was often a front for personal conflicts of a much less lofty nature. If a woman had slept with an official from the other party, you'd hear later that she had lost her virginity to the competition!

All these political and personal intrigues were not so very different from what was happening at the same time in left-wing circles in Western Europe; the erstwhile opponents there, however, now hold positions of responsibility, while in Syria they were all arrested and imprisoned without any form of due process. Except for the communist Bakdash, who was willing to conform and can still be seen dragging his withered shanks up the steps of the parliament building.

The personal dramas didn't end when the *mukhabarat* moved in. One of Sahar's friends fell in love with a woman who lived in the house where he was hiding. He let his wife know that he wanted a divorce, but she refused. A few years later he was arrested, and she reported to the *mukhabarat* as his lawful wife; since then she visits him regularly.

Sahar tells us that two hundred Palestinian prisoners have just been released. Since the Gulf War, there have been rumors that Assad is going to release other political prisoners as well; now that Syria has sided with the Americans, the pressure from Western human-rights organizations will probably increase. "We're all just waiting," Sahar says. In the next few months she's planning to fix up her house and have the seamstress make dresses for her and Aisha.

"I'm not going to do anything until I'm sure Ahmed is coming home," Hala says. She doesn't like these conversations – I've noticed that before. Now she looks down at the scraps left on the table, then at us: "Are we finished? Shall I call Asma and Aisha?"

❖

Back at the campground, all TVs are tuned to the Egyptian series 'Layali al-Hilmiyyeh' – 'The Nights of Hilmiyyeh' – about family perils in a Cairo neighborhood; it's been the talk of Syria for weeks. The events in the living rooms where the series takes place differ little from what I see around me: visitors rush in and out with good or bad news, which is then endlessly talked about, wrangled over and discussed on the telephone.

When the neighbors notice that we haven't brought a TV, they spontaneously invite us to come over and watch. The bad news entering the Egyptian living room this evening is that Nasser has died. Asma and Aisha are stunned by the weeping and wailing that ensues. "Was Nasser an important person, Mama?" Asma whispers.

"Yes, very important."

Once the show is over, the music is turned on again. Most of the families sit in a wide circle in front of their tent; here and there people are dancing. Asma and Aisha are reading Arab pop magazines under the canvas lean-to; they talk about their favorite Syrian singer, Georges Wassouf, about Madonna's millions and Prince's empire.

"We know so much about the West," Sahar says, "we keep up with everything that happens there. But does that work the other way too? Do people in the West know what's going on here?" Her voice sounds slightly reproachful. Once the underlying indictment would have left me feeling guilty, but now I carefully say: "I wonder whether people here really do know so much about the West, and the same probably applies to people there." My father in Belgium and Tété in Damascus – what do they know of each other? There is a screen between them which they each look at from their own side.

"We all dreamed of Engelbert Humperdinck and Tom Jones when we were young," Sahar says.

Adamo, Joe Dassin, Richard Anthony – we have quite a few teen idols in common.

"Sylvie Vartan."

"Michel Polnareff!" We raise our voices, singing 'Poupée de cire, poupée de son', and try out a few other hits from the Eurovision song contest. Whiffs of the past waft by, of suntan lotion and freshly mown lawns. At home, our jukebox was kept in the gazebo in the garden, and in the summer the melancholy sound of 'Suzanne' mingled with the roar of the neighbors' lawn mower.

"And what about Leonard Cohen?" Sahar and Hala shake their heads. They've never heard of him. Sahar laughs: "But then he's got his name against him." It's always the same, I think, disappointed: somewhere, halfway, the curtains are drawn again and again.

Sahar tells us she ordered the *Larousse* dictionary not so long ago. The first volume came, the third one too, but the second volume never arrived; it contained the letter 'I', as in 'Israel'. "They should stop that nonsense," she says. "We're supposedly at war with Israel; we pay war tax and schoolchildren have had to wear paramilitary uniforms ever since 1956, but there's no war!"

I'm surprised. Hala always goes on the defensive whenever

Israel is mentioned, and her eyes are on red alert again now. "It's a sentimental problem," she says. "It's hard to accept that Israel exists; ever since we were young we've been taught that Palestine belongs to us."

"But times have changed," Sahar persists. "In 1967, I wanted to go and fight against Israel, just like the Palestinian *fedayin*, but I wouldn't do that anymore. The Palestinians have suffered a great deal, but so have the Jews. When Columbus discovered America, there were already boats full of Jews bobbing around on the sea."

Hala sighs. "Sometimes I think there should be peace too, but what kind of peace? When Sadat signed the Camp David Agreements with Israel, I wept. It was as though he'd gone to bed with a woman in public."

So far we've only bickered about this subject. I arrived here brimming over with the Arab-Israeli peace talks. In my enthusiasm I told Hala about *Arabesques*, a novel I'd just read by the Palestinian author Anton Shammas. Shammas grew up in Israel and wrote his book in Hebrew. Hala looked at me askance – a Palestinian who writes in Hebrew? "I knew someone like that once," she said. They had met at a party; he was a translator who lived in Switzerland. They wrote to each other for quite a while, and he called her every once in a while. "But one day I put a stop to it."

"Why?"

"I don't know, there was something strange about it, I didn't trust him. I think he was a spy."

"But why do you think that?"

"I can't explain. It was a feeling."

Irritated, I say nothing. Our discussions always stray into this kind of fuzziness. I can't understand her, she says, because I'm not an Arab. She's never heard of Israeli writers like David Grossman, who went to Egypt and the occupied territories to find out what makes the Arabs tick. The Israelis are faceless as far as she's concerned, and she wants to keep it that way. "You don't know what's happened here," she says, "the Syrians have often gone hungry because of the wars with Israel."

She was three when the Suez Conflict broke out and her mother sealed off all the windows with blue paper in case of aerial bombardments. Mothers had their little sons photographed in uniform, a short-barrelled rifle in their hands, grenades in their belt. During the Six Day War in 1967 she had to take care of Salim, Shirin and Zahra because her father was on alert and her mother was doing volunteer work, nursing wounded soldiers brought back from the front. After the war was over, Assad – Minister of Defence at the time – appeared on TV and said this defeat didn't mean they would lose the next war too.

In the years that followed, Hala's family never again took the car out on Friday afternoons: her father wanted to stay close to the phone, and he slept in the barracks more and more often. During the 1973 war, Hala was in the garden when she heard a tremendous explosion. All the windows in the house shattered and it was as though her body was being crumpled. A bomb had exploded not far from their house, and there were bodies lying in the street. The cat, paralyzed with fear during the bombardment, crept around skittishly for days afterward.

Her memories of those wars are just like her readings of Sartre and Camus: she talks as though nothing has happened since. Even the Gulf War did nothing to shake her from her dream. Although I came somewhat prepared, I'm shocked by the depth of her suspicion and ignorance.

I tell her about the Syrian KLM ground hostess I met in

Damascus. During one of its flights, KLM lost eight of its passengers' suitcases. One day a telex came in: 'Good morning, this is Tel Aviv'. The suitcases turned out to be in Israel! The hostess called the Ministry of Transport in a panic, and they advised her to act as though nothing had happened. The telex messages from Israel kept rolling in, but she didn't respond. She told me this in a triumphant tone, as though she had performed an act of heroism.

"I wouldn't have answered either," Hala says. "Did you know it's a punishable offence to have contact with an Israeli? If I went to Paris tomorrow and met an Israeli there, I could count on the *mukhabarat* interrogating me when I came back. Assad talks about peace with the Israelis, but on TV they still call them 'the Zionist foe'. We should talk about these things; let people discuss the issues, let them find out whether their ideas are right or not. But we have to whisper about everything. No one asks us what we think – they'll make a peace that has nothing to do with us."

She sighs wearily and peers off into the distance, where a fishing boat is flashing a weak red beacon. "Sadat broke the window between Israel and the Arab world," she muses. "Through that broken window, the Egyptians can look to the other side, but do they see much? Are they so much better off?"

Sahar doesn't reply, and I too realize that it's best to be silent. I know how this goes with Hala – from now on she'll stick to her own ideas. Behind us, Asma and Aisha are still talking and laughing, their legs in the air. Hala glances at her watch. "It's getting late. Shall we go to bed?"

But once we're lying in the tent, we can't sleep. I'm angry at Hala, for her refusal to think about the changes coming to this part of the world. All those false heroics, all those lost wars – how long will it

97

go on? At the same time, I try to think up excuses for her intransigence. She's against this government's politics – that's why she doesn't want to hear about the peace talks. And how can she alter her opinions if everyone keeps talking about the Zionist foe?

The Egyptian pop music blares away down below us. *Matkhafish, ana mabahib tani* – Don't be afraid, I don't love another. How can everyone, from grandmother to grandchild, listen to this nonsense?

But even after the music has stopped I hear Hala rolling and sighing.

"What's wrong?"

At first I think she didn't hear me, then she whispers: "I'm afraid."

"Of what?"

"Of when Ahmed comes home." And I thought she was fretting about Israel! She rolls over onto her back, her arms crossed behind her head. In the yellowish light of the moon I try to make out her face, her small nose, her deep-set eyes. Behind her Asma lies rolled up happily in a little ball.

"If my father was still around, he'd help me."

"But what are you afraid of?"

"I don't love him anymore." The words remain hanging in the air, still pulsing in the wake of the Egyptian pop music. *Matkhafish, ana mish nasiki* – Don't be afraid, I won't forget you.

"I already knew that," I say.

She turns her head towards me, and I see her eyes glisten for a moment, surprised.

"At least, I thought as much." Her gloom when she came back from visiting Ahmed, the letter she left unread for days, the way she reacted when Sahar began talking about the prison – every time the subject of Ahmed is brought up, I feel her creep into her shell. "Eleven years! I'm amazed you've kept it up this long, I would have called it quits a long time ago."

"But you can't do that here! Didn't you see how Sahar is? And that's the way they all are." She tries to meet my eyes in the dark. I'd like to reach out to her, but I don't dare. She's so physically aloof – the only person she touches is Asma.

"You know what my father said on his deathbed?" Her voice is sad. "That he hadn't raised me to be a prisoner's slave." It was only when her father became ill that she realized how much he meant to her. The months leading up to his death were dark ones; there was nothing more to look forward to. For years she'd lived like she was wrapped in a cocoon, closed off to all emotions, and suddenly the wall she had built around her was breaking. She cried for days on end – she didn't know she had been saving up so much sorrow – and because of that sorrow, it was as though she had awakened from her narcosis. She wanted to be touched again, comforted, loved.

During a reception, an older colleague laid his hand on her shoulder. She hardly knew him; he was not an attractive man, his hand was big and rough, but she began to dream about him. In the days that followed, when she walked down the street she felt like a soldier who stares hungrily at women.

During an exhibition of the work of an artist friend, she met Firas – a painter. They talked, went out to dinner. She fought against it for weeks, but finally there was no getting around it: she was in love.

Firas – I should have known. He calls her sometimes. Asma always sits listening, on the edge of her chair. They're difficult conversations; I often hear Hala agitatedly shout, "*Khalas* – it's over."

"It's a disaster," she says.

"Why?"

"Feelings are something to be ashamed of in this society. Love is something to be ashamed of. Can you imagine how people talk about us? They say: see what the communists' wives do while their husbands are in prison?"

"Does Ahmed know about it?"

"I was afraid he'd hear it from someone else, so I told him myself." It's quiet for a moment. "Do you know what he did? He sent his brother Rashid after him. Rashid threatened to slit his throat if he didn't stop right away."

She sighs. "The big monster who rules us has turned everyone into a little monster." But then she seems to reconsider. "Maybe I've got it wrong, maybe all those little monsters actually created that big monster."

Asma rolls over in her sleep, as if she senses what we're talking about, and throws an arm around her mother. "I can't stand to think that Ahmed might walk into my house one day and act as if nothing has happened," Hala whispers. "My feelings for him have changed, he's become a friend, but he can't accept that." He only fell in love with her in prison, she says, because she's the only woman he sees. He recently asked her to buy a red see-through dress when he comes back, for their evenings alone. That's the sort of thing Rashid is interested in, not the Ahmed she used to know.

"And what about Firas?"

"He gave me *Love in the Time of Cholera*, by Gabriel García Márquez. He says he'll love me for as long as the old man in that book. But it's impossible; it can't be, it's not allowed."

"Why not?"

"Ahmed will take Asma away from me."

I hadn't thought of that: when a couple divorces here, the father automatically obtains custody of any children above the age of nine. "But he's in prison, where would she go?"

"To his family. You've been there, can you imagine what would happen? They'd give her food and drink, like a donkey – nothing else. They'd ruin everything I've tried to do."

"But don't they have any ambitions for their children?"

She laughs scornfully. "You don't have to go to school to saw wood."

But even if her affair with Firas was over, she wouldn't want to go back to Ahmed, she says defiantly. She no longer wants to be a prisoner's wife. She'd always said: the *mukhabarat* are not going to rule my life; but they have anyway. "Eleven years on your own – can you imagine how hard that is?"

Asma is awake. She pulls Hala to her. "Go to sleep, Mama. Come on, let's go to sleep." Hala caresses her hair, and talks to her softly. Then everything is still.

I no longer have a clear picture of Ahmed, I realize. The driven young man I once met has been replaced by the proud-looking man in the tinted photo in his parental home, and now I see him in his tracksuit behind the mesh barrier in the visitor's room, looking at the woman who no longer belongs to him. I can imagine his feeling of helplessness, his despair now that all he has left threatens to slip from his grasp, his attempts to curb her freedom. But then – if he had been in her shoes, wouldn't he have done the same? And who would have blamed him?

❖

The morning sun pricks through the canvas. I creep out of the tent; the campground is enveloped in a deep calm. I feel racked – as though I'd spent the whole day yesterday hanging in a jungle gym.

Could it come from the shaky *hob-hob*? And was that only yesterday? It feels as though we've been travelling for an eternity.

Seven Pillars of Wisdom under my arm, I walk downhill towards the bay. My head is full of cotton, even though I didn't drink at all yesterday. Walking down the steps to the beach, snatches of last night's dream come back to me. The baby I was carrying in an earlier dream was now no longer wrapped in plastic. I held it against me and felt infinitely comfortable with it – it was a part of me staring back. It's because of Asma, I suppose. The question of what my life would have been like if I had become a mother like Hala must be playing around in my head, even though I'm hardly aware of it during the day.

I think about last night's conversation. What if Ahmed did have Asma taken away? Would he and Hala still be together if he hadn't been arrested, or would he have asked for the divorce he was planning? Did he really want to have Firas murdered, or was it only a threat? And then he says I should write about freedom! But which freedom? For Hala, there's never been any difference between political and personal freedom; that's why, after all these years and despite all our differences, I still feel a bond with her.

On the beach, so deserted yesterday that Hala called it 'our private beach', a large family is sitting on a rug, eating breakfast. I have my bathing suit on under my clothes, but I suddenly feel shy – the picnickers don't look like tourists, more like people from around here. I sit on the beachside terrace, waiting for the others. The loudspeakers are blaring Fayruz, much too loudly for this time of the morning. Everything here always has to be drowned out by noise, I think irritatedly.

Over the top of my book I watch the group on the beach. A fat matron in a yellow floral dress is making tea on a little burner;

someone else is passing out bread. Two women have stood up and are walking slowly towards the water. Their feet get wet, the hems of their dresses too, but that doesn't seem to bother them. They walk further into the sea, squat down and drop to their knees; the water is drawn up into their clothing like the dark liquid in a thermometer. A bit later they're lying in the surf like beached fish, letting the waves roll over them. The others just go on eating, biting into hard-boiled eggs, tearing off pieces of bread and dunking it in their tea.

Asma and Aisha come along – bashful little nymphs looking very naked in their bikinis. They hesitate when they see the rustic scene on the beach, and then patter over to the far end of the beach where the rocks begin, followed by the curious stares of the children on the rug.

In *Seven Pillars of Wisdom*, Lawrence has just arrived in Syria, which extended at that time all the way from Jerusalem to Beirut. Once it would ı ever have occurred to me to read a book by a white Englishman – a soldier, no less! – about this region. He may have been Lawrence of Arabia, the romantic hero who fought on the Arab side, but he was also the man bound up with the betrayal that followed, a treachery of which the Arabs have always complained.

But now I read him with pleasure, and some passages are actually straight from my own heart. His characterizations of the Syrians secretly delight me, making me realize again and again how little has changed. The Syrians' blindness to their own lack of importance in the world, their discontent with every regime, their inability to agree on an alternative.

When Hala comes down, she has the Arabic translation of *Seven Pillars of Wisdom* with her. I'd like to hear more about what she told me last night, but her look is so dark that I instinctively keep my mouth shut. "Are you already at the chapter about Syria?" I ask.

"Let's see, where is it?" She leafs through the book, searching. The eight pages about Syria have been condensed to one in her edition. Incredulous, we compare the lengths of other chapters and discover that sizeable cuts have been made throughout. My copy has seven hundred pages, hers just over two hundred. All of Lawrence's second thoughts about his dubious role as a British soldier, all the descriptions of tribal conflicts along the way, are missing from the Arabic version. "Now I know why I thought the book was so boring," Hala says, "my version only talks about battles!"

In the distance, Asma is floating in an inner tube; her soccer ball bobs along happily beside her. Hala slams the book shut, wades out to Asma and leaves me behind in a daze. No problem overcoming the desire to read around here!

Sahar comes over to me, a mischievous twinkle in her eye. "Have you seen how the women here swim?" The matron in the yellow flowered dress has now entered the water as well – even her headscarf is wet. "Brrr, all that soaking-wet underwear, I don't even want to think about it," Sahar shivers. She grew up in Lattakia, the biggest town on the coast. Her grandmother used to have a special white dress to wear when she went into the sea, but no one was allowed to look. "I don't understand it, especially not that old woman," she says. "If you're so puritanical, you're better off staying on the beach."

Three village women are walking across the rocks, picking their way uneasily in plastic slippers. They're wearing long dresses, and their heads are covered too. Now they stand still, sniff up the briny sea air and stare inquisitively at the fat women in the waves, at Asma and Aisha playing with their soccer ball.

The matron has come out of the water; her wet clothes reveal her figure so sharply that she seems naked. Sahar sniffs in disapproval. "See what I mean?"

The only man in the group, an old gentleman in trousers and a jacket, stands watching from the shoreline. His trouser legs are already wet, and when he squats down to roll them up, his coat-tails become soaked as well. The two other women rise up from the water, and the group gradually readies itself for departure.

Only the old man remains behind. Once all the women have disappeared, he carefully takes off his shoes, his coat, his trousers and his boxer shorts, and goes into the water in a long undershirt. We watch him with growing amazement; now that his rank and file have gone, he acts as though he's alone, as if Hala, Sahar and I aren't sitting here with nothing else to look at but his skinny body floating in the water. There's something bobbing along beside him – a plastic bag that looks like it's attached to him by a tube. Sahar squints hard. "I think he's got problems with his prostate," she says.

Once the man has had enough of swimming, he takes an exasperatingly long time to put on his clothes, stuffs the plastic bag into his underpants, rolls up the rug that's still lying on the beach, tosses it over his shoulder and walks off, without giving us a single look – like an actor who has put on a performance and then carries his props off stage. We look at each other and burst into laughter.

❖

I've become reconciled to our campsite by now. We read, eat, hang around on the beach, ogle the inhabitants of Baniyas. But that evening Asma says she's sick of it. I'm amazed: wasn't she the one who wanted to sleep in a tent? Having taken a better look, she doesn't like it here. Every time she goes swimming she has to walk down five flights of stairs. "There isn't even an elevator to the beach!" she protests. Sahar wants to visit a girlfriend in Qadmus, a mountain village close to Baniyas, and invites us to go along.

The next morning we're back in busy downtown Baniyas. It's a long walk to where the taxis leave for Qadmus – five women marching with suitcases and bags under a burning sun. "I'll grow old alone," Hala sighs, "dreaming of a man who carries my bags."

"Your time will come," I console her.

"That's what you think. Do you know who a woman my age can marry? A sixty- or seventy-year-old man. He'd just stumble along beside me while I carry *his* bags!" A few years ago, one of her father's friends said, shaking his head: "What's going to become of you?" He was a widower – it was a thinly veiled marriage proposal. Hala said she wasn't planning to get a divorce, upon which he turned his attentions to Shirin. "My mother would have been happy if he had asked her to marry him. People would have said: oh good, Shirin finally found someone." She walks next to me, defiant. "I want to forget the last eleven years. I can't accept the fact that I'm going to be alone for the rest of my life, I have to fight it."

The driver of an old Chevrolet is willing to take us to Qadmus for a reasonable price. A trip inland, into the mountains – a fertile region of olive trees and orange groves. Around the turn of the century, many people from this area left to work in South America – like the family of Carlos Menem, the president of Argentina. But most of them came back. They drink maté and say '*gracias*' instead of the Arabic '*shukran*'.

Windows rolled open, wind in our hair. At the Valley of Hell, a terrifyingly deep ravine, we stop to take a picture. Everyone laughs, including the taciturn driver – the holiday feeling is starting to take hold.

Sahar's girlfriend's house is on the main street in Qadmus. She has a daughter too, so now there are seven women. Sahar and Hala put on their nightgowns, and the children flop down in front of the TV – I feel completely at home again. Out on the balcony I peer into the heart of the village. The inhabitants of Qadmus are Ismailis, a Shi'ite sect that withdrew into the mountains centuries ago. The village up the road is inhabited by Alawites; we are close to the area where Assad was born.

They turn off the water here three days a week, and there's electricity for only a few hours a day. Damascus often has shortages as well, but rationing is much tighter outside the city. In more remote villages there's no water at all; their supplies come from tanker trucks that drive up and down.

Rana, a neighbor who's heard that there are visitors from Damascus, rings the bell. She's about eighteen: her childlike face is heavily made-up and her pitch-black hair piled high, making her look like a birthday package in her canary-yellow dress – a strange contrast with the sobriety the village radiates when seen from the balcony. She speaks a few words of English, looks at me and gushes: "You are beautiful."

Once she's left, Hala makes an ugly face. Rana belongs to the Futuweh, the young pioneers of the Ba'ath Party. "Another of those ideas Assad brought back with him from North Korea," she grumbles. We regularly see the youngest pioneers, the Talaeh, on TV. The little girls wear white bridal gowns; they wave little flags and sing in high, pathetic voices while the president – framed in a heart-shaped insert – floats across the screen and waves to them approvingly. Rana has already won two prizes for the poems and stories she writes. Hala doesn't have to read them to know how saccharine sweet they are. "And now she wants to become a writer and asks me for advice. What am I supposed to tell her?"

"To read a lot," I suggest.

Hala laughs. "But what if the only thing she reads are the writings of Assad?" Rana's mother is very active in the Ba'ath Party and pushes everything her daughter does. She's taught her to flatter the world around her – Hala also got to hear how beautiful she is. Hala has no trouble imagining Rana getting a job with a magazine in Damascus and assuming a position of responsibility within a few years. That epitomizes the country's mood: the more you idolize the Party, the greater your chances of success. She's seen it happen so often: young women who came to work for a company with no knowledge of the business at all and who now run the show. They have affairs with government officials, are picked up from work in black Mercedes, and talk about clothes all day. "Great shoes! Where did you get them?" "Beirut." "Expensive?" "Naw . . . two thousand five hundred pounds, I think." "Oh, not bad!" Hala wonders where the money comes from – they only earn two thousand pounds a month! Are they working as prostitutes?

"I've seen so many people change, people who used to have ideals," she says. "Most of them are bound to the regime by small favors. The price of a man isn't high: offer him the prospect of a car and he stops thinking. I can understand it, but I can't accept it."

At dusk we take a walk through the village. The streets that were so deserted this afternoon are now full of people. Peanuts are being roasted in huge pans of hot sand; young men on motorcycles sit at the intersection, waiting for passengers – it's the only taxi service in the area. Shops are nothing more than a hole in the wall with a steel shutter that's closed at night. The assortment of goods for sale is limited, but there are huge piles of sanitary napkins everywhere: Aziza, Delilah, Leila. According to Hala there was a shortage of sanitary napkins for years in Syria, until everyone came up with the idea of producing them at the same time.

Along the way we run into Rana with two of her girlfriends. They're eating *bizr* from paper sacks; they stop to greet us and then shyly walk on. I suddenly feel sorry for her, and I can understand her mother's passion for the Ba'ath Party – it's probably the only chance to escape from such a remote corner of the country.

After we've walked for a while, I realize that I haven't seen a single photo of Assad. Our hostess smiles knowingly. "That's right," she says. Qadmus is devoted to Assad's brother Rifa'at, who set up a charity for the poor here a few years ago. Rifa'at is in exile in France, but his followers have made a great many promises to the local population; some of them remain secretly true to him and await his return.

The story of Assad and his brother Rifa'at would surely have provided T. E. Lawrence with material for a fascinating chapter: it's a textbook example of the machismo which reigns in these mountains. Rifa'at, Assad's younger, rebellious brother, was given command over a special army unit in the 1970s and became increasingly powerful. He especially had it in for the Muslim Brothers. When Assad barely escaped an assassination attempt in 1980, Rifa'at sent his troops to the Tadmor prison in the desert, where they took revenge by shooting down more than a thousand Muslim Brothers.

Rifa'at was extremely popular with the young people he trained in parachuting and other paramilitary activities. Not long after the massacre at Tadmor, Hala was going home in a bus when a group of girls in paramilitary clothing stormed on. A bit later the bus was filled with the frightened shrieking and howling of women whose veil or headscarf was being yanked off. The girls had received instructions from Rifa'at; during the next few days, they sowed panic throughout Damascus.

The way those women were attacked – Hala talks about it with horror. In her neighborhood, Rifa'at's campaign generated enormous aggression. Men who weren't fundamentalists at all suddenly announced that they were prepared to shoot to defend their women, and from that moment on the women began veiling themselves more heavily. Close to her live four women who she sometimes sees driving by in their car. They're wrapped up like mummies. The woman at the wheel wears black gloves, holds the tips of her headscarf between clenched teeth and never goes without sunglasses. You never used to see things like that.

Rifa'at and his men became increasingly lawless, and a power struggle with Assad soon flared up. While Assad was lying in a completely weakened state in hospital in 1983, Rifa'at's supporters spread out through Damascus and replaced all posters of the president with those of his brother. The conflict escalated to such a point that, in 1984, the brothers' tanks faced off in the streets of Damascus. Their sick old mother had to intervene to frustrate Rifa'at's attempted coup.

The atmosphere at the university was feverish in those days. Rifa'at's adherents acted like cocks of the walk. Rifa'at had money, they contended; he would make the country's economy flourish. Hala was afraid. She couldn't bear to think of him coming to power, he was capable of slaughtering anyone who opposed him. "You would have been amazed to hear me talk in those days," she laughs. "Whenever the discussion turned to the president and his brother, I always stood up for the president!"

The next morning Hala, Asma and I stand at the intersection in Qadmus, waiting for the *hob-hob* to Baniyas. Half the village has gathered here, and it's open season on anything that moves: the pick-up that brings in vegetables and threatens to leave unloaded, the taxi that drops off a family. There's still no water in the village, a fact that's evident from the waiting people – lots of grimy clothing, sleepy, unwashed faces and frizzy hair.

The pick-up we finally end up in is packed. Two wooden benches have been knocked together under the canvas top; ten pairs of eyes look out at us from the semidarkness. Once we're actually moving, I have to struggle not to panic: I can't see a thing, but I can feel we're going downhill fast. The nose of the pick-up must be pointing straight down.

Hala has Asma on her lap and looks a bit anxious too. "I wonder how our driver got his license," she whispers. According to her you can be a champion driver, but if you don't have the right connections you won't get a license. "And the opposite applies as well: as long as you pay enough bribes, you don't have to be able to drive at all."

"Stop it," I plead. We're roaring towards the Valley of Hell. There are four husky boys standing on the back bumper; I have the ominous feeling they're going to push us into the ravine.

"Let's be optimistic," Hala says in a soothing tone, "maybe only the front wheels will go over the edge."

At Baniyas we transfer to the *hob-hob* to Lattakia. Sitting, hanging and standing, we continue our journey. Children wipe their snotty noses on my clothing, a mother breast-feeds her

111

baby, a man presses himself against me. I couldn't care less – I'm glad to be alive.

❖

As we drive into Lattakia along the broad boulevard with potted palms, other Arab coastal towns cross my mind. Casablanca, Algiers, Alexandria – the faded glory of white colonial buildings with peeling walls. The road is full of potholes, the palm trees look neglected, and here and there garbage is piling up.

Lattakia lies at the foot of the mountain range that has been home to the Alawites for centuries. After Assad came to power, many of them came down from the mountains and made Lattakia their local capital. Just like in Ceausescu's Romania, it is the president's brothers, nephews and cousins who run things here. One of Rifa'at's sons has a chic restaurant in Lattakia, and Assad's brother Jamil controls the city's commerce. Jamil's son Fawaz terrorizes the town: assault, rape, murder – the stories about Fawaz that go the rounds are as gruesome as they are unproven, because it's always his bodyguards who end up in prison. If a new-model Mercedes in the streets of Lattakia catches Fawaz's eye, his bodyguards have to steal it for him.

We go looking for Ghassan, a friend of Hala's who was born in Lattakia and is spending the summer with his family in an apartment on the boulevard. He's sure to have a *wasta* to help us find a chalet. I've already heard about Ghassan; he recently made a number of controversial radio programs, after which he was put on non-active duty for an indefinite period of time.

With one phone call, Ghassan arranges a chalet for us on the outskirts of Lattakia. He takes us there in his car. The holiday village – neat bungalows with patios and little gardens – is run by a member of Assad's family. Ghassan looks at Hala, who is walking in front of us, loaded down like a pack mule. "We call her Ayyoub," he says.

"Ayyoub?" He's referring to Job, the biblical figure known for his endless patience.

Our chalet is big enough for an entire family. Kitchen, living room, shower, two bedrooms – soon our things are scattered everywhere. Asma wants to go swimming, but Ghassan offers to show me the town; I take him up on it immediately. To escape for a while from the weight that sometimes oppresses me when I'm around Hala, her prejudice against this city, her unwillingness to explore. Ghassan has travelled; when we arrived and Hala told him I had written a book about Hungary, he brought out a bottle of *pálinka*, Hungarian brandy.

After the rocking and rattling of the last few days, it's pleasant to sit in a comfortable car, next to a man who drives through the streets with a sure hand. If I already miss this, what must it be like for Hala after eleven years alone!

On our way to the center of Lattakia we pass the prestigious sporting complex built for the 1987 Mediterranean Games. At the entrance stands a statue of a trim Assad – a lithe, athletic fellow. There isn't a living soul in sight. Ghassan carefully drives onto the grounds, past the Olympic-sized pool, around the stadium to the racetrack and then back again, swerving from one parking lot to the next, his hands barely touching the wheel. He seems to derive almost sinister pleasure from our solitary drive. "The only things moving around here are the birds and the wind," he says.

Once a year, during the Festival of Peace and Friendship, the complex seethes with activity, he has to admit. "I think I saw that on TV. The one Basel Assad rode in?" Ghassan nods. Assad's son had sat high on his horse, a young man with a full beard and a proud look. When his horse took a difficult hurdle, the crowd roared: "*Bi rouh, bi damm, nefdik ya Basel* – with our soul, with our blood, we protect you, Basel."

Asma finds Basel attractive and imposing. He always wins, even when a famous Turkish equestrian champion recently took part in the meet. Some people say there were *mukhabarat* in the stands who clapped enthusiastically whenever the Turkish rider was about to take a hurdle, so that his horse was startled and fell; a financial settlement was probably arranged afterwards. Only the Jordanians had the audacity not to let Basel win – it was definitely held against them.

We've driven into town. Ghassan tells me that all of Lattakia's public squares were designed by acquaintances of the Assad family. The result is childlike and clumsy: the statue of a little boy holding a fish is much too small for the square it stands on; a vague configuration of arcades is supposed to elicit the city's Roman past, and a concrete breakwater down at the harbor has even been awarded the status of statue. It reminds me of the works of art I saw in the Gulf states: gigantic sandalwood burners and Arab coffeepots with matching cups.

Idle cranes poke their orange heads into the air around the harbor, where oil tanks glisten desolately in the sun. "Is it always so quiet here?" Ghassan sighs. "I'm afraid so. But you should have seen it! Once there were a great many cafés here, places where men came to smoke the *nargileh*." He laughs dolefully. "Everyone in Lattakia used to promenade past those beach cafés at night. My parents met like that." About fifteen years ago, the city government decided that Lattakia harbor should be moved to the center of town, and the cafés were torn down. "We did everything we could to stop it, but it didn't help. A tradition that went back generations disappeared, but those mountain people couldn't care less – they have no respect for city customs."

The only remaining beach café is on the other side of Lattakia, high on top of a rocky promontory. Ghassan glances around quickly when we get there, and heads for a table with a view of the sea, as far as possible from the other customers. "Did you see those guys in the corner?" he whispers as we sit down – there's no need to say more.

Ghassan says this café has the best *nargileh* in all of Syria. The tobacco is light; it comes from Egypt and is permeated with the odor of the apples in which it's cured for months. "It's the only advantage of our improved relations with Egypt," he says.

"Tell me about Hungary," I ask. "When were you there?"

Ghassan thinks about it – he's been there so many times. After some calculating, we discover that we were both there in the summer of 1989, at the start of the revolution. "Were you there when Imre Nagy was reinterred?" Ghassan stares at me. Imre Nagy? No, no, the name doesn't ring a bell. "The leader of the 1956 uprising who was executed. He was restored to honor," I prompt him. It comes back to him vaguely. "And Gábor Demszky, he ran an underground press, did you know him? He's the mayor of Budapest now!"

Once again Ghassan shakes his head. "Who's the president again? Isn't it Pozsgay?" he asks.

"Pozsgay? No, he only got the ball rolling!" He's never heard of Árpád Göncz, the former opposition leader who's now president.

He asks about a man I don't know, and the rest of my search for common acquaintances proves equally fruitless. For years, it turns out, Ghassan was a member of Khaled Bakdash's communist party – that was the only way a Syrian could travel to Eastern

Europe. In all those years, his sole contacts were with Hungarian communists. "The Hungarian opposition consisted of people educated in the West," he says. "They'd been living abroad for years, then they suddenly popped up everywhere."

"That's not true," I protest, "that's what the communists said at first to discredit the opposition. They weren't able to keep that up for very long."

This isn't the first time I've made the mistake of assuming that people who are against Assad's regime automatically share my views on all kinds of other subjects. In Damascus, Hala took me one evening to visit Fathia, a psychologist she said I absolutely had to meet. She was one of the Syrian intellectuals who had signed a letter of protest against American involvement in the Gulf War; all of those who signed have been in trouble ever since.

A lovely house, furnished in Damascene style. Fathia apologized for the garden, which had just been torn up. She used to have a swimming pool and a lawn with garden chairs, but after the Gulf War she had decided to put in an Oriental garden with tiles. *After the Gulf War!* I should have felt it coming. Her daughter studied in France and had always been very fond of the French, she said, but since the Gulf War she had come to hate them. I knew what she was talking about: before I left for Syria, I had met a lot of Arabs in France who said the same thing. I cautiously ate the French crepe with cheese that Fathia served us on gilt-edged plates, and enquired about the book she was writing.

Somewhere in the course of the conversation, East Germany came up. Fathia had been there a few times; she said that things there weren't nearly as bad as people claimed. There was no unemployment, everyone had a place to live and there was enough to eat – after all, why should every shop carry twenty varieties of jam?

"The whole revolution there was organized by the West," she said. I looked to Hala for help, but she was examining the old Damascene scale on an antique table and wasn't listening to us. Taken aback, I allowed the Stalinist wind rushing through the room to blow over me. I didn't know such people still existed!

I made no attempt to argue with Fathia, but on the way home I could no longer contain my indignation. "Did you hear what Fathia said about East Germany?" Hala had told me how relieved she was when Ceausescu was executed; he and Assad had been good friends, she had hoped he would drag Assad down with him. I imagined she would hold the same views on East Germany, but to my amazement she began defending Fathia. "So what was wrong with East Germany? Are things any better in the West?" I thought of Hungary, a country that was so much more middle-of-the-road than East Germany. The suffering the Hungarians had told me about resembled what I was seeing here, the misery in which Hala was entangled. Why couldn't she see that resemblance? I sensed that I would say something ugly if I opened my mouth, and remained silent. Hazem, an Arab acquaintance I had visited in London before I left, had said: "The views held by Arab dissidents are even more extreme than those of the governments they oppose. I should know, I used to be a communist." I had a good laugh about it at the time, but after visiting Fathia I knew what he meant.

I have to gulp when Ghassan vents his views on the Hungarian opposition, but to my amazement there's no trace of the rage I felt when I visited Fathia. I'm becoming accustomed to this country's peculiarities. We've both ordered a *nargileh*; the sea breeze is blowing through our hair, and the scent of apple tobacco tickles our nostrils. I gaze out across the water. We're better off talking about something else.

And so we talk about Ghassan's daughter, who wanted to study architecture but had to choose chemistry instead, because of the point system they use here for admission to the university. Not in Damascus, as she'd hoped, but in Lattakia. They went to the campus yesterday to have her enrolled. They were so nasty to her that she started crying in the car on the way back. "Don't let it get to you," Ghassan comforted her. "Just try to imagine that we had emigrated to Australia. You would have been surrounded by Aborigines, and you wouldn't have liked that either. Maybe you'd be homesick for Syria already and wouldn't care whether you studied in Damascus or Lattakia."

That's how he tried to calm her, and he saw that it worked. But he himself often dreams of moving to Australia. "For twenty years I've fought to make respectable radio programs," he says gloomily. "Every year I've tried to push the limits just a little further. But since they put me on non-active, the whole thing's just collapsed." There's subject matter galore – from mounting drug abuse at the universities to the mass unemployment among college graduates – but no one wants to talk about those problems.

"Where in the Arab world do you think the situation is better?" I ask. Ghassan drags reflectively on his water pipe. I expect him to say Egypt, which is known for its relatively liberal press, or Jordan, but after some hesitation Ghassan says: "Maybe Libya."

"Libya? What makes you say that?" But he's serious, and after his comments about Hungary it may not be such an illogical choice.

"And what are your plans now?"

Ghassan sighs. "Twenty years ago I still had my dreams. Now

I've realized that the only thing I can do for my children is to make money." He and a friend are planning to make down payments on a walk-in cooler for storing fruit and vegetables. "It's too bad I waited so long to do this, otherwise I'd be rich by now!"

The air around us is permeated with sweet apple. Ghassan looks at me and laughs for the first time since we sat down. "I try to stay optimistic." His mouth twists into a crooked grin. "About Australia anyway!"

❖

That evening Hala, Asma and I take a taxi into town. We pass a motor scooter with no less than four people on it: a father, mother and two children, holding each other in an iron grip. A bit later two Mercedes with tinted windows race by. That must be Assad's clansmen, terrorizing the city. When we get out of the taxi we see them leaning against their cars, talking and laughing – husky men in sunglasses.

The white colonial-style building on the boulevard is Assad's old high school. The square in front is dominated by an imposing statue of the president, surrounded by illuminated fountains.

"Is that the same statue as the one in Damascus?"

"No," Hala says. "Take a good look: his coat's hanging open, because it's warmer here." In front of the University of Damascus is a statue of Assad in a long, billowing robe. "Like Superman about to take off for a spin in the clouds."

Across from the school is a row of small shops selling contraband whisky and cigarettes, and a couple of cafés where the old men of Lattakia meet these days; they drink Arab coffee and watch the passers-by. There's a poster of the president: he's sitting at a desk with a pile of newspapers, glasses in one hand. In Damascus you never see him in such a domestic pose. "He's at home around here," Hala sniffs.

Asma wants to know where we're off to now. "Life is looking around," philosophizes Hala, but Asma doesn't know what she's talking about. If we only had a TV in our chalet, she moans, then she would have stayed there. "When I was her age I tried to stay away from my mother," Hala says. "I went off somewhere to read whenever I got the chance."

"What did you read?"

"Oh, *Reader's Digest*." Some of the articles made such an impression on her that she's never forgotten them: a mother who donated the eyes of her child, who had cancer, to a little blind girl; an American prisoner of war who was mercilessly beaten in a Japanese camp.

We have dinner in an Italian restaurant. Hala looks suspiciously at the framed posters of fish on the walls – the way she stares at all things unfamiliar. "Look at that! All those fish are dead!"

She's been to Lattakia a few times for her work, but it was hard to do research in a city like this – she was always running into obstacles. "Assad's family has many talents," she says cynically. "One of them works in politics, another one's a trader or runs a restaurant." Assad's wife is from the Makhlouf family. The manager of the local tobacco factory is a Makhlouf, which makes him invulnerable. The Ismaïl and Osman families are above the law for similar reasons.

"It's becoming increasingly difficult to publish the truth," Hala says. "That's why I don't go to the countryside anymore. Agriculture and industry are in a bad way, but I can't say that; they'd only accuse me of rancor because my husband's in prison." These days she's more interested in culture, but that doesn't make things any easier. The Egyptian writer Yusuf Idris died recently. She admires his work – he didn't let himself be dictated to by religious or social codes, and she could tell he was a free spirit. When she told an Alawite colleague that she was sorry about Idris's death, he replied: "But we still have Hassan Sakr, don't we?" Hala sighs. Hassan Sakr is a minor Alawite writer – no one's ever even heard of him!

"Do you know that I can never say 'you Alawites' to my colleague? But he can say 'you Damascenes' whenever he wants – because they're in power." She looks at me sadly. "Someone should write about that, but you can't here." She absentmindedly pushes the salad around with her fork. She's always seeing new Alawite singers on TV. Have they suddenly become the only people who can sing? Where are the singers from Aleppo? It's got to the point where she's started liking the famous love poet Nizar Kabbani, who she never used to like, for no other reason than that he comes from Damascus.

"Why don't you ever publish in an Arabic-language magazine outside the country?"

She looks at me, annoyed. "And who do you think finances those magazines? If the publication was hostile towards Syria, I'd be in even deeper trouble before I knew it."

There's a wedding party going on in the restaurant at our holiday park. Vacationers peer in through the windows to where music booms from the loudspeakers, and a group of women in white headscarves are sitting on a low cement wall behind the restaurant, like birds on a telephone wire. They chatter indignantly when we walk by: we're blocking their view!

Hala grins. She was here once with Ahmed's family. There

were twenty of them sleeping on the floor of the chalet, and every evening they would sit outside. The wives of Ahmed's brothers acted much freer here than they did in Damascus, because there was no one around who knew them. "You should have seen them when there was a wedding in the evening – they danced on the patio like they'd paid for the orchestra themselves!"

We sit down on the wall next to the women and take our turn at peering inside. The bride is sitting in a high-backed chair, immovable, wrapped from head to toe in a cocoon of pink tulle. Two bridesmaids help her to stand, and she moves, rigid as a doll, to the podium where she dances a few steps with the groom. Her face is drained, tense. "You wanted to get married? *Tant pis*," Hala says sarcastically, "tonight you'll find out what it's all about."

The men on the dance floor are doing the *dabkeh*, the same dance I've seen performed by men from the mountains of Lebanon: hands on each other's shoulders, stamping their feet. Others spin around the women with arms raised. Hala watches in amazement – the men in Damascus rarely dance, and certainly never with such a display of masculinity. "Look at those body-guards dance," she says. "They can pay for a restaurant and a party, they're in power." Her voice is bitter, as bitter as Ghassan's was this afternoon. There's an undercurrent of jealousy in it that I've noticed before – as though she distrusts anyone who isn't bogged down like she is.

"How do you know they're Alawites?"

"Can't you tell?"

"How would I recognize them?"

"They're badly dressed and the backs of their heads are all flat." She has to laugh about it herself. "In Damascus they say that's because when they're born their mothers smack them on the back of the head and say: 'On to Damascus!' But there are so many ways to recognize them. They like to wear white shoes and socks, look for yourself."

Asma is tired of the spectacle. "Are we going to the Côte d'Azur now, Mama?"

The Hotel Côte d'Azur is down at the other end of the boulevard; Hala and Asma stayed there once when a wealthy uncle rented an apartment with his family. The plush lobby of the hotel is filled with music and people in evening dress, making me think for a moment that there's a disco party in progress. But I'm mistaken. Accompanied by the strains of the schmaltzy 'Wallah, heek eldunieh' – 'By God, That's Life', people are parading through the halls under the eyes of hotel guests sitting at little tables in the lounge.

Women in traditional long dresses and headscarves walk through the crowd, looking around with just as much interest as the others. I think of the three village women in Baniyas who couldn't contain their curiosity, venturing out onto the rocks in plastic slippers to stare at what was happening in the waves.

Even out on the hotel beach, people are walking like would-be movie stars past the tables with thatched parasols. They bask in this decor, so familiar to them from American TV series. But what goes on here has as little to do with America as the books of Sartre and Camus have to do with Hala's way of thinking.

Hala was very unhappy when she stayed here: she couldn't read, she always had to take part in the activities her aunt and uncle organized. But Asma enjoyed it, and now she looks around ecstatically at the girls in their glimmering dresses, the tall glasses with fake cherries on the little white tables. "Mama, why don't we stay at this hotel? It's a lot more fun here!"

I look at her eyes, shining with excitement. Madonna with her millions, Prince and his court, the frivolous atmosphere in this hotel lobby, and her father in prison – how can she reconcile all those things? Now she tugs at Hala's sleeve: "Mama, can I have my birthday party here next year?"

Hala laughs. "Asma is such a dreamer – she'd better marry a Gulf Arab when she grows up!"

After a few days in Lattakia, Hala begins to worry about the home front. How is Salim's marriage proposal coming along? Has he been able to rent a car yet? If he has, he's probably waiting for us to come home so we can make a trip together. Asma is peeved about not knowing what's happening with Captain Majed, and she's missed 'Layali al-Hilmiyyeh' several times as well. A couple of snails, I think maliciously – they'd rather take their house with them wherever they go.

Early one morning we start the trip back. We stop in Tartus to take a boat out to the island of Arwad. Before we get on the ferry, we go looking for a safe place to leave our bags. The pharmacist, the grocer and the café owner all look at us suspiciously and shake their heads.

"They're afraid the bags have got explosives in them," Hala explains. The fear dates back to the early eighties, when the Muslim Brothers planted bombs everywhere.

Across from the harbor is a little stand selling sun hats, dolls and souvenirs. While Asma tries on a cap with blinking lights, Hala and I look at each other: shall we give it a try? The salesman looks us over from head to toe. "What's in the suitcases?"

"Clothes," Hala says.

"You sure about that?"

"No, weapons." The salesman laughs, takes our suitcases and puts them under the table. Relieved, we head for the ferry.

"Nice man," I say.

"Must belong to the *mukhabarat*."

"Why do you have to suspect him right away of being *mukhabarat!*"

"He has a perfect view of the harbor. If he didn't work for the *mukhabarat*, they wouldn't let him have his stand there."

She's probably right; I suppose I'm the naive one. How long will it take me to start picking up on things like that? And won't everything be so permeated with treachery by then that I won't be able to stand it anymore?

A group of young people from Aleppo are on board the ferry. They join our conversation as soon as they hear us speaking French. They have an easy way about them that I'm not used to. "That's how people are in Aleppo," Hala says when we disembark, "much more open than anywhere else. You'll see that when we go there."

We walk out to an old fort where the French kept their prisoners during the Second World War. The road is lined with souvenir stands, but the island is teeming with flies and behind the little stands I see nothing but poverty. In a dusty alley a boy is pulling a piece of broken glass along behind him on a string. A piece of glass! The souvenirs are a sorry hodgepodge: plastic sandals smuggled in small boats from Lebanon, shirts with Hawaiian prints. Hala goes off looking for a pair of Bermudas for Ahmed. She hasn't talked about him since that night in Baniyas, and I haven't forced the issue; I'm grateful for every light-hearted moment on this trip.

In the fort we stop before a copper plaque that tells the history of the island. The Phoenicians settled on Arwad, and even

125

Alexander the Great landed here. "And then came the Ba'ath Party," Hala reads aloud.

"Does it say that?"

"No, of course not."

That evening, all three of us are relieved when we see the lights of Damascus looming up in the distance. Hala feels like an unwashed goat. "As soon as we get home, we'll all jump in the washing machine!" she laughs. A bit further along, traffic has come to a standstill. In the middle of the road an army jeep is lying on its side; the car it hit has been thrown across the road. We look out through the window of the *hob-hob* and say nothing.

CHAPTER 3

WHEN WE turn on the light back at the house, cockroaches shoot off in all directions. "Shhh!...Shhh!..." Hala clacks her heels angrily on the floor and waves her arms to shoo away the fruit flies drifting through the hall. We throw open all the doors and windows, toss our dirty clothes in a heap and soon the boiler is hissing away, the washing machine rumbles and water comes splashing out of all the taps.

Asma lies in her pink tub, making a call, the shower head pressed against her ear like a receiver. "*Keefik Tété? Mniha? Alhamdu lillah. Wa Salim? Inshallah mnih. Wa Zahra?*" I listen in amazement – it's a perfect echo of the conversations Hala always has with her mother – "How are you, Tété? OK? God be praised. And how's Salim? Be it God's will, fine. And Zahra?"

But Hala doesn't want to make any phone calls yet. First the house has to be scrubbed, swabbed, mopped – she won't have a moment's rest until everything is squeaky clean. We put fresh sheets on the bed and spray insecticide into every nook and cranny. "Whenever I go away for a few days the place is full of bugs," Hala complains. She once came home from a trip to the east of the country and found strange bits of fluff in the hall. Where did they come from? There were a few in the front room as well. The blanket on her bed was all chewed up. When she lifted it, she caught a glimpse of something she'll never forget: on the sheet was a rat, lying in a nest of fluff and blood, making gagging sounds as it gave birth to its young. Hala ran out of the room screaming, and felt the rat whizzing past her legs into the hall. By the time she came back with a neighbor, the rat had raced off to hide in one of her new boots. The neighbor beat the boot with a stick until the rat was dead. That evening Hala wrapped the boot in a plastic bag and put it out with the garbage – she still has the other one.

"How does an animal like that get in here?" I ask, filled with disgust.

"I don't know. Through the toilet, maybe – I forgot to shut the door that time." Hala laughs when she sees me grimace. "But it'll never happen to me again, you can bet on that!" She has a French-style toilet, a hole in the ground with two footrests on either side; when she goes away for a few days now, she covers the hole with a stone.

Later that evening I go out shopping in the neighborhood. My skin is tingling from the hot bath, my hair is still damp and I'm slightly euphoric to discover that not only Hala and Asma, but I too, have come home: I know my way around by now, I know where you can buy grapes at this hour, bread and *labneh*.

The cigarette sellers are standing on the street corner as usual. The boy in the leather jacket had seen us climb out of the taxi, loaded down with suitcases and bags. Leaning against the wall he had watched us, his head tilted back slightly, a questioning look in his eyes. Now that I walk past him alone, I don't know which way to turn my head. I'm ashamed of my shyness – I feel like a sixteen-year-old, afraid to be whistled at but at the same time hoping I won't go unnoticed. What's he saying now, what did he say? "*J'adore les Françaises!*" By the time the words sink in, I'm standing at the gate to our house, my heart pounding, and I break into nervous laughter. From behind my wet hair I steal a glance up to the end of the street and see him standing there, legs apart, hands in his pockets, his head turned in my direction.

Asma is lounging in front of the TV in her bathrobe, a plate with a fried chicken drumstick on her lap, watching a weekly program about the heartfelt friendship between Syria and Lebanon. I take off my shoes at the door and put on slippers, and as I walk to the kitchen I notice that I've begun to shuffle like everyone else here. Hala is sitting on the bed, cutting her nails. She's cheerful, the way she always is when she's just taken a bath and everything around her is clean.

"The Prophet said to take a bath every day," she says. She clips on thoughtfully. "But then he also said you shouldn't cut your nails at night."

"Why not?"

"I think it was because in those days people cut their nails with a sword. Imagine doing that in the dark – before you know it you'd be missing a finger or toe!" Then she tells me about Aisha, Mohammed's most beloved wife, who was nine when he married her and twelve when he slept with her for the first time. During an armed campaign, when she was thirteen, Aisha spent the night in the desert with a young man. She claimed that the caravan had left her stranded, but no one believed her. Ali, the Prophet's son-in-law, said he should put her away, but Mohammed loved Aisha so much that he chose to overlook her alleged unfaithfulness. That was the start of the quarrel with Ali, which would cause Islam to split into two branches.

I look at Hala and laugh. The Prophet lived thirteen centuries ago! She talks about it as if it all happened yesterday. When we were in the Italian seafood restaurant in Lattakia and they brought the wine, she asked: "Didn't Jesus say that wine is good for you?" I could imagine that he had said something like that, but I wasn't exactly sure. When I lost my faith, I also lost the traditions that came with it – it would never occur to me to tell someone an anecdote about the life of Christ.

Hala stands up with a sigh. "And now I'm going to call my mother." Tété, Salim, Shirin, Zahra – she has them all on the line, and when she finally hangs up they call back, because they've forgotten all kinds of things. Hala gets told off for staying away so long; it's a good thing we came back before Salim's second cousin Nihal replies to his marriage proposal – tomorrow Nihal and her mother are coming to visit.

Salim is angry at us for taking the *hob-hob*: why didn't we wait for him, he just rented a car! Shirin announces that her mystery lover will be there tomorrow too. Hala puts down the receiver, laughing. "You know everyone is jealous because I took a trip with you? They say it's as though my husband had come home!" She'll start work first thing tomorrow morning; Tété's house has to be scrubbed before Nihal and her mother come to visit. I'm seized by a slight panic: what about me, what am I going to do? I'm certainly not welcome at such a sensitive family gathering. But Hala laughs at me. "Of course you're invited; after all, you're my husband!"

The next day I feel feverish and sick. Gastroenteritis is Hala's diagnosis: "What did I tell you? That's what happens when you eat out." Asma doesn't feel well either. It will last two days, Hala predicts, and then it will be over. Salim comes by to take us to the *souq*. He wants to buy new coffee tables for Tété's living room, and plastic to drape over them, so they won't get covered with fingerprints.

He says nothing about the visit this evening, he only talks about the man Shirin has suddenly come up with. He wants them to get married within the month.

"Why so soon?" I ask Hala.

"Because then Salim can be at the wedding." He still hasn't received his exit visa for Qatar, but by now he's no longer in a hurry.

I buy a pair of shiny mules to wear at Tété's house. Flashy to be sure, but Hala likes them: I can even wear them to a wedding. At the house, Tété is sitting on the couch moping: has it taken us so long to buy a couple of little tables? All the floors in the house are wet, the chairs are up on the dining room table and Shirin is walking around in her slip, a rag and bucket in her hand. She wipes a lock of hair from her face and winks conspiratorially in Tété's direction. "Storm's on its way," she whispers, "keep your distance."

Hala shrugs. Her mother is like a child, she sighs: if she doesn't get enough attention, she starts pouting. During the first months after she married Ahmed, she always dreamed that her mother was standing between them.

Shirin walks me out the door resolutely. "We don't need you around here for the time being." Even under the citrus tree in the garden, the heat is stifling. The branches are bent under the weight of the green, grapefruit-like fruit – Tété will preserve and bottle them before long. I drop down onto a lawn chair, unfold the newspapers I bought this morning, put my legs up on the table and nod off.

After lunch I fall asleep again in Tété's room, as if I had

knocked back a bottle of whisky, and I don't wake up until dusk. The visitors could come at any moment, but Tété is still wearing her dressing gown and no one knows where Salim is. Hala grumbles: the whole house has been cleaned, but her mother lets her cigarette ash fall on the floor as though she were sitting in the garden!

"You're one to talk!" Tété snaps. "If you hadn't stayed in Lattakia so long, you wouldn't be in such a rush today!"

Zahra is standing in front of the closet, fretting. She has a pretty yellow blouse, but no shoes to match. She tries on one pair after another, walks out to the living room and turns around for all to see, but none of them are quite right.

In the garden, which has been hung with lights, Shirin is sitting with a man I don't know. When Asma sees me peeking at them, she pushes me teasingly in their direction. Shirin shyly introduces me to Farid, a young man of about thirty in beige summer trousers and a light-colored T-shirt. He speaks neither English nor French, she explains, while he squeezes my hand and grins broadly. Then he sits down again, legs wide, puts his right arm around Shirin and rattles his keys in his left hand. Shirin looks at me expectantly. "Well, what do you think?" is the question I read in her eyes, but I act as though I haven't noticed. He's the type women here find attractive: sturdy build, sandy hair, green eyes.

Meanwhile Tété's cousin has arrived with her two daughters. Uncle Yassim and his sons are here too, so the room is full of silence and sheepish smiles. In a solemn tone, Tété says: "*Ahlan wa sahlan* – welcome, welcome" – an expression she will use to fill many an uncomfortable silence that evening. She still hasn't dressed, and where is Salim?

The sprightly girl with short hair must be Nihal. She's about eighteen; she wears white pants and a blouse with an anchor embroidered on it. Her eyes twinkle like stars and her cheeks are flushed with excitement. I feel sorry for her. Salim is already going bald – what does she see in him? But her mother, a poor widow who has worked hard all her life to give her daughters a decent education, must consider him a good catch.

In the kitchen, Hala is putting tall glasses on a tray. "Have you seen him?" she hisses through her teeth.

"Who?"

"Farid!"

"Sure I did."

"That smile!" She contorts her lips into an imbecilic grin. I have to laugh, but I'm also shocked by her virulence.

"He's a bodyguard, that's what he is!"

"What do you mean?"

"Didn't you see? An Alawite! He looks like the guards in Ahmed's prison." She angrily fills the glasses with lemonade.

"Now wait a minute," I try to calm her, "you're not giving him a chance. Maybe he's nice to Shirin."

"Bah . . . an Alawite! He's happy enough to get a Damascene!" He's a simple fellow, she noticed that right away. Did I see the keys he was rattling? She wonders what they are for – he doesn't have a car, and he certainly doesn't have a house. And the way he looked around when he came in, as though he were entering a palace!

"You should be happy – an Alawite with no money for a change."

"He's too stupid to earn money." Hala shoves a melon and a knife into my hands and points to an empty dish on the counter. When I've finished, she grimly tells me to cut up another melon. "The dish has to be brimming, you know that, don't you? Not only because we like to eat so much, but also to show that we're not stingy."

She's furious with Shirin. How dare she show up with an Alawite while Ahmed is in prison! "Now we won't even be able to speak our minds at home. Maybe he's from the *mukhabarat!*" She hisses like an angry cat, but when Tété calls her she runs a hand quickly over her flushed cheeks, picks up the trayful of glasses, signals to me to carry a dish of fruit and walks in front of me to the living room. "Oh great," she grumbles when she sees that everyone has gone outside, "I clean the house, we buy tables and everyone moves out into the garden!"

They're all sitting together under the citrus tree, except for Tété who's spraying the flowers and bushes with a garden hose. Her dressing gown has fallen open, revealing a slip stretched tight across her stomach. Salim comes wandering in nonchalantly, as though none of this has anything to do with him.

Asma marches around showing off her new things, the way she always does when she's feeling shy. She has put on the cap with blinking lights we bought at the harbor in Tartus, and her red Walkman is clipped to her shorts. She guzzles down a glass of milk, then a can of cola, and then flops down in a chair with the Milka chocolate bar she bought this afternoon.

Uncle Yassim's sons, sitting at their father's side like sentinels, watch her every move but say nothing. Uncle Yassim is the brother of Nihal's father, who passed away. This evening he's here in the role of Nihal's guardian. The romance between Shirin and Farid, which he can't help but witness, must be no unqualified pleasure for him after having courted Shirin for months.

Hala keeps walking back and forth between the kitchen and the garden. "They're not eating," she whispers in passing, "that's a bad sign." For Salim's sake she hopes Nihal will say yes, but she also feels sorry for her: she's a pretty girl; who knows, maybe someone else is in love with her, or maybe she's in love with someone else.

Nihal's older sister, who sits next to me, says she's studying English at the university. Although her English is quite good, our conversation doesn't run smoothly. She seems accustomed to being silent; she answers my questions without looking at me and then turns her gaze back absentmindedly to the ground. Yes, she has read Shakespeare. When I enquire what she thinks of him in comparison with Arab writers, she says: "I don't know, we don't make comparisons, we just study English literature."

"But if you've read Arabic books you can make your own comparisons, can't you?"

"No, I don't read to compare; I read to learn English." That stumps me. Hala had warned me: the academic level at the university has dropped sharply in recent years. Learning by rote is the motto – don't stop to think about it. When one of Hala's acquaintances, a professor of art history, recently showed his students a slide of a piece of clothing and compared the collar to a Mao collar, they looked at him in bafflement. A Mao collar? Never heard of it. He explained that the collar was named after Mao, then received his second surprise of the day: they didn't know who Mao was. The last time he showed a slide of a painting depicting a naked woman, an indignant buzz ran through the classroom. Those were the fundamentalists; since then he doesn't dare show any more nudes.

Meanwhile the garden is dripping wet, but Tété is nowhere in sight. A fight is raging among the foliage. "Wedding day for cats," Shirin laughs. Until now I've mostly seen her slogging away around the house like Cinderella, but this evening she's wearing earrings that look as heavy as citrus fruit and she's

135

surrounded by an air of childlike gaiety. Farid's family comes from Qirdaha, the village where the president was born, she says proudly. "That's not just an ordinary village, you know, it's Syria's second city!" As long as Hala doesn't hear that, I think in alarm. Could it be that Shirin doesn't know what Hala thinks of all this? Is she really that naive? But a bit later she whispers in my ear: "Farid isn't like other Alawites. He's very sentimental, just like me."

"*Ahlan wa sahlan!*" Tété comes out of the house in a blue-gray satin dress, a theatrical smile on her face. She smells of the bath she's just taken, and her lips are done up in deep-purple lipstick. She steps from one guest to the next, placing plums, pears, peaches and pieces of melon on their plates. "*Tsalla, tsalla,*" she says. Hala looks at me and laughs. '*Tsalla*' literally means 'amuse yourself' – the traditional form of encouragement when guests are served sweets or fruit. "Do you hear that? We eat to amuse ourselves."

Now that Salim has arrived, everyone is more relaxed. He's the man of the house and he has something to say, because he lives far away. He talks about Qatar in his usual woolly fashion. All the Gulf Arabs agree that it's the most boring country in the region, but Salim doesn't mention that. He talks about the *souq* in Doha where the vegetables are cheaper than in Damascus, even though you earn ten times as much in Qatar. He describes the fantastic roads the government has built so that you can easily drive from one city to the next. I refrain from saying anything. Qatar is a tiny place – you can drive through it in a couple of hours and then you've only seen a lot of sand, because the whole country is one big desert.

Nihal's mother peels an apple – eliciting a meaningful glance from Hala – and tells us about the life she has led with her daughters since her husband died. They prefer staying at home – all three of them are pleased when they can shut the door behind them in the evening. This is a secret message for Salim, Hala explains to me in the kitchen: she wants to make it clear that her daughter has grown up in the shelter of the home, that she doesn't go out and that she has no contact with men. Could it be that Nihal doesn't have a boyfriend after all?

Nihal occasionally looks at Salim with a sparkle in her eyes and laughs at his jokes, then stares thoughtfully into space. One moment I think she'll say yes, the next moment I think it will be no. Salim in turn tosses furtive glances in her direction, causing her to blush deeply. How differently they look at each other. She takes him in with undisguised curiosity, like she would a toy that's suddenly within reach. His glances are much cooler: she is a feature of the landscape in which he has planned his future, a landscape with car and house. For the time being he will stay in Doha to earn money, but he hopes to return to Damascus someday and find a job, preferably with a foreign firm.

He makes a brief attempt to capture Nihal's gaze, which confuses her so that she pulls Asma onto her lap, cuddles her and whispers something in her ear. She's wearing three plastic bracelets and black button earrings. "If she says yes, Salim has to buy some clothes for her right away," Hala said in the kitchen just a moment ago. "This is the third time I've seen her in the same pants and blouse."

Zahra is the only one not paying much attention to what is going on around her. She has put on black shoes, but without much conviction: she keeps hiding her feet under her chair all evening. Sometimes she says something, or plaintively calls someone's name, because she can't keep up with the conversation. But no one pays her any attention – the same way we always forget Hildeke on such evenings at home, so that she starts laughing and talking to herself while rocking her torso back and forth. But Zahra sits straight as a ramrod at such moments, a severe frown wrinkling her brow – just like a police officer. I can suddenly imagine her pulling too hard on Hala's legs during the delivery, out of pure clumsiness.

When Hala and I come out of the kitchen with the coffee, Salim is sitting next to Nihal. Tété looks on from across the table, a loving gleam in her eye. That blue-gray dress looks good on her and her mood has also improved considerably after taking a bath. Could Nihal have already said yes?

Asma comes out to tell us that 'Layali al-Hilmiyyeh' has started. Tété wants everyone to stay and watch, but the three women decide that it's time to go home; Uncle Yassim offers to accompany them. I expect Tété to burst into speech after they leave, but nothing happens: she only watches TV, and Salim's face betrays no emotion either.

Ali, the sympathetic main character in 'Layali al-Hilmiyyeh', has become a Muslim Brother while in prison. When he is released, Sadat appears on TV announcing the Camp David accords. This documentary footage elicits a hiss of condemnation from Tété and causes Hala to brush away a tear. Asma reacts just as shocked as she did in the movie theater: "Mama, Mama, what's wrong?"

Zahra asks us to spend the night, but Hala shakes her head resolutely; as soon as the series is over she begins gathering her things. Tété, still playing the role of hostess, walks us to the door. She presses her eyelid to my forehead to see whether I still have a fever, then sternly orders me to go to bed.

"Well?" I ask once we're outside.

"Sweet as can be," Hala says. "Nihal said yes. But her mother wants them to get to know each other better." She sighs. "That means a lot of family visits back and forth. You'd better brace yourself."

❖

And visits there are, and discussions, and incoming and outgoing telephone calls. Salim insists that Shirin hold her wedding party at the Engineers' Club he belongs to, but Shirin doesn't want a party at all. The tragic end of her last affair – her lover rushed head over heels into marriage with a wealthy woman – made a sizeable dent in her self-confidence. She has put her heart and soul into Farid, and would like to keep him safe from the eyes of the world. They met a year ago at an institute where they were both taking English classes. "English! Have you heard Farid speak a single word of English?" Hala mocks. She's right: even simple expressions like 'good evening' are too much for him.

Farid has some vague job with a state-owned company. Hala can't imagine what he does there, except spy. "You should hear him talk, he couldn't produce a grammatical sentence if he tried." The *mukhabarat* she often meets at other companies are just as dumb, she says scornfully. They can't even spell their own name, but rise to become head of their department in no time. They're always calling up other petty bosses; they're the buffer between the workers and those in charge. But she says Farid isn't even smart enough to work his way up to a job like that.

Since his official introduction into the family, Farid spends his afternoons on the couch in Tété's living room, one arm thrown around Shirin, an exaggeratedly broad smile stuck to his face. I suspect that he's not sure of himself, but Hala is on the warpath and refuses to show any understanding. When the news broadcast shows a meeting between Assad and King Hussein of Jordan, Farid looks blankly at the screen and, after a slight hesitation, says: "*Siaseh* – politics."

"*Siaseh!*" Hala parodies him in the kitchen, "he talks like a washerwoman!" He enrages her by constantly referring to Assad as 'Mr President'. Yesterday he went with Shirin to her father's grave. He asked Hala to go along – who does he think he is? He also suggested taking Asma to Qirdaha for a few days. "Just to show that his future in-laws trust him completely!" She wouldn't dream of letting her daughter travel with him.

Salim is also none too pleased by the prospect of an Alawite being admitted into the family. Assad is carrying out a demographic offensive against the Damascenes, he says; he wants as many Alawites as possible to move to the capital, so they can support him in the event of an uprising. But Salim doesn't want to oppose the marriage – like the others, he realizes that Shirin doesn't have much choice at the age of thirty-five.

Shirin spends a lot of time shopping lately, and one day I go with her. We look at material, walk for hours through the covered gold *souq* and stop at every shop window, so that I see golden pendants and filigree earrings dancing before my eyes when I go to bed that night. Shirin laughs mysteriously when I ask about her future with Farid. "I'm going to swim in the sea of honey," she says. I can imagine that she's happy to escape Tété's house, but where is she going to go? Farid lives in a slum on the edge of Damascus, and it won't be easy for them to find anything else with his salary. According to Hala, Farid is counting on Shirin to solve this problem. He would probably have no objections to moving in with Tété – after all, the house is big enough, isn't it? The name Wadi al-Nakhleh has also been mentioned. But Hala adamantly states that she will oppose that to the bitter end; her flesh crawls at the thought of what her mother would do if deprived of the dream of Wadi al-Nakhleh.

In all the hubbub surrounding Shirin, the budding ties between Salim and Nihal are almost pushed into the background. Hala says it's because that union is less urgent – Salim is not planning to get married right away. The visits back and forth have begun, however, and Salim insists that Hala go along with him when he takes Tété to Nihal's house. She dreads it like the plague, and never asks me to go along – sacrificing herself is bad enough, she assures me. She's never had much contact with this branch of the family, and now she understands why. The silence that reigns in that household! No one has anything to talk about, and if she wasn't there to chatter away the hours – she doesn't know what Tété and Salim would do. Salim and Nihal went out onto the balcony last time, leaving their mothers sitting across from each other on the sofa, trying to keep from falling asleep.

"They're Ba'athists," Hala says when she comes home one evening, "the mother and the daughters." She knew about the mother already, because she had run into her at a Ba'athist training camp when she was holding a survey in college. The mother spent the whole time trotting around after the wife of the camp leader, and couldn't understand why Hala wasn't as deeply impressed with her as she was.

Hala sighs. "What are we bringing into our family? A Ba'athist and an Alawite! If my father knew about this, he would roll over in his grave." For years the family had succeeded in keeping such influences at bay, but now there seems to be no stopping them.

The next time I see Salim and Nihal at Tété's house, I notice some progress in their relationship. Salim is able to catch her eye and hold it longer, and later in the evening they sit next to each other on the couch and he touches her arm, sending a blush to her cheeks.

How long ago did Salim announce that he was looking for a wife? A month? How unreal and disastrous such a bond seemed to me at the time. I suddenly realize that I no longer find it strange, and I even follow the course of events with a certain curiosity. Hala has also reconciled herself to the way things are going. Nihal's mother has apparently prepared her for a marriage of convenience with a man like Salim. Nihal wants to know where they'll live and how large a dowry Salim plans to pay. A house, a car, financial security: these are important things in Nihal's life.

But Hala is not at all pleased with Salim himself. She thinks he's become so conservative. One evening she overheard him asking Nihal if she ever wore a bathing suit. "Yes, at school," she said shyly. "And do the teachers see you then?" He didn't seem at all pleased with the idea. Her own brother! She would never have expected him to come up with something like that.

A few days ago he took her to task about Asma. "I don't understand how you can allow her to play at a boy's house, don't you know what that leads to?" One morning when Hala is out, he comes by to pick up Asma. He gives my sleeveless T-shirt a rather annoyed look and says brusquely: "Fortunately, my sister has not left her daughter alone, that's not the custom here."

"What business is it of his?" Hala grumbles when I tell her.

"That's the way they think in Doha," I say.

"But that doesn't mean *he* has to think that way." She's highly critical of the Gulf states for their capitalist bias and pro-American attitude, but the fact that Salim works there, and thereby indirectly supports part of his family, doesn't seem to bother her. On the contrary, she sometimes thinks about going to work in the Gulf herself. Doesn't she realize that Salim's stay there has affected his way of thinking? I've seen it happen so often to foreign Arab workers in the Gulf: keeping their wives at home gradually becomes a status symbol, because that's what the Gulf Arabs do.

"You all look down on the Gulf Arabs, but you're not averse to their money," I say.

Hala doesn't like such digs. "When a woman is ugly and has only one eye, but is basically a good person," she says, "do you tell her right away that she's ugly? You could also start by saying that she has a good heart."

But we don't have much time to get wound up about such things. The wife of Ahmed's brother Rashid is about to have a baby. The doctor wants the delivery to take place in hospital, because the baby is turned around the wrong way, but Ahmed's mother believes that, with God's help, everything will turn out well, and calls in a midwife. Halfway through the delivery they have to rush her to hospital. The child is born by Caesarean section.

Rashid's wife isn't allowed to eat anything at all for the first few days, but when Hala goes to visit she sees that Rashid is busy feeding her *sfiha*, a rich dish of bread, ground beef and onion. Ahmed's mother, who is diabetic, is also eating *sfiha*. On the table next to the bed is an enormous plate of *baqlawa* – incredibly sweet pastries with walnuts and pistachios. "Too bad you missed it," snickers Hala, who knows by now how disgusted I am by the way people here stuff themselves.

Ahmed's mother was in the same hospital recently after an operation. Each room had an extra bed for family members who wanted to sit up with the patient, and her whole family sat fidgeting on that bed all day long. One afternoon Ahmed's father pointed at the oxygen mask hanging above the bed. "What is that?"

"That's fresh air," Rashid said, and pulled the thing down to him, "who wants to take a little walk?" The mask was passed around; they all wanted to try it, and they attracted more and more curious passers-by. A few weeks after Ahmed's mother left the hospital, the bill came: the oxygen they had innocently used cost five times more than the operation itself. "They come from the city," Hala laughs, "but they're not city people."

A bit later she becomes serious again. She has to iron shirts, because tomorrow she's going to visit Ahmed. Salim will take her there and this time I'm allowed to go along too – as far as the prison gates.

❖

Besides clothing and two kilos of sugar, Hala also takes a pile of books about the theater. Since she's become interested, Ahmed wants to read everything about it. "He wants to know more about it than I do, so he can one-up me," she says resignedly, sliding the books into a bag.

Every once in a while he gets to see one of her publications. "It was good, but you should read Roger Garaudy," he says then. Always that paternalistic tone! Once he has read these books, he's sure to come up with some kind of advice – that she should read Stanislavsky, for example, because he's the best theoretician. But she's already chosen the path she wants to follow, she knows what she's interested in. She likes the theater of the absurd: Genet, Ionesco, Beckett. She loves *Waiting for Godot*, every last word of it. "I've tested my ideas in the light of experience; he hasn't. He envies me for that," she says flatly.

I find her callous when she talks like that, and feel sorry for Ahmed on the rebound. That laborious attempt to control her from behind prison walls – why begrudge him that? But I can also see her point. After all these years alone, she's no longer willing to accept his interference.

"What would have happened if he hadn't been arrested?" I asked her once.

"He would have destroyed me," she said without the slightest hesitation. "He couldn't tolerate me doing anything well, being successful."

Salim arrives fifteen minutes late and Asma still isn't ready. "My daughter's dawdling is beginning to take on serious proportions," Hala says. Salim stands in the doorway, looking distant. No matter how often I see him, he remains a mystery to me. Each time I'm amazed by the contrast between Hala's clarity and his fuzziness. I sit next to him in the car. In the back seat, Asma lays her head on Hala's lap and falls asleep immediately. The heavy traffic on the road to the prison infuriates Salim. "Syria is a sinking ship," he mutters, "and I'm not just talking about the traffic."

"Where in the Arab world do you think the situation is better?" Ever since I asked Ghassan that question in Lattakia, I've resolved to do it more often.

Salim thinks about it for quite a while. I try to trace his thoughts. Egypt, perhaps Tunisia?

"I suppose Qatar."

"Qatar! But that's not a real country!"

He searches desperately for the right answer, as though this were a question on an exam. "Then I guess it would have to be Syria." I give up. Syria and Qatar, those are the only countries he knows.

145

We've turned off onto a sandy road. There is the impoverished village we saw from the *hob-hob* – a drab landscape of dust and rocks partly separated from the road by a wall. "A leper colony," Hala says. Further along is a Palestinian camp that was bombed in 1972, after the assault on Israeli athletes during the Munich Olympics. Hala tells me this in a listless tone. The prison mood is already upon her.

"They've put all the outcasts in one place," I say.

"Oh, that's not all. Behind the prison is an insane asylum. Salim will show you later on." She went there one time, not long after Ahmed arrived here. She wanted to get to know his new surroundings. "It was winter – all the windows were broken and it was cold as ice inside. The attendants assured me that the crazy people couldn't tell the difference between warm and cold, but I didn't believe them. I think the staff were stealing the heating oil. There was no use fixing the windows, they claimed, because the patients would only break them again."

Salim has gone down another side road. 'Damascus Prison' is written above an iron gate that has paintings of both the Syrian flag and a large dove. Painted on the back of the gate, Hala tells me, are two horses galloping to freedom. People are standing in little groups at the entrance. Most of them are women and children; they all have bags with them. A taxi driver is sitting on a beach towel in the shade of his vehicle, waiting.

Hala and Asma walk over to a woman who has been smiling at us from a distance. "Ahmed's mother," Salim says. I would never have recognized her in her brown raincoat and headscarf. Nor do I recognize the two girls with her in their black *abayas*.

Salim and I remain standing by the car. It's as though an invisible wall separates us from the others. Only Asma runs back and forth once to pick up the blinking cap she wants to show her father.

The names of family members are called out. The gate slides open and I see a row of trees surrounded by low buildings. Ahmed is in one of those buildings. I'll never get closer to him than this. Hala steps quickly through the gateway, with Asma right behind – two anxious little figures.

The walled asylum we drive past a little later is in a state of total neglect. Weeds rise high above the walls, behind which are the vague contours of what looks like a ruin. "Our cuckoo's nest," says Salim, who must watch a lot of videos at night in Doha. In Arabic, crazy people are called '*asfouriyyeh*', he tells me, a reference to the *asfour* – bird – in their head.

The air is filled with dust, and the hills in the distance are enveloped in mist, as though the sun that was shining so profusely in Damascus this morning has no hold on this landscape. We drive past cement factories and quarries, a school for Palestinian orphans, an army dump, a lot full of wrecked cars. Sand trucks drive back and forth, and a flock of sheep crosses the road. Truly exhilarating surroundings, just like Salim's company. He raises his voice above the roar of the traffic and leaps from one subject to the next, as though his thoughts are rattling around loose in his head.

We've just passed a rusty road sign for Baghdad – a meaningless indicator, for the border crossing at the end of the road is closed. "Saddam has turned the Arabs into the Indians of the world," Salim remarks cryptically. I think he means that Saddam has given the Americans a pretext to exterminate the Iraqis like Indians. He watched the Gulf War on CNN in Qatar and one day suddenly stumbled on a program about San Francisco in which the city was referred to as a 'mecca for homosexuals'. "A mecca for homosexuals! In Mecca even normal people aren't allowed to go to bed together if they're not married!"

147

"But that's not what they were getting at," I say. "It's an expression, it means . . ."

"I don't care! What do the Americans think, that we're barbarians? They have no respect for us." And for that, he says, Saddam Hussein is partly to blame.

I'm glad when we turn back and drive towards the prison, where two little dots stand pushed up against the prison gate, waiting for us.

Hala and Asma climb into the back seat without a word. They've both been crying. "I'll tell you later," Hala whispers when I look at her questioningly. Asma nuzzles up against her, a plastic bag of chocolates in one hand, the blinking cap in the other. Salim says nothing.

Back at the house I retreat to the bedroom and hear Asma sobbing in the living room while Hala talks to her. Later, we eat in silence. Asma tosses Hala warning glances – under no condition is she to tell me what happened at the prison. For the first time since my arrival I feel like an intruder in this house, and I wish I had a place to go to at moments like these.

But after dinner one of Asma's girlfriends calls and, after a bit of hesitation, she runs out onto the street with her soccer ball under one arm and a whistle around her neck. We clear the table without a word. In the kitchen, Hala produces such a heartfelt "Ufff!" that we both break out laughing. I put my arm around her. "So what happened?"

"We made a horrible scene." Ahmed's family has known about their marital troubles for some time. One of the girls with Ahmed's mother this morning was an unmarried cousin the family had once hoped to marry off to Ahmed. The message was clear: if Hala wants a divorce, a new candidate is waiting.

Hala stayed in the background at first while Ahmed talked with his mother and cousins. Asma was closer to them and heard him tell his mother that she shouldn't leave Asma with Hala if anything happened to him in prison. When Asma told her what she had heard, Hala burst out crying and ran outside, Asma right behind her. Ahmed's mother came to get them and stayed out of it for the rest of the visit. At first the accusations flew back and forth, but soon all three of them were crying. I try to imagine the commotion such a scene must cause in the visiting room at the prison. "Aren't you embarrassed to cry in public?"

Hala looks at me with compassion. "There's so much crying going on there, no one notices."

Through his tears, Ahmed begged her to stay with him. "I'll fall apart if you leave me," he said.

"You're not a rifle that can be broken in two," she countered, "maybe it would do you good, it might make you more human."

We've moved to the bedroom, the coolest spot in the house at this time of day; when it's quiet for a moment, I can hear the shrilling of Asma's whistle out in front. "So all you did was fight and cry? And you left him like that?"

"No, no, at the end we calmed down and talked about all kinds of things." Asma told him about the campground in Baniyas, Ahmed asked whether they had been following 'Layali al-Hilmiyyeh' and whether they had thought of him when the main character, Ali, ended up in prison. "My God, he's becoming so childish," Hala sighs. When she raised her sleeveless arm for a moment, she saw him looking at her underarm with a gleam in his eye. He asked whether she still loved him. "What am I supposed to say? I can't come up with the words anymore. I've tried to, but I just can't."

Once they were outside, Ahmed's mother put her mind at

ease. The family had talked about Asma and decided that she could stay with Hala as long as Ahmed was in prison. She also told her that they had bought an apartment for Ahmed which he could move into as soon as he got out.

Hala sighs once more. Since Ahmed has been in prison, he has had much closer contact with his family than he did before. When she married him his family was very poor, but now they've become quite wealthy; he's taken money from them regularly during the last eleven years. She's afraid it will be a millstone around his neck once he's released: he's become dependent on them. She tries to talk to him about it when they're alone, but he always says that his family is the salt of the earth, that he has nothing to fear from them. Hala shakes her head in concern. "If they're the salt of the earth! They're more like a swamp that sucks you down. They keep you from living your own life – you can't change them; they change you."

And now they've even bought an apartment for him. When his mother mentioned the name of the street, she was shocked. It's a closed neighborhood: women there never go out without covering their heads, children never play in the street. The more she thinks about it, the more impossible it seems that she will ever live with Ahmed again. Would she go to bed with him out of pity when he's released? That would be prostitution, wouldn't it? "I hope you're here when he's released," she says quietly, "so you can help me."

We're woken up by the sound of Asma's clear voice in the courtyard. Hala pricks up her ears. "She's talking to herself," she whispers. She has made a drawing on a slate: a house with the kind of tiled roof you don't see around here, a wisp of smoke coming out of the chimney and little curtains in the windows.

Yesterday's sadness seems forgotten, and Asma pulls me into the front room where a present from Ahmed is waiting for me: a palm-resin pendant with the mosque of Jerusalem on one side and a palm tree on the other – Hala told him I had been to Africa. For Asma he made a pendant from the two halves of a peach stone. Three names are written on the inside in calligraphy, in the shape of a sickle. "That's the three of us," Hala says mournfully, "lost and bobbing on the sea in a little boat."

The chocolates Asma got from her father have different colored wrappers that promise fruit and nut fillings, but the first two I open have no filling at all and taste exactly the same. Disoriented, I continue my search and taste the walnut, the cherry and then the hazelnut varieties, until I've had them all and my mouth is filled with the same bitter flavor of unsweetened chocolate.

When we take a walk through the neighborhood that evening, Asma hangs on Hala's arm. She wants to know where she'll go when her mother dies; she doesn't want to live with Ahmed's family, but not with Tété either. Couldn't Hala write a letter saying she should go to Uncle Salim?

"The things a child comes up with," I say, running my hand through Asma's hair. She smiles at me, nuzzles up to Hala and says: "*Ana wa mama* – Mama and me," – words she'll repeat often in the next few days and even sing to the tune of Fayruz's newest hit, 'Kiefak enta'.

That night Hala dreams about her father. He is working on a letter he has to write for her; it has something to do with Ahmed, but she's not sure just what. "I need him," she says, "he would have known what I have to do."

Tété calls: Farid's family is coming tomorrow from Qirdaha for the engagement party, and she needs more chairs. Hala gives it some thought. There are five old chairs out in the courtyard; what if she had them reupholstered? They're covered in spider webs and are in a deplorable state, but before long they've been scrubbed clean and a man comes to pick them up with the promise that they will be ready that same evening.

When we go to the workshop around dusk, there's little movement to be seen. Inside, in the semidarkness, we make out the man who came by this morning. He's kneeling on the floor, giving a rubdown to a fat, groaning man who must be his boss. The chairs are standing untouched in a corner.

The following afternoon we hail a little Suzuki taxi-truck with an open bed and go to Tété's house, the five chairs loaded in the back. The dark-brown leatherette upholstery is stapled underneath – Hala is pleased as can be.

Shirin is lying in her bedroom with her hair up in curlers, pouting: she used a medicinal cream and now her face has broken out in a rash. When Hala hears that Shirin is planning to wear a white dress she's borrowed, she becomes angry. "A white dress? You're not getting married! You shouldn't throw yourself at Farid like that, you don't even know if his family wants to have you."

In the kitchen Tété is grinding meat for the *kibbe*, ground lamb with rolled wheat. Her legs are terribly swollen. "It's her own fault," Hala murmurs, "she shouldn't have walked to the tailor's to try on her new dress." She hiked for kilometers, just to save the taxi fare. When I embrace Tété, she lays her perspiring head on my shoulder. "Why don't you take me with you to Holland?" Everyone leaves her alone to do everything, she sighs. But a bit later she shouts that her children cling to her as though they had claws, that she'll be glad when they're married and she can shut the door behind her. The name Wadi al-Nakhleh also pops up in her lamentation.

Hala shrugs it all off. "My mother is just like the regime in this country," she says. "She claims that she does everything for us, but the truth is that we do everything for her."

Once we're seated at the table, Tété isn't hungry. She pushes her plate away: how can she eat now that Salim and Shirin are about to leave her? Despondent, she puts her head down on the table and begins weeping. "Zahra and I will be left all alone. What do I have to live for? I want to die, I want to go to my husband!"

Salim pulls a pile of the local bread from under her head. "Then you'll go to hell," he says coldly.

"You should be ashamed of yourself," Hala rebukes him. Everyone knows that Salim had no respect for his father.

Zahra sits across the table, looking miserable. She also fears the day when Shirin and Salim leave home: soon all of Tété's grievances will come down on her.

Hala and Shirin say nothing; they're waiting for it to blow over. Now Tété dries her tears, pulls her plate back in front of her, tears off a piece of bread and begins eating the raw *kibbe*, which is swimming in oil. Hala looks at me and winks. But on the way to the shop to buy four kilos of ice cream for the party, she suddenly explodes: "Did you see how they act! Sometimes I feel like I'm surrounded by defectives. And I'm the one who has to take care of all of them." She feels especially sorry for Zahra. After the meal she came to Hala with a worried expression: what will happen to her when Tété dies? I laugh – Shirin is getting married and all anyone talks about is dying!

"What did you tell her?"

"That she could live with me."

"Do you mean that?"

153

"Yes, of course, where else could she go?"

I think about home, about what would have happened if I had stayed there. I too would have regularly been dragged onto the high seas of family emotions. But doesn't Hala bring this on herself? Isn't this the easiest way for her to give her life meaning? The perfect alibi for not devoting herself to anything else? It's a thought that's kept popping into my mind during the last few days.

"Some people can't live without problems," I say, "and troubles are one thing a family always has enough of."

"But if it's not your family complicating things, it's the state, or your job." She walks next to me with angry little steps, searching for the ice-cream parlor someone has recommended. "Here you can go out into the desert and still run into problems! Well then, I'd just as soon have them with my family."

She's right, I think contritely. Who could she turn to if she left her family behind? In Lebanon she might have been able to live a life of her own, or in France. But that's exactly why I came here, because she didn't go away. And now I want to blame her for that?

I've distanced myself from my family, but haven't I paid the full price? Since we came back from Lattakia, I've started dreaming about Grandmother again. It's because Tété is around, I believe – the way Hala deals with her, the conflicting emotions it stirs up in me.

I was nineteen when I went to America and left Grandmother behind. She had taken care of me when I was little, and when I grew up I cared for her; but then I left the nest and she remained behind, like a bird with broken wings. In the hospital where they put her, she opened all the doors: she was looking for my father's office. When I went to say goodbye, she walked with me to the end of the hall. We both cried. She slipped me some licorice for the trip. How careless, how flippant that moment was. I thought she would wait for me – I had so much to learn about the fleeting nature of things. Nine months later she died. By the time I heard the news in America, the funeral was over.

But in my dreams she is never dead. I hear her shovelling coal in the back kitchen, I walk through her house and see that she's bought new furniture – fragile furniture, things I am not allowed to sit on. A couch made of crystal, the same kind of crystal her sugar bowl is made from. I'm always aware of our limited time together, and there's always a certain reproof coming from her. It's a sorrow I carry with me wherever I go, that can rear its head at any moment – something I haven't been able to reconcile with the rest of my life.

Hala and I don't talk about these things. I wouldn't know how to go about sharing a suffering that is so minute compared to the prolonged absence of a man in her life, the recent death of her father. But at night we seem to approach each other. While I summon Grandmother to life in my dreams, she is burying Tété again and again.

❖

That evening everything is different, as though a new act of the play has begun. From the chaos something festive has arisen, an illusion of harmony. The house is as shiny as a new penny, Hala has bought a new pair of shoes for Zahra, Tété struts through the house in a blue dress, weeping because she's so touched by the flowers I've brought her. She'd like to give me something too, she says, only my house is so far away. The flowers disappear, wrapping and all, into a dry vase, where they will die an ignoble death.

155

Shirin's long hair has been straightened and hangs down flat, ending in curls stiff with hair spray. She wears a shiny green-black dress with broad padding in the shoulders and a décolleté covered by a swathe of transparent black material. Such a little person in such a big dress – the effect is quite dramatic.

A distant cousin comes in with a stereo, Salim fetches the fan from Tété's bedroom, Hala's old classmate Noura is busy in the kitchen. The front door, always open a crack at other times, is closed now. When the doorbell rings, Shirin shrieks and races into her bedroom.

In a moment the living room is filled with people. They exchange courtesies and nod to each other encouragingly. Farid's parents exude the discomfort of villagers who've just come to the city. Their other children also live in Damascus, but they are married to Alawites. I have the impression that they view their son's adventure with a certain reserve.

In his off-white suit, and white shoes and socks, Farid's father resembles the Alawites Hala has described to me. His mother looks at Shirin out of the corner of her eye, but also tosses inquisitive glances at me, the foreign visitor. "She's very interested in you," Shirin whispers when she comes by with the glasses of berry juice.

Tété has introduced me rather spectacularly as a member of the family, and that's the way I feel this evening. When Farid's mother's gaze stops at two ugly holes in the wall, I silently curse Salim for being so bent on taking down the bookshelf this morning. And when the standing fan breaks on its stalk like a sunflower – an incident which draws effusive laughter from the guests – I can't help feeling partly to blame. The rusty old fan that replaces it makes a sound like a plane taking off.

It isn't an easy evening for Hala. This afternoon she complained that she would like to disappear and go with me to the movies, but as eldest daughter she has a special role to play: she is expected to put everyone at ease. She wears a dress with little red flowers; her eyes are made-up and she's wearing bright red lipstick. I've become used to her bleached hair, but the way she looks now makes her a stranger again. The lipstick makes her mouth look bigger, giving her something of Shirin's dramatic air.

Hala sits down next to Farid's mother, then moves over to Farid's sister and brother-in-law. Her conversation is as animated as it was with the driver of the *hob-hob* to Baniyas, so I start to think that everything's fine. But when we meet in the kitchen, her eyes sparkle ominously. "They're pro-Rifa'at!" she hisses. Farid's brother-in-law told her that he was a sergeant in Rifa'at's army; Farid's brother was a member of his personal militia. "A bunch of bodyguards is what they are!" They are still in contact with Rifa'at, regularly receive the magazine he publishes in Paris, and are all hoping for his return. Hala looks at me defiantly. "If they're for Rifa'at, then I'm for the other guy – you know what I mean?"

Farid's sister asked her why she only had one child. "No particular reason," Hala answered, but when the sister kept on asking if Hala didn't want a son, and whether she was divorced, she said: "No, my husband is a political prisoner."

Hala laughs maliciously. "That made her sit up and take notice!" She has taken the rolls of Arab ice cream out of the freezer and is cutting them into thick slices. I put them on platters and stick curly almond cookies into them.

From the living room comes the sound of clapping and cheering. Farid's mother has opened the little packages she brought with her. Farid has bought golden rings and bracelets for

Shirin, and his mother puts them on her, one by one. With tears in her eyes she hugs her future daughter-in-law, while Noura bursts out with loud cries of '*you-you*'.

Noura had a date earlier today with a new lover she ran into at the mosque, and the excitement of their rendezvous still clings to her. The scarf she uses to cover her head has slid off; she plays with it as she talks, twisting it around her fingers, holding it in front of her face in feigned shyness – seductive tricks she's learned from the actresses in Egyptian movies. The men in Farid's family are not unresponsive: they cast furtive looks at her and laugh when she makes a double entendre.

After the ice cream comes music. Farid's sister dances around the room and drags the unwilling Shirin with her; the others clap their hands. Noura shrieks in terror when someone tries to pull her up out of her chair. Asma has retired shyly to a corner. Tété sits perfectly still on the couch, a cigarette between her fingers and a smile on her lips. The festive mood is a long time coming. When Farid's sister has finished dancing everyone just sits there, lost again in the midst of the deafening music.

Now Hala gets up. She walks over to Noura, pulls the scarf out of her hands, ties it around her hips, looks around, throws back her head and begins to dance. Swaying her hands, rocking her hips, she turns around and around, her cheeks growing redder, urged on by the clapping and cheering. I clap along, uncomfortably. The way she submits to this family ritual is touching and distressing at the same time – I couldn't do this, it's something I've forgotten how to do. For a moment her eyes catch mine. I see her dancing in Baghdad, twelve years ago, in a room full of crystal chandeliers and mirrors; a small, graceful girl. How little I knew about her back then.

That night I have another dream about Grandmother. There's

a party at her house; I can see it from far away, but I'm not a part of it. There are decorations hanging from the ceiling and all her brothers have come. They stand around her in their soutanes: Reverend Uncle from the Congo, Reverend Uncle from Brazil, Uncle Phil and even my late Uncle Gerard, who I never met. Grandmother has her hair done up and looks young; her cheeks are full and she's laughing. She doesn't need me, she's happy without me. So what about me? I run to her – I must be around seven – I throw my arms around her legs, bury my face in her lap and cry. She says that this is the price of the life I've chosen, that I'll never belong anymore, that I've lost her. I weep so uncontrollably that it wakes me.

When I come into the front room with coffee, Hala is lying in bed, staring at the ceiling. She's feeling gloomy – as if she's only just realized the significance of what happened last night. She had a nasty dream that she can't remember. "My family has been kicked into the president's village like a soccer ball," she says. Her eyes still bear traces of mascara and her lips have a faint pink color. Next to her lies Asma, sunken in a sea of pillows, still asleep.

"Did you see that fat brother-in-law of Farid's looking around the room?" Hala whispers. "As though he'd arrived at enemy headquarters! A typical sergeant: fat, stupid and pushy."

"But his parents seem friendly," I say cautiously.

"Yeah, they're fine, I think." Farid's father told her he had taken a military official out to dinner the last time he was in Damascus. It cost him six hundred pounds; he was extremely shocked. "Whatever else they are, they're not rich. Six hundred pounds – even I don't think that's too much." The problem is that a lot of Alawites around them have become rich, she says. Farid

159

in particular acts as though the world owes him a living.

She had been annoyed at Shirin all evening. Her sister is starting to talk just like Farid. She had bragged about a blind uncle who received a personal audience with Assad, and about how she had seen the president twice in real life, when he'd visited the company where she worked.

Farid had playfully tugged on Hala's hair when he said goodbye. I had seen her turn away irritatedly. "When he loves someone, he gets rough," she says, disgruntled. "He'll end up killing my sister!"

We have to get going, as Tété has invited Farid's family over for lunch. By the time we arrive, the table has been moved to the living room and a delivery boy is trotting back and forth with plates of meat and salads. It's Salim's idea – he wanted to save his mother the trouble of cooking just this once.

Tété, Shirin and Zahra are busy with their toilet, and Hala also disappears into Tété's bedroom to put on her make-up. I remain alone in the living room. When I first came here, this house was like a colorless stage setting where a mother, seated under the photo of her late husband, terrorized her children. Who would have ever thought that this room would teem with life, that people would dance here, that the table would be laid for a party?

Farid's parents enter the house like old friends. His father has brought a video. During lunch they put on the tape, a performance by the Egyptian singer Samira Tawfiq. Farid and his brothers beam. Tété watches politely, and Hala has donned her benevolent look, but pokes me under the table: Samira is especially popular with the armed forces.

Then a belly dancer appears on the screen. Salim, who's sitting next to me, gulps. Belly dancing is not an Arab tradition, he says, it comes from Turkey. The performance by the Lebanese

Madonna, a voluptuous lady in a feather boa and a long green lamé dress slit up to her buttocks, doesn't meet with his approval either. I can't help laughing to myself. The Alawites have looser morals than the Sunnis, which is one of the reasons why Westerners often back them up: whatever the Alawites do, you won't find them propagating Muslim fundamentalism. But many Sunni Muslims associate Alawites with dissipation. Stories make the rounds about the followers of the Alawite miracle-worker Suleyman al-Murshid, who held feasts during which entire villages threw themselves into animistic rites and orgies.

Shirin uses her hands to dish big servings of kebab and *kafta* – broiled, ground lamb – onto everyone's plate. Farid's mother is given so much meat that she protests and throws some of it back onto the platter, causing a bit of a scuffle between the two women. Farid's mother wins. I resolve to do exactly the same, next time I get the chance.

Around two o'clock, Farid's parents start making moves to go. The bus for Qirdaha leaves in an hour. "But the bus station is close by!" Salim calls out. "You're there in five minutes!" When they insist on getting up, Tété and Shirin push them back down in their chairs, where they wait like hostages, anxiously watching the clock, convinced they're going to miss their bus.

❖

Hala turns up her nose at the luncheon leftovers that Tété puts on the table that evening. "Come on, let's find something to eat," she whispers. We leave Asma with Tété and slip outside.

Tété's house is in Malki, one of the better neighborhoods in Damascus. Diplomats' wives come shopping here with their Sri

161

Lankan maids, and wisps of French and English conversations drift by. The shops have everything, from French champagne to tropical fruit and Belgian chocolate. The Syrians who do their shopping in this neighborhood are obviously wealthy. Hala sometimes buys something here when she's in a hurry, but she's always horrified by the prices.

"Let's cut through the park," she suggests. The streetlamps around the park spread a soft yellow glow. Children jostle one another around the bulging belly of a popcorn machine, little girls in doll-like dresses are playing on the grass, an old man with a dilapidated baby carriage is picking up empty bottles and trash. A group of veiled women sit on a bench, eating *bizr*. It's a complicated manoeuvre – they have to keep lifting up their veils. The red lights of the shop where Asma always buys her Milka chocolate bars twinkle in the distance.

We eat on the patio of an American-style restaurant – lots of chicken drumsticks and schnitzel, french fries and coleslaw. The restaurant is in the middle of a hum of activity: customers stand talking on the sidewalk, boys in sports cars with the tops down drive by slowly, ogling the girls on the patio. At the table next to us are four well-dressed Syrian women. I discover to my delight that Hala is eavesdropping on them like an old hand. "They're talking about Lacoste," she whispers. "They say it's no good anymore, everyone wears it these days." All four women are on a diet. One of them proudly reports that she has eaten nothing today but a single banana; another woman says she had a pint of yogurt. Hala laughs. "Well, what do you expect? This is a rich people's neighborhood!"

Neither of us want to go back to Tété's. "Shall we have a drink at the café in the Al-Sham Hotel?" I'd been there once before. '*Café Brésil, le rendez-vous de l'élite intellectuelle*', the menu read. Here and there men were sitting and writing, just like in Cairene cafés, but there were also Gulf Arabs looking around blankly.

Hamid, whose bookstore is just a few streets down from here, complained to me about the Gulf Arabs in the neighborhood. Sometimes they come to buy a newspaper in his shop and casually ask whether he can fix them up with a girl. As if every Syrian were a pimp! One day he got so sick of it that he told a Saudi: "I can't help you with a Syrian woman, but there are plenty of Saudi girls around, and they want it so bad it's free."

He finds them arrogant – the way they pull a wad of bills out of their spotless robes, just to pay for a newspaper! I catch myself feeling a certain compassion when I see them. In their own country they derive dignity from the oil money that's come their way, from the high positions they hold. Here they are at the mercy of local sex-tourism, making them seem somehow timid and fearful.

Hala finally lets herself be dragged along. We pass Hamid's bookstore along the way; I peer inside, but he's not there. At Café Brésil, Hala studies the menu with suspicion.

"What's wrong?"

"One hundred pounds for a glass of orange juice! I'm not so thirsty anymore."

"Come on, it's my treat."

At a table next to the window I see a man who was here last time too. He has longish hair and a beard, and there's a large portfolio leaning against his table. People come up to him and exchange a few words. I watch him from the corner of my eye, not entirely devoid of jealousy for the worldly atmosphere in which he seems to move and from which I feel so cut off. I point him out discreetly. "Do you know who that is?"

Hala takes a look and breaks out laughing. "A very bad painter. Why do you ask?"

"Oh, I don't know."

"He must be from the *mukhabarat*."

This one too! I feel the urge to defend this stranger, but Hala cuts me short. "You have to earn a lot of money to sit here every day. There's no way you can earn that kind of money with the paintings he does." She looks at me and laughs. "We just know these things. It's as obvious as the location of the secret airstrip between Damascus and Homs."

"Secret airstrip?"

She laughs again. The story has it that a bus stop was located close to the airstrip. Whenever the bus stopped, the driver would call out: "Secret airstrip!"

"But where do people go when they want to meet?"

"We used to go to l'Etoile, Laterna or Al-Rawaq, but these days . . ." We went to the artists' club Al-Rawaq – The Corridor – together once. A fairly crowded open-air café with a wall around it. To Hala's amazement, they no longer served alcohol. "*Araq* or beer loosens the lips," she said, disgruntled. "It must have taken too many *mukhabarat* to eavesdrop on it all."

According to Hala, the government doesn't want intellectuals to meet at all. A few years after Ahmed and his comrades were arrested, a group of men began organizing monthly evening meetings, at which one of the people present would give a reading on a subject he specialized in. No politics, that was the agreement, otherwise there would be trouble right away. The first evening dealt with theater, the second with oil. At the third meeting, there were two strange men in the audience. They all looked at each other: where did they come from, who were they with? The following month an outsider proposed that he give a reading on a political subject. Then they knew they were being watched, and that it was time to disband.

❖

Hala is sitting cross-legged on the couch, a mirror in front of her, using a brush to smear blue paste all over her face. "What are you doing?" That blue stuff looks pretty nasty. "Don't worry," she laughs from behind her mask. She's thinned the blue powder with hydrogen peroxide; it will lighten her facial hair, and her skin too.

Shirin's objections to a wedding party have faded under family pressure, and by now the preparations are in full swing. Salim and Hala have reserved the reception room at the Engineers' Club, sent about a hundred invitations and ordered thirty kilos of ice cream. Shirin spends her days shopping with girlfriends in the *souq*; in the evening she exercises endless patience by sewing little pearls onto her satin wedding gown and shoes. Farid comes by every day. Hala is polite to him, but that doesn't stop her from secretly imitating him in the kitchen: blowing herself up to bodyguard size and strutting back and forth between counter and stove.

Farid has bought Shirin an imitation-gold hair clip, an incredible piece of junk that she shows me proudly. To everyone's horror, the clip suddenly falls apart when Asma absentmindedly plays with it that evening; after a great hullabaloo, Zahra finally produces the glue from its hiding place under her mattress.

Waxing legs, manicuring nails, dyeing hair – I become so caught up in all the fuss around me that I too make an appointment for a pedicure. And why not go along to the hairdresser with Hala? Asma dribbles along patiently behind us and watches

165

with interest as my feet are put to soak in a bath and my toenails are painted the same shade of pink as my new mules. Cantankerous as she is at home when Hala and I speak French, she easily resigns herself to these rituals. She couldn't care less about horsing around and playing soccer now; she's being initiated into the world of women. While I'm sitting under the hair dryer in the beauty salon, she comes up, stands in front of me and shows me her arms: don't I notice anything? She runs her hands over the almost invisible white hairs; Shirin has treated them with the blue stuff.

Tété has curled her hair and dyed it black. She spends hours on the phone and moves through the house with an aura of importance, giving commands and not tolerating any backchat. But the night before the wedding, when she sinks down onto the couch and I put my hand on her shoulder, she steps out of character. She looks at me pleadingly and says: "Please, take me with you to Holland!"

Hala and Asma have their party clothes hanging in Tété's closet, so the following afternoon I go back to the house alone to change. When I come out of the bathroom, the phone rings. It's Asma: aren't I dressed yet? I hear talking and laughter in the background. "Who's there?"

I can picture her reclining on the couch, the receiver pinned between shoulder and ear, looking around the room in search of people I might know. "Noura, Sahar and Aisha, Uncle Yassim . . ."

"And what about you, are you dressed yet?"

She giggles. "Yeah, come over and take a look." There's still plenty of time. Farid's parents won't be coming for another hour or two, but I can feel the urgency in her voice – she wants the group to be complete, she can't stand anyone being missing at this point.

"So, are you coming?"

Around dusk I pull the door closed behind me and realize to my dismay that I have to walk past the cigarette sellers. I feel vulnerable in my satin dress, with my high heels and short hair. I peer up the street. They're not there. Could they be around the corner, talking to the man who sells *foul*? They'll start shouting things for sure if I stand in front of them waiting for a taxi. I'd better take a side street.

But that doesn't go unnoticed either. They know me around here by now, and curious stares follow me from the half-lit shops. There's the house where five people were killed when a propane tank exploded. The door opens, and a tall boy in a wrinkled T-shirt and jeans steps outside. The cigarette seller! He's barely awake, he still has sleep in his eyes. Without his leather jacket he looks just as vulnerable as I do in my pink evening dress. We look at each other for a fraction of a second, surprised, caught red-handed. His hair, which is usually combed straight back, is mussed. He turns on his heel and walks in the other direction.

Shirin stands next to me in the doorway of the living room and pinches my arm. Seated on the couches with their velvet upholstery, the men are arranging the terms of her marriage. Salim announces that he is giving Shirin to Farid for twenty-five thousand pounds; Farid says he will pay one hundred thousand pounds if he divorces her. The registrar jots down the sums in the same thick book in which he has just noted their names. These are imaginary figures, Hala whispers – Farid hasn't really paid anything, but this is what Islamic law demands. I'm reminded of the ten thousand pounds Ahmed wanted to borrow from his brother Rashid in order to divorce Hala.

The civil servant makes an edifying little speech, slams the book shut, puts it under his arm and leaves. It's Thursday evening, the start of the weekend – he has more marriages to register.

The Engineers' Club is close by: we can walk there. Asma's hand feels clammy in mine. She looks like a doll in her azure-blue dress; her hair is curled and there's rouge on her cheeks. But back in Shirin's bedroom she showed me, with a look of mischief, what she has on under her clothes: a jersey and a pair of underpants with a picture of Captain Majed kicking a ball into kingdom come.

The Egyptian disco music in the reception hall blares out to meet us. We are the first to arrive; the other guests come in one by one. I've seen many of them at one time or another in Tété's living room, but there are also a few new faces. Farid and Shirin take their places on the decorated chairs up on the podium, surrounded by bouquets of red gladioli and white carnations. Shirin sits there with a forced smile. The hairdresser has teased up her hair so that it is thirty centimeters above her head and all to one side – like a towering wave at sea. She tried to push it down in the bedroom mirror, but it didn't help. Zahra, who has a more modest version of the same hairstyle, sits just as stiffly.

Sahar is wearing pendant earrings and carries a matching bag that her husband made in prison. I tried to convince Hala to take one of Ahmed's bags too, but she's not in a festive mood. She's wearing a simple white floral dress and a worried expression: are the families mingling enough, are any of the guests sitting alone, isn't the music too loud?

This is the hall where she celebrated her own wedding. I've flipped through the album with pictures of that evening more than once. She looked like a fairy in her long white dress, light as a feather next to ponderous Ahmed in his black suit and sweater. Their fathers – the distinguished retired military man and the plump woodcutter who had so little to say to each other – stand next to each other uncomfortably; Hala is smiling at them encouragingly.

Salim's future in-laws have made their appearance. Nihal no longer wears plastic baubles, but the golden bracelets Salim has bought her. The video camera he's rented stands on its tripod; it's aimed at Nihal for most of the evening, which prompts Hala to enquire acidly whether he thinks this is his own wedding. When Salim whispers to her in passing that she has too much lipstick on, she snaps: "Why don't you just keep an eye on your fiancée!"

The evening also has moments when everything falls silent except for the music, when everyone looks at each other to see what to do next. The ice cream is served late, making the hours drag by endlessly. Everyone dances, except for Asma. She races through the corridors of the club with her cousins and takes care of the music. After all the girlishness of the last few days, the boy in her has finally won out.

Noura has had a black dress with rosettes made specially for this occasion. The dress makes her look fat, but she doesn't seem to be aware of this. She flits through the hall like a heavy butterfly. At first she sat down next to an unattractive man with glasses, who Hala says is the owner of an olive-oil plant, but now her eye has fallen on a group that I've noticed too: three handsome, well-groomed men, brothers apparently, who look around appraisingly. The woman in the red dress who's with them has raven hair and flashing eyes. They look less traditional than all the uncles and aunts in their exaggerated party dress. I nudge Hala: "Who are they?" She laughs. That's her father's branch of the family – three cousins, two of whom work in the Gulf. The youngest is a customs official; the red fury at his side is his wife.

The oldest brother, the most handsome of the three, has known many women but has always remained a bachelor. He's looking to marry a sixteen-year-old girl; in his opinion, older women can't be trusted. "And he should know!"

Noura has gone over to their table. She's wrapped her translucent pink shawl coquettishly around her shoulders and apparently invites herself to sit down. Hala stands up. "I'm going to say hello," she winks.

I watch them from across the room. Noura has found the right group of men – before long the glances are flying back and forth and the table is a flurry of conversation and laughter. Hala is laughing too, but when she catches my eye she shakes her head doubtfully. Noura's shawl has slipped off, and one of the men picks it up and drapes it carefully over her shoulders. The red fury looks on, frowning, then stands up and walks to the dance floor. She has a strange, stiff way of dancing: she sticks her chin out and swings her arms and legs. Sahar, who's sitting next to me, laughs at my look of surprise. Fatma is a military training instructor at a high school, she says – a staunch Ba'athist who teaches young girls to march and take rifles apart. To her, everything is martial music.

Fatma's psychological warfare with Noura seems to work: the three brothers have turned around affably and are giving her an enthusiastic ovation. Noura tosses me a big wink. The oldest brother is her favorite, she lets me know from a distance, but she's not averse to the second one either.

The first guests begin leaving, but it's almost midnight by the time we go down the steps, bouquets clenched under our arms. The flowers are mounted on cross-shaped, wooden constructions, and seem to me to be more appropriate for a funeral than a wedding.

"*Kafi* – finished," I say to Salim, who's walking in front of me. He looks back at me in alarm. "Who taught you that word? *Kafi* isn't right, it's *kifaya*." The hell with your formalism, I think; I hear everyone around me saying *kafi* all the time.

A pick-up is waiting downstairs to take the flowers. They're going to Tété's house, Hala has decided – it would be a pity to throw them away. While we're loading them into the truck, Hala whispers in my ear: "Fatma and her husband, Hassan, have invited us to drink something at one of the outdoor cafés on Mount Qassioun – how about it?"

"At this hour?"

"Why not? We used to do it all the time!"

Used to – that's right, but that was so long ago. We haven't been up on Qassioun once since I arrived. "If it sounds good to you too, sure." The thought of the cool air above Damascus is attractive enough.

A bit later we're sitting in the car, Asma between us, her cheeks flushed with sleep. Before long the city is lying at our feet. We stop at a roadside café; Hassan goes inside to order something. I would like to hear more about the military training Fatma teaches at school, but she claims that she teaches psychology, so I don't know how to get around to talking about that marching music. She asks interestedly about Hala's work, and talks about the newest book by a sociologist they both know.

Hassan comes back with tea and plates of *foul*. When I ask him why he didn't go to the Gulf to earn money like his brothers, he laughs: "You can earn money here just as well; I can't complain!" Of course there's no democracy here, but Syria isn't ready for that anyway. "Look at what the country was like before the Ba'ath Party took over. One big anarchistic mess." I feel Hala stiffen beside me, but she says nothing.

"Did you hear Hassan talking about democracy?" she fulminates back at the house. "Where does he get the nerve? Knowing that my husband is in prison!" She's not at all surprised that he gets along so well here. He used to be penniless, but since he found a job as a customs official in the tax-free zone outside Damascus, he's put together a tidy little nest egg. He has two houses, plus a farm in the hills outside Damascus.

"I didn't know you had such wealthy relatives," I say. Hala sneers. "Don't ask me how they make their money. They're welcome to it as far as I'm concerned, I'm proud not to be interested in those kinds of riches." She doesn't like being around them. Had I heard how Fatma insisted on talking about sociology? In different company, though, she likes to brag about her friendship with military leaders or key figures in the *mukhabarat*.

"What were all of you laughing about when Noura was sitting at the table?"

"Oh, Noura claimed that she wanted to learn how to play chess. All three brothers announced their candidacy. Then she suggested they draw straws." Hala shrugs. "It never amounts to anything. In the end she's always alone."

Hala feels alienated by Noura's behavior: she acts like she's religious, but she's not at all. She wonders why Noura is always hanging around in mosques; is someone sending her out to spy?

Asma has thrown herself onto the bed with all her clothes on. She moans when Hala tells her to get undressed. "Come on, tomorrow you can sleep in!" Hala sits on the edge of my bed in her nightgown. "It's over," she says tiredly, "or at least, almost over." Farid's parents are expecting a return visit to their hometown: Qirdaha, the president's birthplace! My heart starts pounding faster right away. "Do you think I could go along?"

Hala laughs. "I wouldn't dream of going without you."

❖

"Look how much space this brother-in-law of mine takes up!" Hala hisses in my ear. Farid is sitting in the back seat of Salim's car, his legs spread wide, an arm thrown around Shirin – Hala and I are pretty much crushed into the corner.

We left at six in the morning. We turned off the coast road just before Lattakia and now we're driving into the Alawite mountains. Tété has never been out here before, and she keeps up a running commentary. It's much damper here than in Damascus – she can feel it in her legs, her arthritis is starting to act up.

For the last few days, Tété and Farid have been locked in a bitter struggle. He has more or less moved into her house, and he comments on everything, especially the food she serves. His mother is a much better cook, he claims. I can't help feeling that Tété is trying to get back at him today. As we approach Qirdaha, she constantly rubs her aching legs and sums up the blessings of Wadi al-Nakhleh.

Farid acts as if he notices none of this. I sense that he feels more at ease than he did at first. Could it be because he recently helped Salim out? When Farid heard that he was having problems with his exit visa, he said he had a friend with the *mukhabarat* who could easily arrange it. No one believed he would be able to do it, but one afternoon he came in triumphantly waving the slip of paper for which Salim had been unsuccessfully pounding the pavement for weeks. Since then he's started acting like the man of the family: if anyone has a problem, all they have to do is come to him.

Now that we're off the coastal road, he's completely in his element. This is his territory, he's at home here. He proudly points out landmarks along the way: the villa we just drove by belongs to one of Assad's nephews, a top military official lives in that house over there. With his sunglasses and the way he sits there next to me, broad-shouldered and with legs too long for this cramped back seat, he reminds me of a bodyguard too.

Salim stops to take a picture. Tété stubbornly remains in the car, but we climb out, relieved to be able to stretch our legs. We look around, breathless: golden-yellow broom, purple heather, rolling hills, misty forests in the distance. The air is filled with the tingling scent of pine.

"These are God's chosen people," Hala whispers. "They have everything: beautiful countryside, power, money." Like King Hussein of Jordan and King Hassan of Morocco, Assad has had his family tree traced in an effort to discover a link with the Prophet. But no one has ever heard anything about the results.

Farid beams with self-confidence – as though these surroundings were his own personal property. But when I write something down in my notebook, he becomes suspicious and asks Shirin what I'm doing. I mumble something about a description of the countryside and then put the book away guiltily. I have to learn not to take notes in public; people like Farid make the wrong associations with the written word, they think right away of reports for the *mukhabarat*.

We drive past a walled fortification guarded by armed men. That was the former home of Rifa'at Assad, Hala informs me; the guards are there to make sure nothing is stolen. On the opposite hill, gray palisades stand abandoned in the landscape. That was where Rifa'at was building a city for his followers. Farid's parents were to have a house there as well, but since

Rifa'at was exiled to Europe the project has come to a halt.

"Doesn't it remind you of the mafia?" Hala says. "They always retreat with their followers to bastions like these." In Damascus, Assad has had a new palace built in the form of a bunker, with the homes of his friends and advisers in the same grounds. It's on a hill, surrounded by barbed wire, and dominates the whole city.

There are many wild rumors about the riches of Qirdaha, but at first glance there is nothing spectacular about the village we drive into. The village structure is unaltered, except for the fact that villas have been built here and there between the simple houses, giving the streets a crowded look. Hala shows me the mosque the president is building for his mother. A ridiculous project, some say, because it's not Alawite custom to pray in a mosque. The only places important to them are the tombs of religious sheikhs, the little white stucco houses with lovely cupolas we saw dotting the countryside on our way.

Farid's parents live in an apartment in the center of town. The rituals in the living room are a mirror image of the ones I have come to know at Tété's house. While Farid's sister serves coffee with fruit and pastries, his mother sits forward on the couch and enquires after Tété's health. "*Tsalla* – amuse yourself," she nods to me encouragingly, pointing at the five horrendously sweet pastries her daughter has put on my plate. She has the nervous gestures of one who knows that everything she does will be commented on later.

Shirin behaves like a model daughter-in-law: she helps with serving and takes each empty plate to the kitchen right away. While Salim shows pictures of the wedding, Tété, Hala and I peek around as discreetly as possible.

"It's quiet here," Tété says approvingly.

"Wait until this evening, then you'll be humming a different tune!" Farid's father laughs. Hala steers my glance towards the three photos above the door. After a bit of puzzling I recognize Rifa'at, Assad and his son, Basel. In Damascus, portraying that trinity has come to be regarded as blasphemous, but apparently other rules apply around here.

"*Ahlan wa sahlan* – welcome, welcome," Farid's mother says for the umpteenth time. "*Allah yikhaliki* – may God protect you," Tété replies. When Farid's sister opens the door to the balcony, Hala and I look at each other and slip outside. The balcony looks out onto a square where two men are sitting in front of a store. A woman with a child stops, and the storekeeper gets up to help her. A normal village scene, were it not for the fact that our view is somewhat obstructed by an imposing statue of Assad with four lions at his feet.

A green Mercedes stops at the shop. The driver yells something to the shopkeeper, races off and zooms by again later on. "That car must have been smuggled in from Lebanon," Hala says. The sound of screeching tires tears the morning silence to shreds.

Here and there we see houses with the likeness of Assad stamped in red on the walls. The only time I've seen anything like it was in the war-torn mountains of Lebanon: local militias did it to show who held the village. Every mountain had its own leader, every faction its own mountain. All those men in dark glasses coming down off the mountain in Assad's wake and racing through the streets of Lattakia and Damascus in cars with tinted glass – could that be the way they feel? That they can do whatever they like because one of them is ruling the country? I can imagine them entertaining that thought, even against Assad's will. In Lebanon, over-confident young people slipped from their leaders' grasp in the same way. Rifa'at gave sense and direction to such ambitions – that's probably why his brother wanted to get rid of him.

At the base of the apartment building lies a vacant lot full of waste paper, empty cans and trash. The man in the apartment across the street inspects the grape vines on his rooftop garden, pruning away a rotten grape here and there. Doesn't it bother him to look down on all that garbage from his spick-and-span terrace? Apparently not. It's like everywhere in this part of the world: people don't have much feeling for civic affairs. A little while ago, Tété opened the car window and threw out an empty cola can; I was shocked, but no one else in the car reacted, not even Hala who's usually so neat about her own things.

Asma has come outside. The importance of this place hasn't escaped her. She tugs on Hala's sleeve and asks who's the richest man in Syria: Assad or Akram, a well-known arms dealer? Hala laughs. "I wouldn't know!" Salim also comes out for some fresh air. It's too warm inside, he sighs. We all lean over the edge of the balcony. Three shiny cars are parked further down the street. According to Farid, one of Assad's nieces lives there. A chauffeur is waiting in one of the cars. "Everyone in this village has an official position, like that chauffeur," Salim remarks.

"The presidential family is fond of cars and doctorates," Hala says cynically. Rifa'at took his degree at Patrice Lumumba University in Moscow, which was specially set up for students from Third World countries. Everyone knows it's not hard to get a degree there. Some even say Rifa'at had someone else write his thesis for him, just like Elena Ceausescu.

During Shirin's engagement party, Farid's brother-in-law peered around as though he had arrived at enemy headquarters. But doesn't the same apply to us? Even I feel like a spy here –

to stand so close to that statue of Assad, so close to his niece's house, under cover of the friendly chit-chat in the room behind us, and then to entertain such unpleasant thoughts about everything happening around us.

My visit to Gbadolite, the birthplace of Mobutu's mother, returns to mind. Broad streets with black Mercedes, palaces in the jungle. Someone predicted that the village would be pillaged after Mobutu's death, that all the doors, windows and even the light switches would be taken.

"What do you think would happen here if Assad were overthrown?" I ask Hala.

She looks at me hesitantly. "I have no idea. But if you look at what happened to President Marcos in the Philippines . . . The same thing's not unimaginable here." Once most Alawites were poor, she says. They worked on the land, but many of them had to go down to the cities to earn money. Alawite men cultivated the land of rich Sunni gentlemen, and their daughters went to work as domestic servants for wealthy Sunnis in Lattakia, Homs, Hama and Damascus. It's a well-known fact that those girls were exploited, often raped, by the man of the house. That is one of the reasons why the situation in Hama got so out of hand at the time – the Alawites wanted to avenge their sisters and mothers. But, Hala suspects, those killings will someday be avenged as well.

Farid calls us in. His parents have invited us to lunch in a nearby village. They don't have a car, but an acquaintance who's offered to accompany them has just arrived.

We drive along shady roads lined with pine trees in the direction of Slenfeh. "That's Ghazi Kanaan," Hala whispers almost inaudibly when a gray Mercedes passes us. Kanaan is head of the military *mukhabarat* in Lebanon.

"What's he doing here?" I ask in amazement.

"Oh, he's probably going to lunch in Slenfeh, just like us." It's Friday, the Muslim day of rest – in a car like his it should be easy to cover the distance between Beirut and Slenfeh.

The parking lot at the outdoor restaurant Farid's father has chosen is full. Lots of cars with Saudi, Kuwaiti and Lebanese license plates; here and there a chauffeur waiting, killing time by polishing the hood. We have a hard time finding a table. A band is playing and it's busy on the dance floor. The restaurant obviously caters to large groups, and before long our table is covered with plates of food, *araq* and half-liter bottles of beer.

The music makes it almost impossible to talk and that's probably a good thing, for no one seems to have much to say once all the civilities have been exchanged. Farid's father tells anecdotes about his work in Lattakia, Tété hands out compliments about the landscape. I don't hear her complaining about her arthritis anymore.

"It's not easy marrying into a family you can't speak your mind to," Hala muses.

"But maybe they're waiting until they can speak freely too."

She laughs. "Sure, about Rifa'at you mean!" She's heard from Shirin that one of Farid's cousins was a soldier in Hama during the events there. Since then he's had sexual problems. "That happens to a lot of men who are present during torture or mass murders," she says.

Shirin lays her head on Farid's shoulder; he puts an arm around her clumsily. When our eyes meet, they smile at me. There's something helpless about the way they're sitting there, full of romantic ideas about what the future will bring, even though they're both in their thirties. Their marriage still has so little substance, apart from these festivities. At Tété's they sleep

179

in separate rooms; the only place they can be alone is at Farid's house in the slums. A few days ago Shirin had a dark-red mark on her neck; she was embarrassed when Hala commented on it. "It's all still new," Hala said afterwards, "but what will be left when the excitement has died down?" They still haven't found a house, and now they are talking about having Shirin move in with Farid for the time being. In a slum! Tété and Hala went there not so long ago. Tété cried when she came back: she didn't know such things existed in Damascus. Hala was shocked too. "I don't know how to explain it to you," she said. "You've been to Africa – I think this must be worse. There's no pavement, no lights, no heating; in the winter the moisture must just drip off the walls."

But today everything seems to have been forgotten, and during the meal Shirin actually gets a bit tipsy. When we walk together to the lavatory, she can barely move through the loose sand on her high heels. She leans against me, giggles, and says: "Today I'm swimming in the honey."

After lunch we go back to Qirdaha and say goodbye. Close to the square with the statue of Assad we see the green Mercedes, which has now been joined by other cars. I think I know what Farid's father meant when he said it's not all that quiet here in the evening.

As we drive out of Qirdaha, Hala looks out the window and says: "I don't see any signs for Homs or Hama, everything points straight to Damascus." Farid laughs contentedly – he doesn't notice the sarcasm in her voice.

Hala is in low spirits on the way home. "I talk, I laugh, I eat, I play the comedian all day," she says, "when all I really want to do is escape. But where would I go? The only place I'd be safe is France."

What would it be like if she arrived with Asma in Paris at this moment? Imagine how much money she would have to earn just to survive. And where would she live?

"Do you have family there?" I ask her.

"Family, what do you mean?" She gives me an incredulous look. "The whole reason I'd go there would be to get away from my family!"

We both have to laugh. "The worst is already behind you," I assure her.

"You're right," she sighs. In a few days Salim will be leaving for Doha, then school will start again. This will be the first year Asma has to wear a paramilitary uniform – Hala wonders where you buy something like that. Life is much more regular during the school year, she goes to the university in the morning, comes home to eat, and then she and Asma do homework together.

Is it already time for Asma to go back to school? And what about our trip to the east and Aleppo? I've been so occupied by the family affairs of the last few weeks that I've barely thought about what would happen afterwards. Somehow I knew the vacation was almost over, but I'd pushed it to the back of my mind. But what's keeping me from travelling on my own? The thought has occurred to me before, but the pleasant shelter of Hala's company has always prevailed. We seem surrounded by a minefield of *mukhabarat*, and I've grown afraid of walking into it.

Night has fallen. Fayruz sings 'Kiefak enta' and everyone in the car hums along. We stop in Homs to buy a local confection for Zahra, who stayed at home. A little later we pass Deir Attieh, the village of Assad's private secretary, Abu Salim. When the illuminated statue of Assad looms up out of the darkness, I'm reminded of the statue of Lenin I saw a few days ago in the newspaper, dangling helplessly in the air. But Assad is still firmly on his feet; his arm is raised stiffly, and Asma makes everyone laugh by waving at him.

Along an unlit road on the outskirts of Damascus, Farid climbs out of the car. "What's he doing?" I ask.

"Shhh . . . this is where he lives," Hala whispers. I feel sorry for him: what a way to end a family outing! I can't imagine how he can find his way through the impenetrable darkness. But he walks away from us with long strides, and after a moment there's no trace of him in the night that surrounds us.

CHAPTER 4

"I'M GOING to Tadmor!" I'm standing in front of Hala, beaming. She frowns. Tadmor: that's the town with the most notorious prison in Syria, where Rifa'at's men murdered more than a thousand Muslim Brothers in 1980.

"What are you going to do there?"

"Walk through the desert to an Omayyad palace."

She's completely skeptical. "It's hot there, I'm sure it will be very tiring."

"So what – that's the whole idea!" The Swiss priest organizing the trip said there would be a lot of people from Aleppo among the crowd of eighty hikers – maybe I can travel back with them afterwards. "No way," Hala says resolutely, "you'll be exhausted after walking through the desert. You'd better come home and rest for a few days first."

I heave a sigh of relief: even though I long to stand on my own two feet, the prospect of arriving in Aleppo with a backpack doesn't appeal to me much. Aleppo is famous for its nightlife – a suitcase full of evening wear would be more appropriate.

The night before I leave, Hala and Asma watch me pack: a

pair of Shirin's pajamas, tennis shoes borrowed from Salim, a sleeping bag from the priests. They're just as excited as I am. "Why don't you two come along?" The very idea makes Hala laugh, and when I think of these two little figures out on the desert sand I have to laugh too. Like most women here, Hala doesn't walk any more than absolutely necessary.

I'll only be gone for a few days, but that evening we take the bottle of vodka out of the freezer and lie on the bed, talking as though we won't see each other for a long time. It's Hala's way of travelling with me.

The next morning she flutters around me, the way she does when Asma leaves for school. Do I have everything? Clothing, food, passport? She dreamed about me last night. The *mukhabarat* asked her to look for my passport: someone had been murdered and I was the prime suspect. "All I kept saying was that you would never do a thing like that." She laughs, but I see the worried way she clasps her hands. The woman next door told her I'd become thinner, and she feels guilty: she hasn't been taking good care of me, and of course I'll only get skinnier out there in the desert.

❖

I've been in the car with Father Léon for less than half an hour and the world has already been turned upside down. The regime here isn't as bad as all that, he says. The Alawites are generally easier to get along with than the Sunnis, and are more tolerant towards Christians. The Crusaders spent more than a century and a half in the Alawite mountains. They built their famous stronghold there, the Crac des Chevaliers, high above the coast.

As late as 1940, priests entered two Alawite villages with the

French and converted all the inhabitants. After the French left, the villagers reverted to their Alawite beliefs, but the residences the priests established there are still standing; no one seems to mind.

In his corduroy trousers and plaid shirt, Léon doesn't look much like a priest – with the possible exception of the cheerful smile he wears, even when there's not much to smile about, as though he wants to set things aright even before they go wrong.

Ibrahim, the Christian businessman who's driving us to Tadmor, doesn't say much. His eyes are fixed on the road, a narrow strip of asphalt with the air shimmering above it in the heat. Stretching out on all sides, as far as the eye can see, is a monotonous desert landscape. When the taxi dropped me off this morning at Ibrahim's house on the outskirts of Damascus, I was surprised: I would never have imagined thàt Father Léon had such wealthy acquaintances. A gardener in blue overalls opened the gate of the fenced-in villa. Ibrahim, a vigorous fifty-year-old in sports gear, was waiting for me on the veranda.

"So you don't think things would be better if the president were a Sunni Muslim?"

Father Léon laughs knowingly. "Then we might really be in trouble." Haven't I heard about what the Muslim Brothers were up to around here in the 1980s? There were uprisings everywhere: Homs, Aleppo, Damascus. Not a single Alawite official was safe.

"And then came Hama," I say.

"That's right, but do you think the regime had any choice? That uprising had to be crushed, otherwise we might be living in a fundamentalist state right now."

Ibrahim looks at me searchingly in the rearview mirror, as though he senses that I'm not used to hearing all this. "Do you agree with that?" I ask him. His hands slide hesitantly over the wheel, and he produces a noncommittal laugh. President Assad is a wise man, he says, and perhaps more popular than I realize. If elections were held tomorrow, Assad would definitely win more than half the votes, because the minorities – who make up about thirty per cent of the population – are on his side; plus there are all the Sunnis Assad has won over with privileges.

Father Léon says the Alawites are far-sighted, and less religious than the Sunnis. "Throughout the centuries, the Sunnis have always been more preoccupied with God, so they've lost touch with a lot of other things." Preoccupied with God – I'm amazed to hear that reproach coming from the mouth of a priest, but then Léon isn't your run-of-the-mill cleric. If he were back in Switzerland he would probably be working with drug addicts or the homeless.

The Alawites once belonged to the very lowest class in this country, they tell me, rather like the untouchables in India. Out of fear of persecution, they kept their religion largely secret. They had no mosques and they didn't observe Ramadan; that's why it was easy for them to adapt to other customs. Under the French mandate, the Alawite men served in the army, while Sunnis and Christians tried to buy their way out of conscription. "That's why Assad was able to seize power: there were a lot of Alawites in the army, and they supported him."

"And what happens when Assad dies?"

Father Léon smiles knowingly. "He's got a son, Basel, hasn't he? A fine young man, nothing wrong with him. What's to keep him from taking over from his father?"

Ibrahim nods in agreement. "I've always worked with Muslims," he says. "A lot of them live in my neighborhood, and I consider them my friends. But if the Muslim Brothers were to take power, I'm not so sure my friends wouldn't turn against me."

I knew the Christians in this country felt threatened – they account for fifteen per cent of the population, and the interests of the Alawite regime, a minority itself, are served by keeping alive the latent fears of the other minorities – but I hadn't realized things were so bad. I offer them my most convincing proof of the opposite of all they hold true: Hala – a Sunni Muslim herself – is every bit as afraid of Muslim fundamentalism as they are.

Father Léon isn't impressed in the slightest. "People like that are the exception," he says.

"No they're not," I object, "all the people she knows feel the same way."

Ibrahim gives me another searching look in the mirror. He used to feel the same way, he admits, but after what happened in Hama . . . At first the Muslim Brothers all over Syria had been sure of their victory. In Aleppo they had taken up a collection among Muslim businesses to buy out a well-known restaurant where alcohol was served. None of the business people were particularly devout, but it had taken them only a few hours to get the money together.

While I was packing last night, Hala said: "I bet all the people you meet there will be Christians." I hadn't thought about my trip that way. Did she know I would encounter ideas like these, is that why she sounded worried? I'd said that she was just as afraid of the fundamentalists as Father Léon and Ibrahim, but she never talks about them as a real threat. She says fundamentalism is a way of saying 'no' to the government, just like communism. Is she really as detached from Islam as she seems? Asma hadn't had to go to school a few days ago. "A day off already?" I'd exclaimed, "the school year's barely started!"

"It's the Prophet's birthday," Hala had said, sounding some-what annoyed.

"So what?"

"It's like Christmas," she'd snapped, "you all have the day off then, don't you?" She was right of course, but I was shocked by her fierce reaction – as though I'd intentionally slandered the Prophet.

It's become quiet in the car. The sun has reached its zenith, and hot air is blasting in through the windows. Ibrahim shakes his head hard to stay awake. Next to him, Father Léon has nodded off: he was up before dawn this morning to say Mass.

When we drive into Tadmor, he opens his eyes groggily. "Are we there already?" The dead calm of noon reigns in the streets of the desert town. In the distance rise the ruins of celebrated Palmyra, a Greco-Roman city that stretches into the desert for miles.

The Hotel Zenobia, where we'll spend the night, is located at the foot of the Palmyra ruins and is named after the queen who once ruled here. The hotel lobby is deserted; the rest of the group will arrive by *hob-hob* this evening. Father Léon and Ibrahim have to drop by the *mukhabarat* to report our plans to walk through the desert. I boldly climb back into the car – I've heard so much about the *mukhabarat* these past months; now I'm finally going to see them.

The little building we end up in smells of dust and long hours of indolence. Behind a desk covered in dog-eared dossiers sits a man in pajamas, drinking maté. Two of his colleagues, also in pajamas, poke their heads in the door as soon as they hear our voices. Their boss has risen to his feet, clearly intimidated by this unexpected visit. He offers us a chair, and his assistants sit down across from us.

Father Léon puts everyone at ease, telling little jokes, coyly flaunting the Aleppine accent he picked up during his early years in Syria. He tells them he's been here for twenty years and wouldn't move back to Switzerland for all the money in the world, a statement that wins him the men's unconditional approval. Before you know it they turn into animated conversationalists, complaining about the boredom of this distant outpost.

One of the men goes out to make coffee, grabbing his clothes from the coat rack as he goes by, then returning in trousers and a shirt. The other men follow his example. I peer at the dossier that was open when we entered and now lies closed on the table: what kind of devious schemes might be in there?

Father Léon sips his coffee and tosses me a wink. He doesn't seem at all impressed by this place. This morning in the car, when I told him about Hala's predicament, he suddenly turned around and asked: "Doesn't she have a *wasta*?" I shook my head weakly in surprise. "A *wasta*? No, I don't think Hala has one. Maybe through her job at the university . . . but it doesn't seem to help much." "Well, she does have bad luck then," he said, "that's simply the way this country works: if you don't have a *wasta*, it's difficult to get ahead." It would also be impossible for him to organize these hikes, I suspect, if he didn't have all kinds of people putting in a good word for him. The government is wary: before you know it the Muslims will want to go hiking in the desert too and set up a training camp for fundamentalists. Ever since Hama, only holiday camps for the Ba'athist Pioneers are allowed.

The man behind the desk examines the document Father Léon brought with him from Damascus, and then signs it. A few minutes later we're standing outside, with three attentive gentlemen in our wake. "They're completely baffled by this hiking business," Father Léon grins. "In this heat, they try to move as little as possible!"

At sunset a soft pink glow falls over Palmyra, and Ibrahim and I go for a walk among the ruins. Palmyra was once an oasis on the trade route between the Levant and Mesopotamia – it's one of the cities from pre-Christian and Christian history which are tucked away in Islamic Syria. The cool breeze blowing through the rows of pillars whips up the desert sand, veiling the distant triumphal arch in clouds of dust.

On the landing in Ibrahim's house this morning, the marble statue of a woman caught my eye, her eyes closed, arms folded across her chest. It exuded such serenity that I stopped in my tracks. "Yes, take a good look at it – it's authentic," Ibrahim had said proudly.

Now I look at him out of the corner of my eye. "That statue I saw at your house . . ."

He laughs light-heartedly: "That's right, it comes from around here. Probably from one of the tombs." He doesn't seem to have any qualms about it. No more than the owner of the Hotel Zenobia: the tables on his patio are Corinthian capitals.

To Hala, Palmyra is a faint echo of a deeply buried past, but walking around with Ibrahim I sense that he sees this city as an essential part of his own history. Before long we're back on this morning's topic. I was shocked by the opinions he and Father Léon entertained, but the tone of concern I hear in Ibrahim's voice now compels me to listen anew.

"The Christians here are uncertain about their future," he says, "everything has changed in the last ten years or so." Ten years – that's the period of time Hala always mentions too. Before that, everything seemed possible; then Ahmed was arrested,and Hama followed shortly afterwards.

"The Sunnis think this country is theirs alone. If they come into power, the Christians will become second-class citizens." Ibrahim is kicking a stone along with the tip of his sneaker. "More and more Syrian Christians are emigrating to the West. They don't feel at home here anymore; they no longer feel they have anything to offer their children. France, Australia, Canada – there are entire streets in Montreal where the only accent is Aleppine."

It's getting dark; the air is drained of color, and I can barely make out the expression on Ibrahim's face. "And what about you, wouldn't you like to emigrate?"

"No, not me," he says hesitantly. We've both turned back, as if at a signal; the hotel glistens softly in the distance.

"Do you know why Father Léon organizes these walks?" Ibrahim doesn't wait for my reply. "He wants to give the Christians back their feeling of attachment to their country – he doesn't want them to leave."

"So it's only Christians who come here?"

Again he hesitates. "Not exclusively, but most of us are, yes."

An overloaded *hob-hob*, decked out like a Christmas tree, drives beeping up to the hotel. A group of young people pour out of the bus. Father Léon is standing on the hotel steps, beaming. They surround him, pound him on the back, throw their arms around him. They call him *abuna* – 'our father'.

The boys who had ridden on the roof of the bus begin throwing down backpacks. I sit with Ibrahim at one of the little tables, watching the scene. My attention is drawn by a young woman, the focus of an excited group. Broad cheekbones and almond eyes, thick hair in a ponytail; the red cursive letters embroidered on the back pocket of her jeans read, 'Gloria

191

Vanderbilt'. She has something worldly about her – the kind of natural leader I remember from the summer camps of my youth. When a second bus arrives and a new group pours out, she is greeted and hugged just as enthusiastically as Father Léon.

The two of them come over to us, arm in arm. "This is Louise," Father Léon says, "I'm sure you'll have a lot to talk about." Ibrahim has gone to the car and brought back the cooler full of food his wife gave us for the trip this morning. He painstakingly sets the table with napkins, plates and utensils, then opens the plastic food containers one by one. A Corinthian capital for a table – it takes some getting used to, but I see everyone around me sitting casually with their feet up on them.

I'm starving, but Father Léon has stood up to greet more newcomers and Ibrahim makes no move to start without him. I think of his fenced-in villa, his garden with its antique statuary, his parlor with its polished furniture and antiquities in glass display cases. The only thing he has brought along from those surroundings is his cooler; he handles it as though it contains his entire life. Only when Father Léon has rejoined us does he begin carefully dishing out the grilled meat, tomatoes and bread.

Three men have walked up onto the patio. They look around, searching for something. Their expressions clear when they see Father Léon. Where do I know them from? Once they've settled down at our table, it suddenly dawns on me: these are the *mukhabarat* we met this afternoon. They look around inquisitively, legs wide apart, arms wrapped comfortably around the backs of their chairs. They order tea, wave to the hotel owner and laugh at Father Léon, who trots out his Aleppine accent again.

Louise speaks French fluently, and while the darkness deepens amid the ruins of Palmyra, we're soon talking like old friends. This sudden familiarity – I miss Hala, even though she would probably find this all strange and have a great many more reservations than I do about a woman like Louise.

Louise is one of those well-travelled Christians Ibrahim talked about. New York, Florida – she has family wherever she goes. Her parents spend part of their time in Toronto, the rest in Syria. The people she tells me about seem to have a tremendous urge to make their mark. "The Christians in this country have a great need to prove themselves," someone had told me earlier. "That's because they're a minority. They can't gain political power; the only thing within reach is commercial success." Louise's brother started out selling bread and cakes from his parents' garage; now he has his own confectionary business.

"Can you just do that here? Doesn't the government make things difficult for him?"

Louise laughs. "It would probably be better if they did!" Her brother received an order from Russia not long ago for one hundred tons of jellied fruit. He worked on it all summer. Then something went wrong: Syria halted all exports to Russia. Exporting commodities had once been the ideal way to balance the country's import payments, but trade between the two countries broke down when the Russian economy fell on hard times. Meanwhile, part of the jellied fruit shipment lies rotting in Tartus harbor. "You see why my brother would like to emigrate to Canada?"

She herself would rather stay in Syria. "But I'm afraid I won't be able to."

"Why not?"

"I'm in love with a Muslim," she whispers.

I laugh. "What difference does it make? Muslim, Christian . . ."

"Maybe it doesn't to you, but it does to people around here.

They all say he'll make me unhappy. It would be impossible for me to stay here if I marry him." Something dark has crept into her voice. "Maybe we could live together in Canada for a while, without getting married – then I could see whether it works out."

How can this region ever change, I think irritatedly, if everyone in these situations just flees to the West?

"Why don't the two of you try living together in Damascus?"

Louise shakes her head. "Live together here? No, that's out of the question. And if I marry him . . . you can't imagine the consequences that would have. My children would be raised as Muslims. My parents would never accept that."

"Are your parents that important to you? More important than he is?"

Louise smiles sadly. One of her parents' friends is married to a Muslim. One day their seventeen-year-old daughter went to her Christian grandfather and said he should convert to Islam before he died, otherwise he would go to hell. "You see how loathsome it is? I wouldn't want to do anything like that to my parents." Quietly, she adds: "Especially not after what happened to my sister."

"What was that?"

Louise pushes back a loose lock of hair. She looks at the three *mukhabarat* sitting at our table, then at her friends unrolling their sleeping bags in the distance. "I don't know if this is the right moment," she says hesitantly. But she tells me anyway.

It happened about ten years ago. Her sister was walking home from the university one afternoon. Suddenly a man raced by – an escaped prisoner, as it turned out. The policeman chasing him fired his gun. The man kept running, but her sister sank to the ground. She died on the spot.

"Everything in our family changed after that." Louise stares out across the busy patio, into the darkness. Her mother was inconsolable: she'd lost her favorite daughter and didn't know where to turn with her grief. "Since then she's thrown herself into religion. She goes to church every day, and the rest of the time she's busy with her Bible studies and charity work. It seems to be the only way she can live with her loss." Louise looks at me. "Can you imagine what would happen if I told her I wanted to marry a Muslim?"

A loud yell comes from a corner of the patio, where the first hikers have laid down to go to sleep. Louise smiles apologetically. "I have to go. My friends are calling."

I watch her as she disappears into the darkness. How carefree she'd seemed when she arrived with her friends. I couldn't help thinking: why isn't Hala like that? Toronto, New York, Florida – how quickly the illusion of cosmopolitanism summoned by those names has been dashed, how quickly the world has folded back in on itself.

❖

Abuna Léon walks out in front – lanky, in high spirits, a bandanna tied around his neck, on his head a weird knitted cap that generates at least as much hilarity as his Aleppine accent. We left in tight formation in the early morning, but now trail through the desert in a ragged, broken line at least two kilometers long. It's rolling countryside – every once in a while a section of the ragged line vanishes over a hill. I was worried about not being in shape, but there's nothing fanatical about Father Léon's hikers; I have no trouble staying among the first group of twenty.

A professor from the University of Damascus, who studied in Leipzig, comes to walk next to me. He's big and strong-looking, but it's hard for him to keep up the pace. "I had pictured something quite different," he grumbles, wiping the sweat from his forehead. "Just imagine, the Jews wandered through the desert for forty years after being driven out of Egypt. I feel for them." Biblical references! In my mind's eye I keep seeing T. E. Lawrence, who sometimes travelled through the desert on his camel, sick as a dog, falling asleep in the sand at night with fever racking his body.

The professor is about thirty-five, but he still lives with his parents. "It's not easy to find a wife," he says, "the supplies are limited." He had a number of girlfriends in Leipzig, and he can no longer imagine marrying a girl he barely knows, but that's completely normal around here. "You can't even walk down the street holding hands – everyone would think that was scandalous."

"Didn't you meet anyone in Leipzig you wanted to marry?"

"No, German women . . ." He sighs. "Somehow Syrian women are different." This is the first time he's gone along on one of these hikes. Could he be here to find a suitable partner? It doesn't seem unlikely, and when Louise joins us, I see his face light up. She's clearly the old hand in this crowd: the right walking shoes, cap on her head, day pack strapped around her waist. Last night's distress has disappeared without a trace. She strides along at a good pace, but when Father Léon remarks that some of us are falling too far behind, she slows down. A bit later she's bringing up the rear, her arm around a girl's shoulders.

Ibrahim is walking in front of me. Even though he seems to know many of these people, he doesn't join in their conversations. He has come here with his own thoughts – he prefers to walk alone.

Father Léon is carrying all his baggage, but most of the others have left theirs in the bus that will supply us with water along the way. When we see the bus loom up on the horizon around noon, a cry of relief goes up. We drink, and rest a bit in the shade. The professor plops down hard next to me.

A group of about ten hikers obstinately refuse to leave the bus. They've had enough. At one of the windows I see the girl Louise had her arm around, crying. "She's just been through a period of depression," Louise says. "It all came back to her when she started walking." Father Léon had already talked about that: the desert silence throws many people for a loop. Half joking, half serious, he drags a couple of young people from the bus. They protest loudly, but he's unrelenting. Only the crying girl is allowed to stay seated, along with a father and his young daughter.

"The people here aren't used to living on their reserves," Léon says as we walk further, "as soon as they get tired, they give up. I want to teach them to fight against that, because that's exactly what they do in daily life as well." I can't help weighing his comments against my own experiences. Doesn't Hala also give up too quickly? But isn't that because everything around her is so discouraging? Wouldn't I become like that too if I stayed here?

We walk on and on, and gradually become less talkative. The landscape devoid of highlights, the wind whistling through the hills, the relentless sun – soon the silence has me in its grip as well. My body moves like a robot, and apparently incoherent thoughts roll through my mind, like a concert in a hushed hall.

What must be hours later, I suddenly find myself walking next to Ibrahim. "What do you think, how far do we have to go?" I ask. It's starting to get dark, and here and there I hear grumbling about *abuna Léon*. He claimed it was a hike of around twenty-five kilometers, but we've already walked much further than that and Qasr al-Hayr is still nowhere to be seen. Even I'm starting to have had enough of this mechanical march through the sand: where's that damned palace?

"That's Father Léon for you," Ibrahim grins, "he loves to sow confusion. It's always further away than he claims." The group of teenagers in front of us has struck up a song. I try to place the melody, but can't. It's definitely not one of the popular Egyptian songs of the moment – I would recognize any of those.

"What are they singing?"

Ibrahim listens. "A religious song. Something about the Virgin Mary and her son."

The Virgin Mary and her son – how about that, and completely spontaneous to boot, without *abuna Léon* anywhere around! The singing grows louder, and is picked up by the group in the lead. If only Hala could see me walking here, under the moon that hangs like a glaring lamp in the firmament, behind a group of Syrians singing Christian songs – she'd think it was pretty suspicious. Yet this all seems familiar to me. This is how my father must have sung at scout camp, kerchief around his neck, knee socks pulled up below short pants.

"What are you thinking?" Ibrahim asks.

"About my father. He must have sung songs like this when he was young. But that was at least fifty years ago."

"Would you say that people in Europe are no longer religious?"

"Well, no, not like this anyway."

His experience is different. When he goes to Switzerland with Father Léon, he meets a lot of rather pious people. I think of the Dutch TV programs by the Evangelical Broadcasting Association: the open mouths, the elated warbling. "If you look long enough, you'll still find them," I say hesitantly, "but compared to this . . ."

"That's because this is a spiritual area: the three major mono-theistic religions arose here . . ."

"Look!" The singing out in front of us suddenly sounds happier. A light has appeared in the distance. We head for it, walking fast.

❖

A big pot of soup is simmering on a gas stove. Sitting around it is a group of fifteen happy souls – the group which stayed in the bus after the second break, blatantly refusing to walk on despite Father Léon's vehement protests. Behind them loom the con-tours of Qasr al-Hayr, the palace the Omayyads built here in the early eighth century, during the heyday of their power. Not long before that they had defeated Ali, son-in-law of the Prophet, and made Damascus the hub of the Arab Empire.

We unload our things from the bus, and settle down at the base of the palace to gloat at the hikers arriving in increasingly lamentable states. Father Léon, bringing up the rear, is greeted with catcalls. Beaming with delight, he admits that he underes-timated the length of the hike: we've walked a good thirty-five kilometers. When someone moans that we'll have to walk the same distance back tomorrow, Father Léon promises that we'll do the last leg by bus.

As it turns out, Ibrahim has a tablecloth among his things. He spreads it on the sand, carefully smoothing out the creases. The contents of his cooler smell less fresh than they did yesterday, but he arranges the tomatoes, boiled potatoes and cheese with no less ceremony. I rummage through my pack and place my

199

meager contribution alongside. Father Léon appears with three cups of steaming soup. Ibrahim makes room for him, but Léon has barely squatted down before he's called away once more.

Ibrahim remains sitting motionless. "Shall we just go ahead?" I suggest.

"Oh no, I'm sure he's coming back, he left his soup here."

"Come on, I'm starved!" I start eating, without looking him in the eye. Ibrahim keeps peering into the darkness until he locates Father Léon: he's standing next to the steaming pot, cap on his head, slurping at the dregs of another cup of soup. "He's not coming back," I say, "he's too busy." Ibrahim haltingly follows my lead.

We sleep at the base of the palace, the women in the middle, the men in a wide circle around them. Father Léon says Mass, but I'm long gone by then.

❖

We lie in the red glow of the rising sun like soldiers who've fallen on the field of battle. I sit up in my sleeping bag and look around; some other people are already awake. In this light, Qasr al-Hayr looks like a fairy-tale fortress: high walls, embrasured towers and a narrow gateway. Later we will go in through that gate, the reckless among us climbing to the tops of the walls where they will sing and wave down to the rest.

Today, Father Léon has decided, we will take the route due south; the bus will pick us up once we hit the paved road to Tadmor. We take off in good spirits. I silently bless Salim's tennis shoes, simple Chinese sneakers that prove a great deal more effective than the expensive sports shoes worn by many of the other hikers. One boy has such bad blisters that he walks in his socks.

An Italian nun hikes along with me for a while. She lives in Hassake, a small town in the north-east of the country, not far from the oil fields where Hala was once beset by the elderly Abu Talib. Her stories about the Kurds, Christians, Muslims and Bedouins in that area, which borders both Turkey and Iraq, capture my imagination. When we arrive at the asphalt road, she will say goodbye to us and hitchhike back to Hassake with a few young people. Shouldn't I go along with them? Isn't that my only chance of ever going there?

All morning I weigh the pros and cons of such a change of course, and cover a great many kilometers in the process. But Hala's house keeps appearing in my mind: the cupboard she's emptied for my things, the bed that's always covered in clothes, the evenings when all three of us have had our baths and a pleasant quiet settles on the house. Hadn't Hala insisted that I come back after my walk in the desert? If I stay away too long, I may lose her. What's more, Ibrahim has invited me to join him and his wife soon on a visit to Aleppo, where they have an apartment.

It's already two o'clock, but there's no sign of the bus. My water is finished, and by now I've also consumed the professor's water supply. The murmuring around us increases in volume. "Hey, where's that bus!" "*Abuna Léon*, if this is another one of your jokes!"

We decide to halt at the top of a hill. Human wreckage comes stumbling towards us: there's the guy in socks, and a bit further back there's someone with a bad nosebleed. While we're discussing our next move, a young man in an enormous sombrero, who's been clowning around the whole time, suddenly faints. His friends make a sunshade for him from sticks and a raincoat. Someone pours the last of his water over his face while Louise fans him with his own sombrero. I look at him, lying there like a felled oak, and feel a rush of panic: what will happen if we don't find the bus? The professor peers off in the same direction and says despondently: "Do you remember how thirsty Christ was when he hung on the cross? This is our Calvary – we won't get out of here alive." But one look at Father Léon reassures me. He's lying calmly on his back, his hands behind his head, a dirty handkerchief draped over his face. I have a sneaking suspicion that he's laughing beneath that handkerchief.

Someone is waving wildly to us in the distance: one of the patrols sent out to scout the surroundings has located the bus. Sighing and groaning, the group sets itself in motion.

We reach the Hotel Zenobia around evening. Father Léon is taking the *hob-hob* to Damascus, but Ibrahim offers me a ride. We're hungry, but when we open the cooler, the stench of fermenting tomatoes and over-ripe cheese hits us in the face and we close the lid in horror.

Outside Tadmor we encounter a roadblock. A soldier looks in the car disinterestedly while his colleague remains seated in his chair beneath an awning. "They're afraid of infiltrators from Iraq," Ibrahim says. Further along another soldier jumps out in front of the car, waving his rifle. Ibrahim screeches to a halt, and the man sticks his head and his rifle in the window. To my surprise, Ibrahim scolds him violently. The soldier withdraws his rifle in shock and Ibrahim races away.

"What was that?" I ask astounded.

"Some hitchhiking soldier! Standing there waving his rifle around, who does he think he is!"

"Weren't you afraid? He could have mowed us down."

"Mowed us down? Not him," Ibrahim says grimly, "he knew the score as soon as I yelled at him to keep his rifle to himself.

One look at my car and he knew he'd better not mess with me."

I sit there, still shaking for a while. How different it is travelling with Hala, how much more fearful she is of soldiers and *mukhabarat*. We drive down the unlit road in silence. For two days I've been putting my best foot forward – anything to ward off Father Léon's compassionate little smile – but now I'm suddenly dead tired. Ibrahim is deep in thought.

Driving into Damascus, after the freedom of the last few days, it's as though I'm boxed in again. It's so late that Ibrahim suggests I spend the night at his house. I sleep royally, in a guest bedroom with adjoining bath, in a high bed with a floral spread and matching curtains. In the morning I'm awakened by the sound of the gardener cleaning the pool. Ibrahim's wife, Amira, and the cleaning woman are busy in the kitchen.

We drink coffee on the veranda. Through the slats in the fence around the front of the house I can see mothers in black *abayas* taking their children to school. It's a strange sight – as if they don't belong in these surroundings. One of the children stops and tries to peer into the garden. I'm embarrassed to be sitting here, in the midst of so much luxury, cut off from the street by a high fence.

When Ibrahim and Amira bring me home, it's their turn to look around uneasily; they've never been in this neighborhood before. As their bright blue BMW pulls up in front of Hala's gate, I see the greengrocer peering at us inquisitively.

Amira stays in the car while Ibrahim takes my backpack out of the trunk. "Come in with me," I suggest. Amira hesitates. "Come on, just for a moment." Hala and Asma aren't home. Ibrahim puts my backpack down in the living room, and Amira pokes her head through the door. "Do you live here? All three of you?" I see our furniture turn shabby before our eyes: the plaid couch, the curtains, the wooden cupboard with glass doors behind which stands the photo of Ahmed – all these endlessly familiar things.

Ibrahim puts his arm around Amira. "Shall we be going then?"

CHAPTER 5

S OMEONE ELSE'S things are in the house: school notebooks that don't belong to Asma, a cardboard box of cheap cookies Hala would never buy, a small bottle of Syrian perfume. My cupboard is full of junk, and there's an unfamiliar dress hanging on the line.

Hala comes in around noon, in a hurry, plastic bags full of groceries in both hands. She looks tired – her face is swollen. "I thought you'd never come back!" We hug, clumsily as always. "We have guests," she says.

"Yes, I noticed."

"Sahar and Aisha, they're not staying long." Sahar is a Christian, I suddenly remember, her husband a Muslim. There you have it – the religious differences everyone has been talking about during the last few days don't apply to Hala and her friends.

"Have you heard the news? They say the prisoners are going to be released. Sahar is having her house fixed up; that's why she's staying here."

"What about Ahmed?"

Hala shrugs. "He asked me to bring him his winter clothes. That means he's planning to stay for a while."

She begins peeling potatoes in the kitchen; the children will be coming home any minute. I bring in the folding table from the hallway, pull up a plastic chair and apply myself to the green beans. Hala gives me a searching look. "How was it? Anything interesting happen?" She sounds skeptical.

I tell her about Father Léon's weird cap, the grumbling hikers, the ups and downs of Louise's love life. I suddenly realize that when I arrived in Syria I didn't even know whether Hala was a Christian or a Muslim – we didn't talk about those things back then

"Do you consider me a typical Christian? Have you ever thought of me that way?"

Hala laughs in surprise. "No, what makes you think that?"

"Oh, I don't know, I just wondered."

She says nothing more about it. She doesn't seem at all interested in what's preoccupying me. She tells me about Tété, Zahra, Shirin and Farid. Every name she mentions is accompanied by a heartfelt 'umph!'. Shirin has moved in with Farid. "You know what? The cows wake them up every morning." Hala makes a disgusted face. To wake to rural sounds – as a city dweller, she can't imagine anything worse. "Farid is used to it, of course, but Shirin . . ." She lights the oven, puts in a casserole dish of potatoes, onions and ground beef, and says peevishly: "Just the thing for them, they can drink fresh milk every day."

Tété is worried sick that they'll want to move in with her again before long; after all, how can they make it through the winter without heating? "She's begging me to come and live with her for the next few months," Hala laughs. "She says I can even bring you along!" Asma's school is closer to her house, Tété reasons, and it would save on the heating bill. "The price of oil has gone up again: one hundred pounds for two days' worth. How can a family ever afford that on a monthly salary of two thousand pounds?"

"But everyone here has more than one income, don't they?" It pops out before I know it. That's what Father Léon says, and he's right too, everyone here has something going on the side. But Hala isn't used to having me contradict her – until now, she's been my principal source of information about this country. "No, not at all," she protests, "most people have to make do with just their salary." More and more children are being sent out to work, she says. Every morning on the way to the university she passes a little boy, who must be about eight, selling bread; when she comes home in the afternoon, he's still standing there.

How long have I been gone? Barely three days, but Hala talks to me as if I've just come from abroad, as though I know nothing about what goes on here! Before I have time to reply, Asma and Aisha rush in. They throw their schoolbags on the floor, change their clothes and lock themselves in the front room with a Madonna tape.

Hala tosses my clothes in the washing machine, sweeps the courtyard, scolds the neighbors who have their TV on much too loudly, runs back and forth between the kitchen and the bedroom, and grumbles the whole time about a colleague of hers at the university. He knows nothing about the subject he teaches – what he would really like to do, she says, is become head of the *mukhabarat*.

Gradually I feel my defiance ebb away. The clarity of the last few days, the empty desert landscape, the broad hallways in Ibrahim's house, the cool guest room with its high bed – it all starts to seem like a mirage. I'm back at the school of hard knocks.

After dinner, Hala, Sahar and I lie on the bed in our night-gowns. Asma and Aisha are doing their homework in the front room, and Madonna blares through the walls. Sahar is excited by the rumors about the release of the prisoners. Aisha and she have already been to the tailor's for new dresses.

"You'll never guess who I ran into this morning," Hala interrupts her. "Who?" "Omayya!" Omayya's husband was released a few years ago after fifteen years in prison. "Well?" Sahar asks inquisitively, "what did she say?" "She cried, right there on the street. 'Don't wait for your husbands,' she said. 'I waited so long for mine and now I wish they'd lock him up again.'"

"Why?" I ask.

Hala sighs. "He's become old, he doesn't know how to be happy anymore. The only thing he thinks about is how his friends in prison are doing."

"Did you see Tadmor prison?" Sahar wants to know.

I shake my head. "No, *abuna Léon* wasn't so interested in that."

I tell her about Louise. "By the way, how did you do it? Weren't your parents opposed to your marrying a Muslim?"

Sahar thinks about it. "At first they were, but later on not anymore."

"What if they had tried to stop you, what would you have done then?"

She laughs. "I didn't need their approval, it was my life. We belonged to the same political movement, we didn't care much about religion – we had other things on our minds!" I'm reminded of what a Lebanese acquaintance once told me about leftists in the Arab world. They had done nothing to change tribal consciousness, he said, they had simply started a new tribe: the communist one. There they found the security they had known before among their own people.

That night Hala and I sleep in the same bed again. We both lie dreaming, tossing and turning. In my student quarters in Utrecht I find that three little urchins have moved in with me. I try to explain to my roommates that I can't work with these kids around, but no one understands what I'm so worked up about.

Hala dreams that she's at a reception, where she meets a very bad Egyptian actress. While she's talking to her, she suddenly discovers that she forgot to put on her shoes. She's embarrassed: a faculty member of the University of Damascus without footwear! But a bit later she feels an enormous rage welling up inside her. She looks at the actress with fire in her eyes and shouts that she doesn't even *want* to talk to her.

I'm startled awake by the rasping gutturals of the muezzin in the nearby mosque. It's still dark outside. *Allahu akbar, Allaaaah* . . . It sounds like he's sitting in the corner of the room. How have I been able to sleep through this for the last few months? Once my eyes become adjusted to the dark, I see that Hala is awake too. She looks at me and smiles, but says nothing.

❖

At first, Asma was wild about her new paramilitary uniform. She put it on as soon as Hala brought it home, stuck a toy pistol in her wide leather belt, took her whistle out of the drawer and ran outside. She wanted to keep it on as long as she could at night. It took some getting used to – it was like having a little soldier around the house. After her bath she would lie in front of the TV in her pajamas, her kepi on her head.

But the first morning she had to go to school in uniform, she acted bashful. She turned endlessly before the mirror in the hall, schoolbag strapped to her back. At the bus stop she was reluctant to join her classmates; some of the girls were wearing white headscarves with their uniforms.

By now the novelty has worn off: after school she kicks off her khaki pants in the bedroom, her shirt and kepi fly through the air. One afternoon Hala picks up the pants with a sigh and discovers a tear in them. "Look at this – what a little monkey, these have to last her six years!" Schoolbooks and notebooks with pictures of Assad on the covers lie tossed all around. Classroom stories seep into the house and begin coloring our lives.

Asma would like to be put in a different class, where more of her former classmates are, but when she asked the teacher about it, her reply was: "Do you have a *wasta*?" This same teacher appointed one of the girls to inform her about everything that goes on behind her back. "That's how they teach children to spy, even at this age," Hala sighs.

Sometimes we pick up Asma from school. In the taxi one afternoon she asks: "Mama, are the *ikhwan muslimin* – Muslim Brothers – bad people?" Hala looks at the taxi driver in alarm, signals to Asma to talk more softly and whispers: "Why do you ask that?" Asma says they learned a new song at school. Later, when we sit down to dinner at the kitchen table, she sings it for us. It goes like this:

We vow to combat imperialism
and Zionism, and backwardness,
and that their criminal accomplices, the Muslim Brothers,
we shall destroy.

They have to sing that every morning in the playground. The last line in particular echoes in Asma's mind. "But do you know who the *ikhwan* are?" Hala asks. "Those are the boys in prison with Papa, the ones who sometimes come over to say hello when

210

we visit him. Remember Rafik? Does he look like a bad person?"

No, Asma has to admit, Rafik doesn't look like a bad person. She eats her soup slowly, deep in thought. Then she asks another question. It has something to do with me, although I can't find out right away what it is. Hala answers her quietly, but Asma's voice keeps getting louder. She angrily brushes aside all Hala's demurrals. I listen in amazement: this demagogic tone is so foreign to Asma, it's as if a fourth person had joined us at the table.

"What are you two talking about?"

Hala is visibly embarrassed. "Asma wants to know why you don't become a Muslim."

I laugh. "How did she come up with that?"

"Oh, the things people say around here . . . Christians believe that Mary is the mother of Jesus, they say, and therefore the wife of God, which is impossible according to Islam."

"Where does Asma get these stories?"

"From her religion teacher, apparently."

Asma gives me a fierce look; the fire of this morning's religion class burns on. Islam is the most recent religion, her teacher said, and therefore the best.

"What do you tell her?" I ask Hala.

"What *can* I tell her? I don't want to say things that will get her into trouble at school, I don't want her to become alienated from her classmates. I can only hope she'll eventually discover the truth herself, like I did."

Asma has left the table. Hala follows her with her eyes as she runs outside with her whistle around her neck. This isn't the first time they've had these discussions. Last spring Asma came home from school thoroughly upset. At first she didn't want to talk about what had happened. She just wanted to cry, she said, that's how bad she felt. That evening Hala suggested that they

211

take a walk, like two grown-ups who have something important to talk about. During the walk it all came out, bit by bit. A girlfriend had told her that Mohammed didn't receive his knowledge directly from Allah, the way the religion teacher said, but from Buhayra, a Christian monk he met on one of his journeys. It's a story Christians often tell about the Prophet – Hala had heard it before. "And it's probably true; of course Islam adopted some things from Christianity."

"Did you tell her that?"

"Oh no. I can't tell her everything I'm thinking. To me, Islam is an old carpet: beautiful to look at, but old nonetheless. But if I told her that and her teacher heard it, she'd think I was a communist!" She stares sadly into space. "Who knows, maybe the things they teach Asma at school are a good preparation for times to come. Maybe before long there won't be any place for ideas like Ahmed's and mine."

The TV is on, the cassette recorder is playing and the folding table has been moved from the kitchen to the front room – Asma is doing her homework. Sometimes she calls Hala in to help. They bicker about the law of gravity: Asma doesn't understand it, Hala can't explain it. That evening Hala has to quiz her. Another person takes possession of Asma as she recites her lessons, her legs folded under her, her body held taut as a wire. Sometimes I recognize the rhetorical, hollow tone of the speeches of Arab leaders; at other times, the entreating voice of the imam in the mosque. When she's in a good mood, I'm allowed to test her French. Her textbook was published in 1971. It contains drawings of French children, of cats and dogs and French villages in the snow – 'every Sunday, Delphine and Marinette go to church with their parents'.

I'm amazed at the complicated French sentences Asma is able to recite by heart; little stories by Guy de Maupassant, poems by Victor Hugo. They're delivered in tight little packages, with not a single word left out. Afterwards, when I ask her a simple question that isn't in the book, she laughs shyly and Hala has to translate what I've said.

"Did you learn everything by heart too?" I ask Hala.

"No, at least not that way." A military regime doesn't want people to think, she says, it would rather have them recite everything.

That evening I have to go to Father Léon's house to drop off the things I borrowed from him. "Maybe I'll ask him to come by and visit us sometime," I say. "I'm sure both of you would like him."

When I come home Asma is already asleep. Hala is lying on the bed in her room reading *Le harem politique: Le Prophète et les femmes* by the Moroccan sociologist Fatima Mernissi. Not the Prophet again! Father Léon was right when he said that the Sunni Muslims wallow in Islamic history.

Hala looks up from her book. "Interesting?" I ask. She doesn't fail to notice the irony in my voice – she senses exactly what's on my mind since my walk through the desert with Father Léon. She nods. "But I never thought I'd read something like this."

"So why are you reading it?"

She puts down the book with a sigh. "Did you hear Asma at the table this afternoon? That teacher of hers comes up with the biggest nonsense about Islam, just like the fundamentalists. I want to be able to defend myself when people attack me, and I can do that better with the words of the Prophet himself than with Marx or Sartre. Do you think people understood Ahmed and his friends when they talked about communism? No, they only understand the language of religion." Even the communists

213

realized that after a while, she says, but just when they were trying to find common ground with the Muslim Brothers, to form a united front, they were arrested.

She likes the book. "There's even something in it that will appeal to you." She reads me a passage in which Mernissi explains that, to Westerners, the past is like dessert, while Arabs regard it as the main dish.

Hala is sitting up now and laughs secretively. "Asma and I had an interesting talk after you left."

"About what?"

"How can Father Léon come to visit us, he's a Christian priest, isn't he?" Asma had asked as soon as I pulled the door shut behind me.

"That doesn't mean he can't come to visit us." Hala had said.

"But the Christians don't like us, do they?"

"Who says they don't? Where did you hear that?"

"I can tell at school," Asma said. "The Christian children always play by themselves, they don't like us."

"What about Sahar, she doesn't have anything against us, does she?"

Asma had to think about that one. Sahar, that was different, she said.

"And what about Lieve? She's a Christian too."

Asma thought again. "Maybe she's not a real Christian," she wavered. When Hala insisted that I was, Asma ruled: "No, Lieve is Lieve."

❖

It's growing cooler in the streets of Damascus – Hala had warned me that the seasons change abruptly around here. Close to Tété's house, little stands selling prickly pear have appeared, and Tété has spent days bottling citrus fruit and *makdous* – little eggplants stuffed with walnuts and hot peppers. At home, Hala puts away the floor fan and covers the bed with heavy blankets. She buys fresh olives at the market and pickles them in brine. They taste bitter, but the Damascenes like them that way – it goes with the season.

The smell of autumn is in the air, an intimate, cosy smell that reconciles me to the domesticity of my life in Damascus. The jasmine tree has lost its scent, the leaves of the fig tree in the courtyard have begun to change color and there's a new sound in our street: *Blooopblooop, blooopblooop.* The first time she hears it, Hala pricks up her ears and runs outside. It's the man who sells heating oil; there's a barrel on the roof that he fills to the rim.

The cigarette boys squat down together in the evening and warm their hands at the chestnut-seller's fire. Whenever I get out of the taxi and see them in the distance, my heart begins to pound. Their leader's leather jacket shines under the streetlights. Ever since I saw him coming out of his house with his groggy face and wrinkled T-shirt, I've felt a peculiar bond with him. But he himself seems to have lost his bravura since that meeting. His friends still nudge him when I come by, but he no longer calls out to me, he only looks at me out of the corner of his eye.

His presence imparts a certain wistfulness to our street. One evening when he's not there I saunter home, disappointed, searching for a glimpse of his jacket and his proud head with its combed-back hair. Suddenly I remember Siham's story. She lived in a neighborhood just like this one, in the old part of Baghdad. As she was walking home one evening, a young man came up to her. He pressed his body against hers and she smelled

215

his breath – he had been drinking. He kissed her, hard and desperately. She was too stunned to resist, but before she even realized what had happened, he murmured "Excuse me, excuse me" and ran off around the corner. Only then did she smell his scent – a pleasant, spicy smell. For months the mysterious meeting was on her mind: she kept feeling his body against hers, smelling his scent. She searched for him in every young man she came across. She was twenty-five when I met her; that stolen kiss in the night seemed the most substantial thing that had ever happened to her.

Hala and Asma are taking a bath together. They talk and chortle like turtle doves; I listen to them with a mixture of tenderness and envy. They're discussing who's the best hairdresser in Damascus, Georges or Johnny. Wrapped in her robe, a towel around her head, Hala comes walking into the bedroom – "Oh, are you back already?" Asma calls from the bathroom to ask for a robe, using her sweetest voice. "Coming right up, *ya habibi*." Hala winks at me. '*Habibi*', my dearest, is a masculine form of address.

"My daughter is growing up," Hala whispers laughingly. Not long ago, Asma was looking at herself in the mirror in the hall. "When will the boys start calling out to me?" she wanted to know. "Soon," Hala said, "but only if you start dressing less boyishly. They won't whistle at you if you always wear jeans." Some time after that, Asma asked her about the difference between a girl and a married woman. Hala gave her a vague answer about a married woman usually working more around the house and taking care of the children, but that apparently wasn't what Asma was waiting to hear. Tonight she started talking about it again. "Mama, is it true that girls have something fragile inside them?" She heard that from Leila, one of her girlfriends at school. When a woman marries, Leila claims, that delicate membrane gets broken. "And if a woman is divorced and then marries again, Mama, does it grow back by itself?"

The curse of virginity! The same curse Hala decided to shake off at the age of eighteen. "It all repeats itself," she says. When Asma comes out of the tub she throws herself on the bed and looks at me, eyes gleaming, still under the spell of the chatter in the steam bath. Her hair is wet, her skin glistens, she smells soapy, and when I reach out an arm to her she snuggles up to me. She peers at Hala through her wet hair. "Tell Lieve about Rami," she says. Rami is a classmate she's had a crush on for months. Of course I've already heard all about him, but Hala plays along. Asma shows me the picture she keeps in her wallet, next to the one of her father: a plump little boy with a worried expression – not exactly what you'd call a playboy. But Rami is popular, and Asma isn't his only girlfriend: she's second in a line of five. While Hala combs her unruly curls, Asma announces that she's going to invite him over for lunch next week. When he comes, she says sternly, Hala and I will have to stay out of the room.

That evening she lies in front of the TV and sings along exuberantly with the commercials for Lebanese shampoo, powdered milk and corn oil. She changes channels with her foot. Suddenly, Assad appears on the screen, seated across from a blonde female journalist. They're talking about the peace conference in Madrid. Hala comes in from the kitchen. "This was taped at his new residence," she remarks. "See those enormous vases? Just like in Saudi palaces."

"What's he saying?"

"Wait, they'll translate it in a bit." She's right: later we see the interview again, this time subtitled in English and French.

Assad's shirt is blue, then white, depending on the quality of the reception. The American journalist asks him about political freedom in Syria. Assad smiles affably and points out that there are only two political parties in America, but seven in Syria. "And now the only thing we'll hear for days is how wonderful the Americans think our president is," Hala grumbles.

Tomorrow she has to visit Ahmed; the preparations take up all her time. In the bedroom I find her standing high on the ladder, her head practically hidden in a leather suitcase on top of the cupboard. She pulls out a baggy beige sweater and looks at it lovingly. "I knitted this for Ahmed myself." She tosses it to me resolutely. "Put it on the pile. It doesn't look so great anymore, but Ahmed would wonder why it wasn't there, he'd think something was going on." He still wears the blue shirt he had on when he was arrested, even though it's in tatters by now.

"Maybe I should buy him a shirt," I say.

"You'll probably still be here when he comes home." Hala has turned around. "Don't you think? You heard what Sahar said, didn't you? The prisoners are going to be released. After all, Assad has to show the Americans that he's a real democrat!" She laughs. "Nothing's happened around here for eleven years, then you come along and everything happens at once. The presidential elections are coming up in December. There's no way you can leave now."

"But I can't just wait here until they free Ahmed. Who knows how long that will take? I can't stay away that long. What would my boyfriend say . . .?"

"Why don't you have him come over?"

"And stay in this little house?"

"We could all move out to Wadi al-Nakhleh."

"And take Ahmed along?"

"Why not? Or maybe Ahmed would rather stay here alone."

"I'd have to have my winter clothes brought over from Holland, and send my summer things back."

"I'd wait before sending those summer things if I were you. Maybe you'll still be here next summer."

It's nice to bob along on her sea of fantasy. The air suddenly tingles with excitement again, and the end of my stay fades into the indefinite. Who knows, maybe important things are about to happen here.

Hala has come down from the ladder, and the floor of the cupboard is covered with more plastic bags full of things. Last winter she was in mourning for her father – she hasn't looked at her winter clothes for two years.

"Take a look at this." She sits down in the cupboard and hands me a light-pink compact. '*Amour absolu*' is printed on the lid in graceful letters. I open the little box and carefully pick up the powder puff. "It's at least forty years old," Hala says. "It was one of my mother's wedding presents."

"And from the looks of things she never used it."

"No, she gave it to me just like this." She carefully wraps the box back up in its white tissue. Sighing, she explores further. "All this junk, what am I going to do with it?" She pulls out a muff with a fake gold chain, stands before the mirror and presses it to her side coquettishly. "What do you think?" It's not her style. "I'll wear it when Ahmed comes home." We both know that's not true.

She digs in the cupboard again and comes back up with a black shawl with a picture of St Peter's on it. "Remember that Italian cinematographer in Baghdad? She gave me this."

"And you put it in the cupboard right away."

"Sure, what else would I do with it?" I catch a glimpse of the little bathrobe and the T-shirt with a motorcyclist on it that I brought for Asma. Meanwhile, Hala has run across three flat boxes with silk nightgowns in them. "Look, I bought these when I thought Ahmed was coming home." Pink and light-blue little nothings with bows – she's never worn them and she wonders whether they're still in fashion.

"Why don't you give them to Shirin? I'm sure she'd be happy to have them."

Hala looks at me from between the piles of clothing, total incomprehension on her face. "But Lieve, these are my dreams!"

❖

"How do I look?" She's standing in the doorway, bags full of winter clothes and books in each hand, taut from head to toe, braced for the journey. "Well, those earrings . . ." The silver hoops with tinkling bells and little blue stones are much too heavy for her little face. "Ahmed likes them," she says bravely, "I do it for him."

This time she's going alone. I hug her – now it's as though she's the one going on a trip. But it's only a little past noon when I hear the gate open again. She has his summer clothes with her, and a present for me: a pen box made of wood and palm resin, decorated with copper arabesques and lined with red velour.

She collapses on the couch. "If you knew what I've been through this morning!" She had to wait forever before they let her in, so she started talking to the woman in front of her, someone she'd never seen before. "Is your husband in there?" The woman nodded. "Politics?" The woman turned up her nose in contempt. "No, money." She looked at Hala without a smidgin of curiosity. "What about you?" Hala thrust her chin in the air and said: "Politics." Neither of them said a thing for a moment; Hala was trying to imagine what 'money' could be about. "Bribes?" she enquired. The woman threw her a withering glance: "That's what they say."

The rumors about the political prisoners being released had made everyone nervous. When their names were finally called, they saw that the guards had an enormous dog with them to sniff out any drugs being smuggled in. Some of the women were frightened and started screaming. The dog was as big as a pony, and Hala didn't dare walk past it either. One woman took the bag of sugar she'd brought for her son and threw it at the guards. This caused such a commotion that they had to take the dog away.

Then, out of revenge, the guards began skimping on the food the women had brought for the prisoners. They confiscated Ahmed's mother's homemade *kibbe*, and another woman had to leave behind a plate of fish. "They're afraid to surrender power," Hala says, "they want to show us they're still the boss." But the women protested so loudly that the guards finally had to give in again.

"What did Ahmed say?"

"He doesn't know. He's hoping, but at the same time he's afraid to hope." A smile crosses her face. "He says he'll cook when he comes home, and that he wants at least four more children. I just let him talk, I didn't feel like arguing with him." She looks at me, a gleam of amusement in her eyes. "He even said I should try to convince you to have children!"

The Jordanian spy he had spent a lot of time with had been transferred to the prison at Tadmor, making Ahmed's life a lot less interesting. "In fact, he's desperate. If he were a criminal he'd at least know how long he had to serve, but this way . . . no one knows when it will be over." Some of the prisoners have been called in by the *mukhabarat*. Since then all kinds of rumors have been making the rounds about a document the prisoners have to sign before being released.

"What would Ahmed do in that case?"

"That depends on what he has to sign," she says despondently. "Leaving the prison with his tail between his legs after serving eleven years for his ideals – that's not Ahmed's style."

❖

Campaign posters start appearing in the streets of Damascus. I look around wide-eyed. At the beginning of a busy shopping street hangs a banner reading: 'The shopkeepers of Salhieh say "yes" to President Assad, the true Damascene'. The bit about the 'true Damascene' in particular makes Hala laugh. Armored vehicles with photographs of the president zip by, and amateur painters give their fantasy free rein: from the side of a bank in the center of town, Assad's stern features stare down at us from a canvas twenty meters high. Elsewhere they've given him a baby face and fat little arms – just like a cherub.

Meanwhile, the peace talks are rapidly approaching. One morning in bed I hear the BBC correspondent wonder aloud whether there are enough halal restaurants in Madrid; in the front room, Hala is listening to Radio Monte Carlo. We don't learn much from the Syrian press, and Hala says that's the way it will stay – the journalists Syria has sent to Madrid are notorious dunces. They speak only Arabic, but that doesn't matter – they'll obediently write whatever their editor-in-chief tells them to. On the first day of the conference, Hala and I are out running errands for Tété. Am I only imagining things, or is the city in a more subdued mood than usual? In the taxi everyone listens tensely to the radio; no one says a word. I think of Sadat, who signed the Camp David agreements – two years later he was dead.

Most of the sellers at the *souq* are also glued to the radio. Now that things have come this far, I feel a slight exhilaration, but when I look at Hala I see tears running down her cheeks. "For years they've been stirring us up against Israel, and now they suddenly go over our heads and cook up something completely different!" She takes a handkerchief from her bag. "No one ever asks us a thing, they do exactly what they want." I can imagine her sense of helplessness. Her years of passive resistance have been fruitless; the world has rolled on without her.

"It's all so confusing," she says defiantly. "If only they'd just say what it's all about – but while our Minister of Foreign Affairs sits at the table with the president of Israel, the papers still talk about the 'Zionist foe'. Assad puts on his left blinker, but turns right."

We have lunch at Tété's. Farid and Shirin are there too. Suddenly Tété says: "May Allah punish the Israelis and undo everything that happens today in Madrid." The sentence clatters on the table like a weapon, and no one picks it up. Farid acts as though he has heard nothing. Hala looks at me conspiratorially – even she doesn't harbor such radical thoughts. "My mother has been listening to the radio all morning," she says in an attempt to smooth things over. "The Israelis are keeping up the bombing of southern Lebanon. For her, this conference is unacceptable. It's like . . ." she searches for an accurate comparison, "like someone asking her to walk down the street in a bathing suit."

Back at the house, Hala turns on the TV right away. "Maybe Assad has decided in his infinite goodness to give us back Jordanian TV." She flips through the channels, hoping against hope. Jordanian TV is much more varied than its Syrian coun-

223

terpart, but it's been jammed ever since the Gulf War, because Jordan sided with Iraq. This evening we once again have to settle for the Syrian news.

The camera roams from the Palestinian speaker to al-Sharaa, the Syrian Minister of Foreign Affairs, and from him to the Jordanian delegation. There we have Shevardnadze, then Baker . . . no sign of the Israelis. We sit in front of the TV for the next three evenings. The speeches by the members of the Arab delegation are broadcast in their entirety: endless, numbing monologues that blend in with the monotonous drone of Asma reciting her lessons.

Hala remains on an emotional roller-coaster. At somber moments she says that these talks will cost the Alawites dearly, that they will bear the eternal shame of being the first to make contact with the Israelis. Then she complains about how the Israeli delegation is kept off-camera. "Al-Sharaa is sitting in the same room with Shamir," she shouts one evening in desperation, "why can't I see that, what do they have to hide?" We remain hopeful to the bitter end, but when the conference is over we still haven't caught a glimpse of the Israelis.

CHAPTER 6

"DO YOU still want to go to Aleppo?" Ibrahim asks when I call. "We're leaving tomorrow." Of course I do; everything I've heard about the city so far has aroused my curiosity. As an important trading center between Asia and the Mediterranean, Aleppo has been in intensive contact with the outside world for centuries; the European mercantile families who lived there left their mark on the city's character.

But Aleppo does not impress Hala at all. She's glad I'll be staying with Ibrahim and Amira, because she says the hotels aren't safe. She had to spend the night in Aleppo once, years ago. The hotel clerk accompanied her to her room. While showing her how to lock the door, he fumbled so badly that the key broke and they couldn't get out. There were almost no guests in the hotel and the staff had all gone home. The clerk seemed quite embarrassed by the situation, but Hala was convinced that he had broken the key on purpose. She cursed him up and down, and when that didn't help she threw open the window and started screaming. Before long someone came to let them out, whereupon Hala grabbed her bags in a huff and went looking for another hotel. She hasn't slept in Aleppo since. When she has to go there now, she takes the night train and makes sure she's through by evening.

"It's a strange city," she says, "the people live much more freely than they do here." According to her, the Aleppine Christians are loaded with money and no Muslims are allowed in their private clubs, where strange things go on. "You're a Christian," she says, "try to find out what happens there."

The roads into other Syrian cities are always dominated by a statue of Assad, but in Aleppo I see nothing of the sort. At the entrance to a park modelled on the Jardin du Luxembourg in Paris, my eye is caught by a modest bust. Could that be Assad? "Oh no, that's a poet," Amira, a native Aleppine, informs me. Poets and monsignors are the local heroes. One-fourth of all Aleppines are Christians – many of them Armenians who fled from Turkey.

Leaves are blowing along the street. We drive past a café where people are sitting together under subdued lighting; a restaurant down the block is still serving lunch to a few late customers. A girl in a miniskirt walks past a woman wrapped in a black *abaya*. I press my nose against the window and feast my eyes. Pastry shops, cafés, restaurants – it looks like Paris! Amira laughs. "I knew you'd like Aleppo. All Europeans do." Aleppines are industrialists, she says; Damascenes are traders, a different breed. The Aleppines accuse the Damascenes of swaying with every wind that blows, of compromising with every new regime. "Do you know what we call Damascenes? Tamerlane's bastards." Tamerlane was the Mongol leader who invaded Damascus in 1401.

Ibrahim and Amira's apartment is in one of Aleppo's better

neighborhoods and turns out to be hermetically sealed. Ibrahim needs three keys to open the solid wooden door; he has to turn the biggest key seven times before the lock clicks open. It's pitch dark in the apartment. Once Ibrahim has raised the roll-down shutters, Amira looks around contentedly. "Oh good, the cleaning lady has been." Amira and I fold up the sheets that cover each piece of furniture. Ibrahim removes the heavy stones from the toilet, the sink and all other drains in the house; they too have been startled by a rat when opening up the house after a long absence.

The only bad thing about living in Aleppo, Amira says, is the powdery desert sand that creeps in through every crack and crevice. That very afternoon a sand storm comes up and darkens the sky. The wind tugs at the windows and trees, people are blown along, light as scraps of paper, and before long our footsteps can be seen in a thin film of sand on the floor.

Amira calls her family to say we've arrived. The news must travel through Aleppo like wildfire, because the phone doesn't stop ringing from that moment on. They're all talking about the storm. The sand is blowing in from Saudi Arabia, someone says. "Don't the Saudis have anything better to send?" Amira complains.

That evening we sit in the roomy salon of one of Amira's uncles, Maître Gaston, a retired notary and prominent member of the Aleppine Christian community. Stately family portraits hang on the walls, silver and porcelain knick-knacks rest on little cabriole-legged tables; the stained-glass dining-room doors are discreetly closed. Meanwhile, the storm has passed. Below us, in the center of Aleppo, people stroll past lighted shop windows and the traffic is bumper to bumper.

Maître Gaston went to a Jesuit school in Aleppo, studied at the Sorbonne in Paris, back when, as he puts it, it was still a prestigious university, and has seen a great deal of the world.

227

Despite his age – he's in his early eighties – he's just returned from Switzerland; that's where he got the chocolates he serves us with a glass of Dutch liqueur. He sizes me up at a glance, and a single question from me elicits a torrent of fluent French. Ibrahim and Amira apparently realize what's in store and move to the adjoining room, where Gaston's wife is watching TV with some other guests.

Ibrahim and Father Léon's views concerning the predicament of Christians pale by comparison with those of Maître Gaston. "Did you know they burned down a Coptic church in Cairo? One of the priests was so frightened that he jumped out the window and fell to his death." Maître Gaston looks at me almost triumphantly. As late as 1850, the Christians in Aleppo were murdered and raped in their walled-in neighborhood; the Turks had to step in to put an end to it. A long period of quiet followed, until the late 1950s, when – during the brief union with Egypt – businesses were nationalized and a great many Christians left the country. But since Khomeini came to power in Iran, Maître Gaston says, things have really gone downhill for Christians in the Middle East. "In another fifty years you won't see many Christians around here. Only lots of women veiled in black – and seeing as all Muslims have ten children . . ."

I object, thinking of Hala's friends who rarely have more than two, but Maître Gaston dismisses this with an impatient flutter of his hand. "Those aren't typical people, they don't represent Syrian reality." I listen, amazed. That French refinement on the one hand; those coarse brushstrokes with which he portrays the Sunnis on the other. Louise's impossible love story, as well as older memories of the Christians in the mountains of Lebanon, cross my mind. Always that same deceptive Western facade, masking century-old fears.

Oh no, the Maître corrects me, I mustn't misunderstand him. Of course there are Muslims who are different. There are very fine Sunni families in Aleppo, some of them even belong to the Club d'Alep, although he must admit that the outfits some of the ladies wear . . . At any rate, if they're not fanatically religious, they sometimes swing in the opposite direction. I stifle a laugh: so he's a puritan as well!

The Club d'Alep, that must be the exclusive Christian club Hala talked about so mysteriously. In summer, the members meet in a garden on the edge of town, Maître Gaston tells me; during the winter they move to a building downtown.

"What do you do there?"

"Oh, nothing much – play cards, chess, billiards."

On the way home, Amira also talks about the Club d'Alep. She says it's the best place to show off new clothes. That's why the club is always closed between the summer and winter seasons: to give the ladies of Aleppo the chance to shop for a new winter wardrobe.

❖

Amira and I have passed through a stone archway and are standing in an alley so narrow that we automatically lower our voices. "Now we're in the old Christian city," she whispers. You can still see traces of the heavy gate that once sealed off the neighborhood from the outside world each night. No one went out on the street after dark; people visited each other across the rooftops. Only in 1925, when the French guaranteed the Christians' safety, was the heavy gate opened for good.

Amira raps on a door with a copper knocker. "Distant relatives of mine live here," she says. Moments later we're standing in a beautiful courtyard with a well and citrus trees. An outside stairway leads to the rooms on the top floor. The niche with low benches and a painted wooden ceiling is where the men once smoked the *nargileh*, received guests and listened to music.

The lady of the house serves us berry juice and the first citrus preserves of the season, then leads us down narrow stairs to a cool cellar with an enormous larder. Aleppo has a great tradition of preserving food; every family here makes its own cheese, smoked meat, jam, fruit juice and wine.

In the course of our walk through the old city, we push open a great many doors. Most of the people who lived here have moved to apartments like Ibrahim and Amira's, and their houses are put to other uses now. We visit a school for orphans where the nuns are knitting around a pot-bellied stove, then a house that has been squatted by several families, the wooden ceilings eaten away by time and moisture. But the Maronite cathedral on the square has just been restored and the Armenian church is in mid-renovation. These impressive buildings house a wealth of icons and paintings.

Further along, in the *souq*, are the caravanserais, the large inns which were built around a courtyard for the horses and camels. This was once Aleppo's consular district, where the foreigners lived. They too were sealed off at night from the rest of the city by a heavy wooden gate. Most of the old caravanserais now house small businesses; only the French consulate still operates from the *souq*. One staff member rents the adjoining residence from the famous Poche family, which once handled consular affairs for the Austro-Hungarian Empire; when the merchants lock up their wares at night, the caravanserai is closed as well and he can only go in and out through a little door in the huge gate.

During the first few days of my stay I walk around in a daze, completely under the spell of the city's riches. It's as though I've arrived in a different country; the cares of the last few months have fallen from my shoulders in one swoop. Amira is the perfect guide, and wherever we go she knows people or has memories to share. In the museum for folklore she stops in front of a painted magic lantern and whispers, visibly moved: "This used to be our movie theater." She can still see the old man walking down the street, carrying the box on his back. Whenever he stopped, children would rush up to him. For a couple of piasters they could look through the little windows, behind which colored pictures raced by to the rhythm of the old man's story.

Little cakes and sand tarts, jellied fruit, rose-hip syrup – it's food and drink everywhere we go. Meanwhile, Amira's girlfriends comment on her weight, compliment her on her new shoes, and gossip about the honorary consul of Italy, Georges Antaki, who recently organized a party in the foyer of the Turkish bath. Aristocrats from around the world came to Aleppo. In the course of the evening, some of the guests disappeared into the cupolaed labyrinth of the bathhouse to have themselves lathered and massaged. Over the next few days, many of the partygoers were seen in the *souq* buying Aleppine cloth, leather slippers and satin *jellabas*.

The Aleppines can't get enough of such stories. In the same breath, Amira's girlfriends talk about their work for the Femmes de la Flamme, a Christian organization that runs catechism classes in the outlying villages. They just held a fund-raising bazaar for the handicapped where they sold a lot of crochet work, knitting and embroidery.

While I'm in Aleppo, my church attendance takes an unexpected upturn. Maître Gaston realizes that a Christian might not go to church every day, but missing Sunday Mass is, in his eyes, a mortal sin. One evening we attend a service in honor of an Italian priest who is about to leave Aleppo. The clerics are dressed largely in purple, the women in outfits of silk and linen. Amira, looking natty herself in a copper-colored suit, nudges me surreptitiously during communion: the women strut about with such conviction that it looks like a fashion show.

Afterwards there's a reception in the foyer. Ibrahim listens to the theatrical cackling around him, then abruptly announces he's leaving. We say goodbye to Amira and walk through light drizzle to the car. "Pharisees," he says angrily.

"Shall we go for a drink at the Baron Hotel?" I suggest. I've been wanting to go there for a long time. Since it opened at the beginning of this century, all the great and famous have stayed at the Baron during their visits to Aleppo. T. E. Lawrence once paced its corridors, General Allenby made a speech from its balcony after the city was freed from the Turks, Agatha Christie stayed there while writing *Murder on the Orient Express*.

Ibrahim looks at me hesitantly. "The Baron? No, I don't think . . ."

"Why not?"

He doesn't quite know how to put it. "People here talk so much. Some other time, maybe, when Amira's with us."

I have to laugh. I'm suddenly reminded of the fussy way he took things out of his cooler in the desert. But Ibrahim doesn't bat an eye. "You don't know what Aleppines are like. If someone saw us, the whole city would know about it by tomorrow."

❖

Ibrahim and Amira often go out to dinner with their friends. Aleppo's better restaurants remind me of Rick's Café in *Casa-*

blanca. They all have their own orchestra, and the owner – usually wearing a white suit – keeps an eye on the tables himself. The customers all know each other: they nod, laugh, bow and pay a great many courtesy calls in the course of an evening.

Maître Gaston usually goes with us, and I soon become quite attached to him. He's always up for a night on the town, and never above leading a discussion about some period of Aleppine history, even if it means he has to scream to be heard above the Beatles or Egyptian hits. When I talk to his nephews and nieces I can tell how much has been lost within a brief period. They're not interested in anything but cars, clothing and travelling abroad.

Ibrahim and Amira will be going back to Damascus in a few days, but they've urged me to stay in their apartment for as long as I like. I dream of having Hala and Asma come over for a weekend, but don't dare ask them after all the stories I've been told about Muslims. Amira and her girlfriends talk about *musiciens* instead of *musulmans*: they say they can easily single out the Muslims in a crowd because they sing when they talk. They recognize the women by the way they dress: Christians draw their inspiration from Parisian fashion; Muslim women copy Egyptian actresses – lots of glitter, masses of curls, garish make-up.

Sometimes I try to imagine what it would be like if Hala were with me, but all I come up with is the suspicious way she looks around in unfamiliar surroundings. Her introduction to Aleppo ended with the man who broke the key in the lock of her hotel room. How easy it is for me to enter worlds that have remained closed to her. I sometimes feel guilty about it – after all, it's *her* country. But I'm afraid she wouldn't be at ease here. Asma, Tété, Shirin, there would always be someone tugging her thoughts in another direction. She has no time for casual outings.

"Is something wrong?" Ibrahim tries to catch my eye.

"Oh, no." I laugh, caught off guard. "It's just . . . you don't have restaurants like this in Damascus."

"Of course you do, only no one takes you there." He's probably right. What would I know about the restaurants of Damascus? Damascus is Hala's town.

The evening before they leave, Ibrahim and Amira take me to the Club d'Alep, which has just reopened. I recognize the broad, stately steps from Maître Gaston's photo album: this is where he stood in his younger years, wearing a fez, a watch and chain on his vest, surrounded by ladies in shimmering evening gowns.

These are steps to strut up, but our party's in no mood for that. Amira and I have been wandering through the city all day and our feet are sore; Ibrahim is somewhat withdrawn, as usual – the silence of the desert suits him better than this city's sophisticated bustle. Only Maître Gaston climbs with an energetic step, an expectant look in his eye.

It's quiet inside. The men playing cards at the tables greet Maître Gaston and assess me with a professional look: who is this newcomer? The smell of tobacco permeates the room – right down to the rugs and curtains. The podium, where a band plays on festive occasions, is empty now. Consul Antaki is dining at the far end of the room with a group of friends.

Is this all there is? I look at Amira. She sees the disenchantment on my face. "It's still early in the season," she soothes. But Maître Gaston gazes around contentedly and points to the wooden dance floor, where he's wont to take a turn on occasion. "A tango or the Vienna waltz, of course, what did you think?"

All kinds of acquaintances join our table in the course of the evening. They talk about business and travel, as if their real lives don't take place in Syria; Paris, Toronto and Montreal seem only a stone's throw away. Like foreign workers in the Gulf states, they live here without taking part in the country's political or public life. But they also feel alienated from the places they travel to. Maître Gaston tells us about a retired doctor who visited his son in New York, only to find to his amazement that a hotel room had been booked for him. After a while the son confessed why he hadn't wanted to receive his father at home: he was homosexual and lived with a man. "A black man, no less, and they were married, too!" The old doctor returned to Aleppo, deeply shocked, and has been in bed with a depression ever since.

Maître Gaston shakes his head. Such lunacy is beyond him. The others have been listening sympathetically: this must be the nightmare of every Aleppine family with a child living abroad. A heated discussion concerning the rights of inheritance of married homosexuals follows. Someone cries out: "Oh my God, and then their children will be black as well!" The others all burst out laughing.

That night I dream that Hala has come to Aleppo. The dress she's wearing is covered in stains. I try to wipe them off with a washcloth, but the harder I rub, the more they spread. To my dismay I see that the stains have become holes. But Hala doesn't mind. She runs a hand over her dress and says: "You'd never see it from a distance."

❖

As soon as Ibrahim and Amira are out the door, I phone Hala. Her voice is even higher than usual in the morning.

"I miss you," I say.

"I miss you, too," she admits. "Even Asma misses you. We've become used to you."

"Aren't the two of you coming to Aleppo?" We've talked about this before.

"Not yet. Maybe later."

"I dreamed about you."

"I dreamed about you, too."

"What did you dream?"

"I was trying on a bra and slip in a secondhand-clothing store. They were too big for me, but I thought: let's buy them anyway, maybe they'll fit Lieve." She laughs. "That's because it's getting colder and you don't have any winter clothes."

She's turned on the heating, she says; the house will be warmer when I come back. I hear Vivaldi in the background.

"What are you doing? Don't you have to go to work?"

She hesitates. "I'm writing." It's still early, so she must be sitting at the table in her nightgown. She may even be smoking a cigarette – she does that sometimes when she's working. In the cupboard with the glass doors, behind the picture of Ahmed, is an open pack.

"What are you writing?"

She hesitates again. It's an old habit: she doesn't talk freely on the phone.

"Is it for the university?"

"No, no, it's a story, just a story for myself." It's about a meeting between two women, she says. One of them thinks and does all the wrong things, the other one is much braver. "But I'm that other one too, only . . ."

The words are faint, but I think I understand. "It's like looking in the mirror."

"Something like that, yes."

"And then you see yourself."

"No, I see you!" It's quiet for a moment. I wish I was with

her, but at the same time I realize that if I were, she wouldn't have said this.

"The same goes for me." Now we're both at a loss. The invisible third party who may be listening in – would he be able to follow our fuzzy dialogue?

"Are you enjoying yourself?" Her voice is suddenly lighter. "Have you found what you were looking for?"

I tell her about the exhibition by a Lebanese artist I attended with Amira. Huge paintings of horses and madonnas, lots of red. I thought it was kitsch. The show has moved to Damascus – Hala has seen it too. "He has nothing to say," she scoffs, "it's rich people's art." I'm taken aback by the anger in her voice. *Rich people's art!* I hadn't thought of it in those terms. It's a qualification from another world, and I can't help but feel the silent accusation it contains.

I tell her that I bought a pillow for Asma's collection at a charity bazaar. A strange little thing with a cat and mouse sewn onto it, but Asma is sure to like it. Then I remember something else. "How's Ahmed?"

I hear Hala sigh for the first time. "The same. But the rumors are still flying. His parents say they'll slaughter a camel when he comes home. Don't stay away too long, otherwise you'll miss it!"

❖

Ibrahim took me aside just before he left. Last night he heard me talking to Maître Gaston about the Arab-Israeli peace talks. It's a subject to which Gaston takes a very pragmatic approach: military spending accounts for seventy per cent of the Syrian national budget; three wars having been lost, he thinks it's reasonable to put an end to that. According to him, the Israelis would only benefit from a peace agreement; they're the best business people in the region, and the Arab market is enormous.

"It's no problem, of course, to talk about things like that within the family," Ibrahim says, "but if you meet other people it's probably better not to ask questions about Israel. You never know who's listening."

So Hala's not the only one to see this system's incongruities! I had to laugh to myself at Ibrahim's secretiveness, but I was also a little annoyed. "I'm aware of that, Ibrahim, I know I can't talk to whoever comes along."

He kept his worried gaze fixed on me. "You can't be too careful."

And so I stay close to Gaston for the time being; at least nothing can go wrong with him. When he hears that I want to go to the Baron Hotel, his eyes light up: he's been meaning to visit his old friend Coco – as he refers to Krikor Mazloumian, the Armenian owner – for quite some time.

Maître Gaston's way of commenting on what he sees is both concise and imperative. As soon as we step outside he points his cane at a rather grimy building across the street. "St Joseph's. A top-notch school. Until they nationalized it. That was the end of that."

We have to cross the street. Old Buicks drive by, as well as noisy little carts with souped-up motors. Gaston holds his cane straight out in front of him, marches into the traffic and exhorts me to do the same. His cane works like a magic wand, as though the drivers deduce his unrelenting character from the figure he cuts.

The wooden shutters on the school building sag on their hinges. Through a hole in one of them we look into a classroom.

The chairs are worn and the steel cupboards rusted, but the posters of Assad on the walls are new, as are the streamers with Syrian flags hanging from the ceiling. Election propaganda. Maître Gaston takes it all in without a word.

By now, elsewhere in the city, I've come across the inevitable statue of Assad. The president holds his hands pressed against his body, his head slightly bowed – a subdued pose, as if he knows the setting in which he's being viewed. The first campaign posters have also appeared in the streets. They disrupt the graceful lines of Aleppo's buildings, marking the uneasy presence of a military regime in this city which prides itself on its good taste. Smack in the center of town, a Ba'ath Party office is under construction. An ugly, cumbersome thing with a thick wall around it – a real fortress.

It's getting dark. Outside a movie theater, a group of unkempt, sultry-looking men stand around the poster of a scantily clad woman. They're wearing long robes and have woollen scarves wrapped around their heads. When two girls walk by, they hiss lewdly.

Maître Gaston sniffs. "Bedouins! Back home they've never seen a woman's bare arm, but the first thing they do here is go to a pornographic movie!" This street, with its torn-up sidewalks and countless coffee houses, was once a sort of Champs Elysées, he tells me, with lovely cafés and casinos where couples sat together in the evening. Now men smoking the *nargileh* peer at us from the darkened storefronts.

"Aleppo is becoming *Bedouinized,*" Maître Gaston says irritatedly. The city once had a French Cultural Center and a Goethe Institute. Now they're in Damascus, where it's easier to keep an eye on them. "And we've got Bedouins instead." Hala's brother Salim also complained about the villagers overrunning

239

Damascus. "Do you mean the Alawites?" I ask. Maître Gaston shakes his head in vexation. "No, we had them too, but there are hardly any left. They left town, at least those who weren't . . ." He stops for a moment and looks at me quizzically. "Haven't you heard about that? There was a time when one Alawite official after the other was being shot dead in Aleppo. Out on the street, in their offices. Just like that, pow!" The sound he makes is abrupt, disdainful.

"By Muslim Brothers?"

"Of course, who else?" We've come to another intersection – Gaston sticks out his cane again. Once we're on the other side, he says: "All right, we're almost there." He's looking forward to seeing old Coco – the prospect has made him forget what we were talking about.

"*Voilà – l'Hôtel Baron.*" Maître Gaston has stopped before a majestic Arab-Italian building. Broad steps, a spacious patio, 'Baron Hotel, Mazloumian & Frères' written above the entrance. In the lobby with its black-and-white tile floor, beneath a poster depicting the hotel in its former splendor, an old waiter in a grimy jacket sits dozing. There's no one at the bar. A lone tourist is reading a book in the salon. The piano, the red leather couches, the French prints in gilded frames on the wall – Maître Gaston leads me around as if it all belongs to him.

"Is your father here?" he asks a middle-aged man at the desk. The man nods, leads us down the hall and stops at a door in front of which a dog lies sleeping; the dog has clearly seen better days. "Well, Caesar!" Maître Gaston bends over and strokes the animal's dirty white fur. He's mistaken, as I discover later: this isn't Caesar. Caesar died long ago.

Inside, amid a jumble of telex rolls and stacks of paper, sits a quite peculiar-looking little man. He's wearing dark glasses with leather flaps on the sides, and a bright blue shirt beneath a safari suit with oversized pockets. Long hairs protrude from his ears, and on his head he has a little, green paper visor with the name of a laundry detergent. He looks like a flying ace from a comic book.

It takes a minute for Mazloumian to detect our presence, but when he recognizes Gaston his greeting is hearty. He clears a space for us and pours little paper cups full of *ararat*, Armenian brandy. When Maître Gaston enquires after his health, Mazloumian's face takes on a pained expression. "My eyes, Maître, my eyes." It turns out he's half-blind, and the light hurts his eyes terribly; hence the flaps.

Mazloumian goes on shuffling through the papers on his desk for a while, but when he starts talking his hands gradually grow still and his attention shifts to his memories. His mind is clearer than I'd expected – he has reached that merciful age when things that happened in his younger years are clearer and closer than what he's been doing in the last few hours. When his son comes in to ask for a telex that should have arrived this afternoon, Mazloumian becomes flustered and sends him away empty-handed. Then he returns without a hitch to the year 1912, when his father and uncle festively opened the hotel with a brass band and a ball.

Back then the Baron Hotel lay on the outskirts of Aleppo, in unspoiled surroundings, close to a little river where young Coco hunted wild geese; a servant took him to school every morning on horseback. The railway from Berlin to Baghdad was built in those days – the city was full of Germans – and the Orient Express arrived in Aleppo twice a week; the hotel staff would worry when the train was late.

It was a hotel in the colonial tradition. There was no need to

241

feel uprooted, for everything was imported from Europe: the china, the furniture, the chairs with 'Baron Hotel' carved on them. Only the carpets came from Izmir. During the banquets in the ballroom, the cooks – who had all worked aboard luxury liners – trotted back and forth with dishes of *canard à l'orange, pommes sautées* and *marrons glacés*. The ladies and gentlemen at the hotel parties walked around with a *carnet de bal*, jotting down the names of those with whom they would dance the next polka or waltz. The German maître d'hôtel fell in love with Coco's Protestant kindergarten teacher, and put a bullet through his head when his love remained unrequited.

The men always dressed in suits, the women wore long dresses, hats and jewels. In their free time the owners of the hotel accompanied their guests on trips to the Dead Cities – the ruins of Roman and Byzantine towns outside Aleppo – or took them hunting. Liman von Sanders, Jamal Pasha, Atatürk: all the top German and Turkish military men who visited the city during the First World War sat at the same table and were welcomed in the same fashion. "In wartime one asks no questions," Mazloumian says. Syria's King Faisal received the military salute on the balcony of room 215, Nasser and Tito gave speeches from the patio. When he mentions the name Nasser, Mazloumian falls out of character for a moment. "That swine," he snarls. Nasser was the man behind the nationalizations – no wonder he isn't too fond of him. His uniform had to be pressed three times a day, he recalls. "That's how the Egyptians fight their wars!"

Gertrude Bell, Freya Stark, Patrick Leigh Fermor – the names roll effortlessly off Mazloumian's tongue. Sitting there in his safari suit and strange little hat, he seems to have taken on something of the adventurous character of his illustrious guests.

Lawrence never bought a carpet without consulting Mazloumian's father.

But now Mazloumian waves his hand, as if shooing away the ghosts of the past. "Ah, that's all gone and done with," he sighs. The woods where he once played have been chopped down, the little river has become an open sewer and the street is filled with thundering traffic all day long. He recently discovered that two pages had been torn from the hotel's *livre d'or*. Even Lawrence's hotel bill, on display in a case in the parlor, is a copy: the original was stolen.

The days of the French, that was his favorite time. After independence, things went downhill fast. "Damascus has been pushed to the forefront," he says with regret, adding in a whisper, "we've been kept on a short leash ever since." He is convinced that the electricity and water are never turned off in Damascus, and looks at me dubiously when I say that's not the case.

"What's more, the big bosses there know nothing about tourism," he adds stubbornly. A German TV crew making a documentary about the Paris-Beijing road rally stayed at the hotel some time ago. They wanted to film the hotel from the street, but were soon brought back into the lobby by two *mukhabarat*: they had inadvertently filmed a torn poster of Assad that was hanging on the low wall in front of the hotel. Mazloumian acted outraged, assuring the *mukhabarat* that he would have gone out and removed the poster himself if he had seen it. "I offered them a glass of sarsaparilla." His smile is wily, but also a bit compassionate. "And a lighter with the name of the hotel on it." He searches through the pockets of his safari outfit, pulls something out and hands it to me. "Look, one of these. Take it." It's a cheap disposable lighter made of green plastic. "They were quite pleased with it."

Tourists come in groups these days, he complains; they're always in a hurry and even eat the local cuisine. A *ragoût de boeuf à la jardinière* would be wasted on them, so he and his British wife, Sally, and their son Armen dine by themselves every afternoon in the big hotel restaurant. They're served by an incompetent waiter who steals things as soon as they're not looking. The dust is piling up in their house behind the hotel: the cleaning lady ignored their instructions and stuck her hand in the washing machine. Now she's missing a thumb.

Mazloumian begins leafing through his papers again. Now that he's arrived at the present, I feel his attention dwindling. He looks at us absentmindedly from behind his thick lenses; there's his old friend Maître Gaston, but who is that woman next to him? And what got him talking about the past like that?

His son reappears in the doorway: has the telex turned up yet? Maître Gaston clears his throat and stands up. "Well, Coco, it's time for us to be going." There's no one in the corridor, but three gentlemen are sitting in leather armchairs in the bar, conversing in hushed tones. The old barman who was dozing away on the couch when we came in is now listlessly polishing glassware.

It's drizzling outside. The car tires stick to the asphalt and the dust of the last few days runs across the street in dirty rivulets of mud. All of a sudden I feel sad, and Maître Gaston too is quieter than usual. He picks his way carefully along the slick sidewalk – as if suddenly more aware of the finite nature of things.

Mazloumian told us about the English travel writer Freya Stark, a distinguished lady who visited all of the Dead Cities on horseback in 1939. He kept up a correspondence with her, and about ten years ago she came back to Aleppo. She was well into her eighties and had trouble walking, but said she wanted to ride out to the Dead Cities, just like in the old days. Mazloumian had his misgivings about that. One morning, while they were inching along through the *souq* on their way to visit the Poche family residence in the caravanserai, she had a bad fall. She ended up with a black eye and some nasty scrapes on her knees. "From now on we're only going places by car," Mazloumian said, but she protested: why not take the car to the Dead Cities and pull a horse trailer along behind them? Of course, they never did anything of the kind.

Those two old-timers walking the cobblestones of the *souq* – they belong to this city's colonial past, which has almost gone now except for a few glorious memories. They lived at such an energetic pace, they couldn't reconcile themselves to the sluggishness that followed.

My thoughts are interrupted by Maître Gaston's voice: we've arrived at his door. "Would you like to come up for a moment?" I shake my head. "No thank you, some other time." He waits with me on the pavement until a taxi turns the corner, then fixes his gaze on the license plate. "Give me a call when you get home," he whispers, "in Aleppo these days, you never know. I've got his license number."

❖

Ibrahim made me promise never to leave the house without lowering the shutters and turning the big front-door key seven times in the lock. The gnashing sound of that key in the silent hallway – if anything frightens me, it's that. The electricity is usually turned off during the day, so I have to grope my way to the shutters. It doesn't take me long to tire of this creepy little ritual, so I decide to lower them only at night. But when I sit in front of the window to read, the passers-by stare in so unabashedly that it makes me feel like I'm doing something improper.

The shutters in the apartments around me are rarely open. The tenants have left their houses in the old city, but apparently go on living the way they used to. One day I go to visit some of Amira's acquaintances. It's only four o'clock, but inside night has fallen. The light from the pink lamps on the side tables is so unreal that I feel like I've walked into a theater just as the performance is about to begin. Floors of Italian marble, Aleppine brocade rugs, a sofa covered in local fabric to protect the velour underneath – everything is so clinically clean, I'm almost afraid to sit down.

My hostess is wearing a red and black suit, and her husband sits stiffly in the chair across from me; at five o'clock they're going to a recital in the Latin cathedral. The wife brings me a cup of coffee. "Aren't you two having anything to drink?" "No, we've already had something." She goes to the dining room, opens the buffet – I can smell the furniture wax – and takes out a little dish of bonbons. The tapestry above the buffet is covered with a sheet of plastic.

"Do you keep the shutters closed all the time?" I ask casually.

"Yes, of course!"

"But why?"

"The dust! Haven't you noticed how dusty it is in Aleppo?" But she has to admit that it's the light as well: she's afraid the carpets will fade.

Fear: the air here is redolent with it, and before long our conversation is too. Aren't I afraid of the Muslims overrunning Europe, don't they pose a threat now that Christianity is on the decline? My hostess looks at me askance: I'm probably one of those watered-down Christians. If there's anything she admires in these Muslims, it's their unswerving faith. This morning her Sunni cleaning lady was standing on a ladder to wash the walls.

When she told her to be careful, the cleaning lady laughed: "If I fall, it's God's will!"

They try to convince me to go along to the recital with them, but I politely refuse. Once outside, I heave a sigh of relief. I look up to find the apartment where I've just been, but can't locate it: a smooth facade of closed shutters stares back at me. I slip into the stream of shoppers. Since I've been alone in Aleppo, I constantly feel I'm being looked at: the Aleppines notice unfamiliar faces in the streets of their city and do their best to place them.

In Maître George's drawing room I encounter a group of French archaeologists. They're sipping from crystal glasses, oohing and ahing over the monuments they've visited. A Maronite dignitary, invited over for the occasion, has smugly settled into the best chair and is playing with the big cross hanging around his neck. Maître George draws contentedly on his pipe and runs through the same stories he's been telling me for the last few days.

These French people in search of the rich Levantine past, that cleric with his purple socks, Maître George with his anecdotes – and outside the window a city where the traffic honks and blares and where blue-eyed Bedouins stand staring at pornographic posters. The longer I watch the group in the drawing room, the more anachronistic it seems. Frozen figures who have lost their ties with the landscape in which they find themselves. I suddenly realize why Hala is so little impressed by Aleppo: all this nostalgia, what good is it?

❖

Just when I've started thinking that the ideas of everyone in this city are hopelessly outdated, I run into Walid. He's one of the

247

Syrian intellectuals who condemned Khomeini's *fatwa* against Salman Rushdie. The petition wasn't published in Syria, but everyone knows about it and all those who signed it got into trouble with the *mukhabarat*. "Assad couldn't just let something like that go," Walid says, "the fundamentalists might think the government is on our side!"

Walid works for a state-owned company and writes in his spare time. He's close to sixty, but his eyes are so lively and what he says is so refreshing that he seems much younger than that. He has to laugh at my somber impressions of Aleppo, and disarms me with ease. He travels a lot, but he's always glad to come home. "Try looking at Aleppo as an arabesque," he says circumspectly, "it's a five-thousand-year-old city. There's a school here for iconic art, we have our own music and in every family someone plays an instrument. It's not easy to steamroll a society like this."

We're sitting in his office, a bare cubicle with faded posters on the walls. Walid lights his pipe and puffs on it contentedly. Of course, sooner or later the *mukhabarat* will ask him a few questions about my visit, he says with a smirk. "The *mukhabarat* are part of this country's folklore!"

I would expect something like that from Father Léon, but I'm surprised to hear it from a Syrian. "You're not afraid like other people," I say, "why not?"

Walid laughs. "I don't have much to fear. I have no desire to be rich, and no ambition to rise through the ranks of this company. That makes me pretty much invulnerable." Walid grew up in a liberal Sunni family. His father was a sheikh. Not one of these fanatics you run into so often now; no, in his father's day the sheikhs still engaged in heated debate. He remembers a sheikh at his school who once offered a gold piece for the student who could prove the world was round. His father was incensed when he heard about it. He went to the man and said: "You shouldn't promise the children a gold piece when you don't have one. Besides, my son can prove that the world is round for ten piasters!"

When Armstrong landed on the moon, a sheikh in the mosque said: "If you ask someone whether Armstrong went to the moon and he says yes, ask him again. If his answer is the same the third time you ask, you may kill him." Walid laughs sneeringly: "What idiocy!"

His father's friends were outraged when he wanted to send his daughter to a Christian school: was he trying to make a Christian out of her? His father laughed in their faces; he felt that a Muslim should find out as much as possible about what the world has to offer.

Later, his sister married a Christian. Walid was called up by a Christian patriarch who fumed: how could you give your sister to a Christian? "He was afraid of losing one of the flock," he grins. Walid told him that his sister had chosen her own husband, and that he'd had no say in the matter.

"In my father's day, social change started at the universities," he says, "but these days everyone clings to the mosque, where they certainly aren't preaching change. I'm starting to feel more and more like an oddball in my neighborhood. My wife is the only woman who doesn't wear a headscarf, and I never go to the mosque, I drink alcohol and smoke a pipe, even during Ramadan. Some people actually think we're Christians!"

Things haven't improved since the Gulf War. When Assad sided with the Americans, Walid was appalled at first. "But our president may very well be more realistic than most Syrian intellectuals," he admits. "We're dreamers. I'm a dreamer too, but that's just part of me; the other part says . . ." He leans back in his chair and looks at me laughingly. "Saddam Hussein claimed he had modern arms, but his enemy hit him with weapons he'd never even heard of!" He takes a contemplative tug on his pipe. "We Arabs invented algebra, but what good does that do us now? Even Einstein has become passé. Everyone talks about our great poet al-Mutanabbi, but I may actually be fonder of Gabriel García Márquez."

Walid recently gave a reading in the Lebanese port city of Saida. He had always seen Lebanon as the land of freedom, so he spoke open-heartedly about Arab culture's need for new stimuli. He used the example of hybrid plants being much stronger than those whose reproductive cycle remains unbroken. He was stunned by the vehement criticism after the break: the room turned out to be full of supporters of the pro-Iranian Hezbollah Party. He made his getaway that same evening, to Christian East Beirut.

"I'm getting old and impatient. I'd like to see something change in this part of the world during my lifetime, but I'm afraid . . . Take the Syrian elections. If I were free to choose, I'd probably vote for Assad, because I don't see any alternative. But I don't feel free." *Masiras* – marches – are being organized all over the country: everyone is obliged to demonstrate their loyalty to the president. Walid's company also took to the streets a few days ago, and the next day his colleagues commented on his absence. Walid beams. "I told them: but I was with you in spirit! I saw it all on TV, I had a much better view than you did!"

During this campaign, Assad is often referred to as *abu Basel* – the father of Basel. It's a way of promoting his eldest son and likely successor. "It's fine with me," Walid says, "but why not be straightforward about it? Let them proclaim a monarchy, preferably with the right amount of pomp, so we can finally put an end to this farce!"

He's afraid of what will happen when Assad dies. Someone recently predicted that a river of blood would flow through the country – they could very well be right. "If the Muslim Brothers came to power, I'd probably be killed. I smoke a pipe, which is a symbol of Westernization – that's all the reason they'd need." The Muslim Brothers are out for destruction, he believes; they offer no solutions for the real problems of this country. "Within ten years the Syrians would be hungry for bread, not prayer!" If the fanatics do take power, he'll emigrate right away. "A job in Rotterdam harbor," he laughs, "that sounds like just the thing."

For the first time I sense how much anxiety is hidden behind his laugh. Travelling is probably all that keeps him optimistic. The worst thing for him would be to become part of a group, unable to maintain his distance. He's been to Japan a few times – he'd like to live there for a while, to find out what the modern world is all about. "I believe in a cosmopolitan civilization," he says, "I believe in science. We don't need new politics here, we need a new culture."

❖

"Shawqi is in town," Walid announces one afternoon, "and he's giving a reading tonight. Do you want to come?" Shawqi – his name is like something from a distant past. He's the poet who is the focal point of the group of friends that meets each week at the Café Havana in Damascus – a gathering Hala thought it wiser for me not to attend. So fate has placed Shawqi in my path again! I eagerly accept the invitation.

That evening the audience trickles in. By the time the reading is about to begin, the room isn't anywhere near full. A sixty-year-old in a Syrian-tailored suit walks out onto the podium and sits down at a little table. He doesn't start reading, the way I'd expected; he starts speaking. A friend of Walid's sits next to me and translates.

Shawqi talks about his life. He used to be a communist; he went to Moscow and held Stalin's military power and firm countenance in such high esteem that he wrote epic poems about him. During the union with Egypt he was imprisoned for his communist ideas. He considered himself a hero at the time, but now he's ashamed of that period in his life, of his adulation of that one man, of having taken part in such hero worship

I was prepared for anything but this old-fashioned stint of communist self-critique. Talk about an anachronism! But you could hear a pin drop in the hall. Everyone is staring at Shawqi, and as he speaks I feel the tension rise. I look at him again. An ageing intellectual in an unseasonably light, ill-fitting suit. Then I notice the portrait of Assad behind him, prayer beads held loosely between the fingers, a smile playing on his features.

Suddenly I realize why the audience is so quiet. As Shawqi talks about Stalin, the portrait on the wall seems to come to life. Assad gazes down with his all-knowing smile on the penitent, who in turn looks increasingly oppressed. I feel a mixture of admiration and pity for Shawqi. Not only does he have those two eyes prying at his back, there's also someone from the *mukhabarat* watching him from the audience. My interpreter pointed him out to me: a man in a cobalt-blue suit, staring noncommittally into space.

Now Shawqi speaks directly to his audience. He's pleased, he says, to see a few young people here tonight, for having lost contact with them is the one major regret in his life. Somewhere, something has changed: young people are no longer interested, their minds are empty. He reads a poem he wrote after visiting a school where a tyrannical teacher was railing at his students. The poem ends with the line: 'If you can't choose your father, at least choose yourself'.

I think about the Arab friends I visited in London and Paris before I left Europe. How much fiercer they were in their attacks on this regime. But if all the dissidents left Syria, who would keep an eye on its moral integrity? Suddenly I think of Hala. She admires Shawqi for his courage to say the things others keep to themselves; he's a man who walks the thin line between freedom and imprisonment.

After the reading we all end up at a friend's house. It's a balmy evening, and in the courtyard the guests are eating, drinking and talking. Shawqi asks around interestedly about the score of this afternoon's soccer match. Just one of those good-old-boys' conversations about sports, I assume at first, but soon discover that there's more to it: one of the teams was Jableh, an Alawite club. During one of Jableh's recent matches against a Sunni team, rioting broke out in the stands; one person was killed, another wounded.

Later that evening, when Walid tells one of his famous anecdotes about the idiocy of sheikhs and I ask someone to translate, Shawqi says: "You'd have to live here at least a year to understand it." I turn my head away in annoyance. The wind from Damascus is blowing, the close-mouthed wind. Walid winks at me and says: "A year? You mean a century!"

I try to calm myself, thinking of the tragic course of Shawqi's life. A former communist, to be sure, but didn't Walid say, "You need the communists to balance out the religious fanatics"? Like Hala, Shawqi is restricted in his movements – how could he know what a foreigner does or does not understand?

When we say goodbye, Shawqi invites me to the next gathering at the Café Havana, and I hear myself telling him I'll be there. Hala, Ahmed, the elections, the Café Havana – there are suddenly so many reasons to go back to Damascus.

CHAPTER 7

H ALA OPENS the gate with a knowing smile. "Have you seen them?" She throws a meaningful glance at the hodgepodge of campaign slogans in our street. The poultryman, the barber, the greengrocer, all scream their support for the president from every wall and window. The down-at-heel young man who sold Captain Majed stickers from a hole in the wall during the summer is now peering out from under a fan of heart-shaped stickers of Assad. Up by the little shop where they sell what Hala calls 'fifth-hand clothes', a sheet covered with closely written text has been slung across the street.

"The poorer they are, the harder they shout," Hala says. "Shall we put up a sign too? What about: 'Hala and Asma say "yes" to President Assad'?" She pulls me inside laughing.

I put down my suitcase in the hall and look around in amazement. Winter arrived while I was away. Rustic flowered carpets on the floor make everything look heavier and darker than before. There's a roaring fire in the round iron stove in the front room and my bed is covered with an eiderdown. I can't stop looking at the rug in the bedroom. Where have I seen it before?

"Don't you remember? Think about it. You're the one who gave it to me." A caravanserai in the *souq* – Hala bought me some blue glassware, and the little statue of Leda and the swan. In a shop nearby I chose a gray, handwoven carpet with a simple pattern for her. It's pretty, but it doesn't go with the Turkish carpets in the rest of the house – she must have put it down just for me.

Asma comes home beside herself with excitement: she spent the whole morning dancing to the song the school is going to sing at the big parade for Assad. She jumps up onto the bed in her pajamas and starts singing about *abu Basel* and Assadna (our Assad).

"It sounds like you're in love with him," I tease.

"Of course I'm in love with him!" she shouts.

"But why?"

"Because he threw my father in prison!"

I look at Hala and see that she's laughing. "Any news from Ahmed?" She puts a finger to her lips. "Later."

Sitting on the floor, I unpack my suitcase with Asma at my side. I've been gone so long, she says; did anyone teach me to play cards in the meantime? The Aleppine marzipan with pistachios, the chocolate, the little cat-and-mouse pillow – she puts them all in her cupboard, where she hoards things, just like Hala. She thinks the red leather slippers I bought for myself are much too big; she prefers the shiny mules I wear at Tété's.

Hala is sitting on the bed watching us. "How was Aleppo?" I recognize that tone of voice – no enthusiastic stories, please. And so I tell her about my visit to the quiet Club d'Alep, about the decline of the Baron Hotel. "Guess who I ran into? Shawqi!"

"Shawqi? In Aleppo?" It's the first time she shows any interest. "He's a good man," she muses, "that's someone I respect."

"So why don't the two of you ever get together?"

"What would we say to each other? That everything's just fine? We both know that's not true." She smiles. "Everything we say is new to you, but he and I have nothing to talk about, we know it all already."

As it turns out, she knows Walid as well. "He doesn't seem too worried about things," I say.

She shrugs. "He can afford to be that way, he's from a prominent family – they wouldn't dare do anything to him." According to her, even Shawqi has protection.

"Shawqi? What do you mean?"

"If they arrested him, all the poets in the region would be up in arms."

"And you," I ask, "do you have protection?"

"Me? No, you know I don't. That's the whole problem."

While Hala is listening to Asma recite her homework after dinner, I suddenly feel lost: I'm home again, I've unpacked my bags and put away my clothes, but what now? The rhythm of Aleppo is still pounding in my head – if I were there now, I'd be about ready to go into town.

Hala appears in the doorway. "Aren't you tired? Don't you want to take a bath?"

I make a gesture to fend her off. "No, maybe later." Whenever I've been away I always have to take a bath. I'm not even dirty! And why should I be tired? The only thing I'm tired of is the lethargy in this house. I look at Hala. "Just leave me alone."

She hesitates for a moment, then comes over to the bed and sits next to me. "I know how you feel," she says softly. "I used to be like you. I wanted to know everything, discover everything – I was so much more optimistic. But now ... when I think about

257

what goes on here, about what's happening to Ahmed and all the others, and that I can't fight it, that I can't do anything about it – it makes me feel so discouraged."

I stare at the rug lying at our feet. I wasn't the only one who liked it at the time; she was drawn to it right away too. But it needs a lighter, more spacious home. So much grief and regret well up in me that I throw my arm around her. I'd like to hold her against me, but I hesitate as usual.

"You came here," she says, "and you're amazed at everything. I've lost my curiosity. Can you understand that?"

I nod and pull back my arm, feeling lumpish and clumsy. "What happened to the story you were writing?"

"The same as always, it's lying around here somewhere."

"And what about Ahmed?"

"I don't know. They say Assad is going to release all the prisoners before the elections. I have to go to the *mukhabarat* soon to pick up a new visitor's permit – it's been years since I had to do that. I told myself I wasn't going to hope anymore, but the waiting has started anyway." She looks at me hesitantly. "I wish they'd let him go, then I could get on with my life."

"What are you going to do when he gets out?"

"File for divorce, right away." She sighs. "It's over. If he came in here and started acting like my husband . . ." She shudders at the thought. "He'll just have to go to his parents. He wants a woman – not me, not Hala."

She sits silently staring into space. Then she says: "I saw Firas again." She laughs at my amazement. "It's because you weren't here – I felt weak and alone." She hadn't heard from him for weeks, it was like he'd disappeared from the face of the earth. Then she went looking for him. She found him in his studio, which she calls his 'helicopter' because it protrudes from the building and has lead-glass windows with a view of the city and Mount Qassioun. It was so cold that their breath turned into clouds that floated through the room. On one of the windows he had written: 'Love hurts'.

"I need someone to think about me," she says abashed, "and I want to think about someone too."

"You don't have to explain that to me, I know exactly what you mean."

"But no one here seems to understand! A colleague told me recently that it was my patriotic duty to remain faithful to Ahmed!" She looks at me in despair. "Remember what happened in France when *Madame Bovary* was published? People said it was scandalous, they couldn't stand the idea of a woman breaking her family ties and following her feelings. *Madame Bovary, Anna Karenina* . . . I believed those stories when I read them, I thought I would follow my heart too. And just look what's come of it." She shrugs despondently. "Sometimes I wonder what's crazier: loving Firas, or not loving him."

"Mama, Mama, come here!" We hear the sound of footsteps and shouting outside, as though everyone's hurrying in the same direction at once. We run to the gate. Hala sees what's happening at a glance. "A *masira* for the president," she says. I peer over her head at the broad street in the distance. "What are they doing?" "Oh, nothing special. Go and take a look."

I walk up to the corner in my Aleppine slippers. It's a student demonstration: the marchers are wearing paramilitary outfits and mechanically chanting the same sentence over and over. They must have walked a long way, there's no spring left in their step. The torches they're holding have gone out and their feet shuffle over the asphalt – they look more like apparitions on a death march.

The people crowded together along the street look at me. I shiver in my light clothes, but just as I'm getting ready to go back I see the sheen of a leather jacket close by. The cigarette seller! His friends aren't with him; he's alone and looking at me with a calm, faintly amused expression. I turn my head the other way, timidly. A few moments later I feel a hand searching for mine in the crush. It's Asma. She and Hala have coats on over their pajamas.

The three of us walk back together, suddenly a family amid the anonymous, prying eyes. At home Hala makes a soup of crushed wheat, powdered milk, onions and mint. She's put a stool in front of the iron stove; this is her spot in wintertime, where she sits when she's taken a bath, a towel wrapped around her wet hair, where she listens to Asma recite her homework, watching TV from the corner of her eye.

"Oh, I forgot to tell you: Shirin's pregnant."

"Already?"

"A little Farid," she says gloomily. She's argued with Farid quite often lately. She and Tété have decided to stop keeping their thoughts to themselves when he's around: he's part of the family now, he just has to realize that what they say isn't necessarily aimed at him. But Farid feels as if he's landed in a den of spies.

"You're dangerous," he said to Hala recently.

"Go ahead, report me," she snapped back at him.

"He believes in the system; he thinks the *mukhabarat* are there to help people, that they're fair," she fumes. "He hopes to get ahead by being loyal to the regime, but he doesn't exactly know how to go about it." A few days ago he went shopping with Shirin in the *souq*, a list of official government prices in his pocket. Those prices are absolutely unrealistic, no one sticks to them, but every time Farid wanted to buy something he would pull out the list and give the merchant a dressing-down. They came home empty-handed. Shirin could have died.

"I don't think they're happy together. Yesterday Shirin cried when she had to go home."

"And she said she'd be swimming in honey!"

"Swimming in muck is more like it!"

❖

Not a single street, square or building in Damascus has escaped the election fever, and everywhere I look I see men busy hanging posters, flags and portraits. When I stop in front of an office building where a new banner is being hung up, I receive such penetrating stares that I walk on, feeling guilty. Those looks: they have something shamefaced about them, but also something aggressive, as if what's happening here isn't meant for foreign eyes.

I stop by Hamid's bookstore to buy a newspaper. His familiar face behind the cash register – it's good to see him again. When I point out the Assad stickers on his door, he grins and holds up his hands in a sign of surrender. "I didn't put them there!" A few days ago two men visited all the shopkeepers in the street: stickers on every door, a poster in every window, they decided. "As you can imagine, I couldn't do a thing about it." A friend of Hamid's discovered that a poster of Assad had been stuck to the side of his car. "You think he dared take it off? That would have cost him at least a year in prison." A man in his neighborhood whose son is in prison recently tore down a poster that had been stuck on his front door. They arrested him that same evening; no one's heard from him since.

"It's never been this bad before," Hamid says worriedly. "But of course we know why." He gives me a conspiratorial look. "Assad wants to show the Americans that he can force anything down our throats, even a peace agreement with Israel."

I have an appointment with Hala. She's decided that we're going to buy winter clothes for me. Secondhand clothes, just like in her dream, for she doesn't think Syrian fashions would suit me. On the way to the *souq* I pass a banner announcing the Damascus Film Festival, a biennial event that Hala has been looking forward to. But when I asked her about it yesterday, a shadow crossed her face. A heated controversy had broken out around the festival, she said. It began with rumors about a Tunisian film that presented a Jewish character sympathetically, while all the Arabs were portrayed as unpleasant. Someone said the film had been co-financed by the West; another claimed it had been made with Jewish money. Now everyone was talking about the danger of co-productions.

"Tunisian film-makers have the reputation of being the best in the Arab world at the moment," I ventured.

Hala turned up her nose. "Oh yes, you mean in the West!"

I sighed – why disturb the domestic peace on my first evening home? Hala didn't push things either, but I noticed that she'd been pretty busy gossiping about the controversy. To smooth things over she told me that when the festival started, I should go with her to hear for myself what was really going on.

I've been waiting for Hala at the entrance to the *souq* for twenty minutes. Just when I become worried, I see her pop up out of the stream of people, looking even smaller than usual in the big black cardigan she wears as a jacket. "Oh, what a mess!" She laughs. "Come on, let's go." She walks next to me, taking quick little steps and blowing off steam as she goes. Tété's heating oil is

262

almost finished. The oil vendors usually drive up and down the street, but a while ago they seemed to have disappeared. She finally called a supplier and brought her position at the university to bear. He'd promised to come by the day after tomorrow. "If it takes two days even with a *wasta*, imagine how long people without a *wasta* have to wait!"

Her own supply of heating oil is almost finished too, but she didn't dare ask the supplier for two favors at once. On the way over here she suddenly saw an oil vendor drive by. She ran after him, but he just kept on going at full speed. She finally took off after him in a taxi. "Just like in an Egyptian TV series!" The taxi driver was very helpful; he finally forced the oil vendor to stop and hopped out, like he was chasing a criminal. But the vendor refused to go to her house, even after she offered to pay for his gasoline. "Something strange is going on," she says. "It's as though there's a shortage of heating oil." The vendor wasn't at all interested – as if he knew a crisis was on its way.

Suddenly Hala interrupts herself. "Did you listen to the news this morning?"

"No, why?"

"They're going to disband the Soviet Union." She heaves a deep sigh. "If you only knew the kind of tumult that would once have caused! The Soviet Union – that was our guiding light, something we could look up to. But now no one's interested in what happens there. The only thing they talk about on the radio is the elections."

The shops Hala pilots me through that afternoon are deeply depressing. Dismal cellars filled with the smell of mildew, where women with scarves around their heads claw through piles of clothing. Everyone thinks I'm Russian. "They're the only foreign women who ever show their faces here," Hala whispers.

I feel increasingly older and uglier, and before long the smell of the clothing clings to us even out on the street. "Enough is enough," I say, "this is hopeless." Father Léon had suggested that I come and pick something out of the pile of sweaters in his closet; pious ladies have knitted them for him, but he never wears them. I'd laughingly refused his offer, but after what I've seen this afternoon it suddenly seems very tempting.

A young man is standing on a street corner selling Chinese tennis shoes from a big plastic bag. "A soldier stationed in Lebanon," Hala whispers.

"How can you tell?"

"It's the neighborhood. You can buy anything here," Now that I'm paying attention I see more vendors: a man with a sack full of soccer balls, a boy displaying a row of Nikes on the sidewalk. You're not actually allowed to sell these things here, but Hala says it's the way they placate the badly paid soldiers in Lebanon.

A woman with orange lipstick, a bouffant hairdo and a bright yellow dress is leaning against an alley wall. The smell of cheap perfume wafts our way. "Do they stand right out on the street these days?"

"It's the neighborhood," Hala repeats curtly. It's been a long time since we've walked through the city together, and I realize how much less I see without her. I could wander around for hours, but Hala's eyes have taken on a harried look: Asma is at Tété's house and the cartoons are over – she's probably getting impatient.

Tété is sitting as still as a statue next to the big iron stove, beneath a clothesline hung with nightgowns. "You two are late," she says. People have been calling all afternoon, asking about Ahmed. Blood rushes to Hala's face. "What did they say? Has he been released?" It happens often enough that a prisoner suddenly shows up at the door without notice. But Tété has no idea. "Probably another false alarm," Hala decides. But she gathers Asma's things with more than her usual haste. "Come on, we have to go home. To wait for Ahmed."

The taxi driver has the radio on. Hala listens with raised eyebrows to the announcer's whining voice. "What a bunch of nonsense!" she sputters. It hasn't rained for a long time, the announcer says, but soon God will send rain and the rain will say 'yes' to Hafez al-Assad. I burst out laughing. "Did he really say that?"

"Just be glad you don't understand the rest of the nonsense he comes up with!" We drive past a fountain spouting green water. "Before you know it, he'll say: 'I drove past the Central Bank of Syria and asked the green fountain what it thought, and it replied that it too would say "yes" to Hafez al-Assad.' "

We hear the telephone ringing as soon as we push open the gate. It's Sahar. A friend of Ahmed's has been released; he says Ahmed has been called in to see the *mukhabarat*, which means they plan to release him too. The telephone keeps ringing all evening, but we find out nothing more. Then Tété calls. The oil vendor says he's coming by tomorrow morning – could Hala be there to open the door? Hala slams down the phone. "That's just great! She wants me to come over right away."

"You're not going to, are you?" Asma has homework to do, and we were planning to . . . But Hala is already collecting her things. She looks at me resignedly. "Didn't I tell you I come from a family of invalids?" I keep sputtering objections. "Come with me then," she suggests, but that appeals to me even less.

I ask myself what disappoints me more: the thought of staying here alone, or the fact that Hala doesn't have enough guts to stand up to her mother? How can she ever decide her own future if she lets her family blackmail her so easily?

I suddenly remember a passage from *Arabesques*, by the Palestinian writer Anton Shammas. The narrator is nine years old when he has to clean the bottom of the well behind his parents' home. Trembling, he lets himself be lowered down on a rope, along the cold, slippery wall of the well, scared to death of the darkness awaiting him. But once his feet are resting on the muddy bottom, his fear vanishes; for the first time in his life he is alone, and that solitude exudes a special magic.

It's an innocent little scene, but the symbolism has great power: at the bottom of the well, the boy discovers that there is a world beyond his family, a universe where he can be alone and make his own rules. But how could Hala ever grasp this symbolism? Shammas wrote his novel in Hebrew – for her, that has only negative connotations.

❖

Shawqi seems genuinely pleased to hear my voice. In Aleppo I had imagined that he gave readings often, but the enthusiasm with which he looks back on that evening tells me that there's a good deal less going on in his life than I had supposed. "What have you been doing for the last few days?" I tell him about my walks through Damascus, my outing with Hala. I automatically address him as *ustaz Shawqi* (Master Shawqi), like his friends in Aleppo.

"Damascus has changed a great deal since I was last here," I say. He laughs. "Yes, what did you expect?!" The word 'elections' is never mentioned.

"And what have you been doing?"

He's silent for a moment at the other end. Then he says: "I eat, I sleep, I wait for a miracle." It's a variation on what Walid said: "I'm waiting for an earthquake." Shawqi's laugh sounds shrill now, a bit derisive. He must assume that the line is tapped. "Will you be coming by this afternoon?" He doesn't mention the location.

The Café Havana has heavily tinted brown windows that block any view of the interior – I've walked past countless times without noticing it. Somewhat timidly, I push open the door to this darkened world. Fortunately, Shawqi and his friends have already arrived. The other patrons watch unabashedly as I walk over to their table. All men, I ascertain from the corner of my eye – not a woman in sight.

In Aleppo I talked to Shawqi about Hala's objections to my visiting the Café Havana. He reassured me: now that we have met each other at a reading, he will have some kind of explanation should they ever ask him about it; he'll tell them that I'm interested in Arabic literature.

Shawqi stands up, lays a hand on my shoulder and introduces me to his friends: a writer, a lawyer, an economist, a couple of journalists. Later, to my great relief, a young woman joins us.

I look around, somewhat amazed. A marble floor, light wooden tables, bare walls – is this the legendary café where the Ba'ath Party ideologists once met? I had imagined something scruffier. "It's just been renovated," Shawqi says, and points to the cozy little alcoves on the mezzanine; since the renovation, the café has also become a popular meeting spot for lovers. He smiles discerningly. "They've made it more touristy."

Give him the good old days! In the 1950s this was the site of heated discussions. The French colonials had just left – it was up to the Syrians themselves now. Arab nationalism was in its heyday, and Ba'athist ideals flared up in both Syria and Iraq. The intellectuals met in the Café Havana; the Café Brésil, across the street, was for the civil servants. There was a lot of tension between the two groups – on rare occasions someone would cross the street to report on what the others were cooking up.

Shawqi points to an old man at a nearby table. "That's the former mayor of Damascus," he whispers, "he's often here with his friends." One-time communists, Ba'athists, socialists – they run into each other at the Havana just as they did in the old days, and nod knowingly. The relationship with Iraq turned sour long ago, their dreams are shattered and many of them have been put on the sidelines; they come here to warm themselves in the glow of memory. "And because they have the cheapest coffee in town," Shawqi admits. "Wealth is one thing that awaited none of us."

The Arabs have no foresight, he says. Had I read *1984* by George Orwell? He read it in the fifties. At the time he thought it was an imperialist book, with all that whining about 'Big Brother'. But he read it again not long ago. What foresight Orwell showed! This country's government doesn't represent any social class, it's a coalition of intelligence services. "I'm not against the president," he says cautiously. "But he should allow more political parties, he should let people speak their minds. The world changes, Syria can't lag behind."

"Haven't you ever thought of going abroad?" It's a question that's been on my mind for some time. Shawqi shakes his head. "What would I do there? Here, I'm known as one of five writers who, when a microphone is put in their hand, dare to talk about what's going wrong. I wouldn't be able to play that role abroad."

Two years ago, a speaker at the annual writers' conference in Damascus launched a vehement attack on Iraq. Shawqi stood up, asked for the floor and said: "We know by now that there's no democracy in Iraq, but is this a democracy? Doesn't everything we write have to be passed by the censor?" The audience was silent for a moment, then applauded hesitantly.

Later that week he took in his column to the newspaper for which he'd been writing for years. The editor-in-chief told him that his services were no longer required. Since then all the papers have blackballed him, and he's no longer allowed to travel abroad without permission from the *mukhabarat*. "I don't write anymore," he says sadly. "The only thing I do is read."

The man next to us has been listening dejectedly. Shawqi takes him by the arm and says paternally: "This is Khairi, another one of us who's not allowed to write for any newspapers." I've heard of Khairi before – he was one of the writers who signed the notorious petition supporting Salman Rushdie.

More people have come to our table. Some of them drink a cup of coffee and then leave, others just stop to pass on the latest news. Shawqi shakes hands, accepts a package someone has brought for him, looks around contentedly and, after a while, suggests that we go somewhere to eat.

When we walk outside – a rowdy group, laughing, gesturing, talking, moving down the street slowly to make sure we don't lose anyone in the crowd – I become infected by the euphoria that seems to have Shawqi and his friends in its grip. Yet at the same time I feel vaguely uneasy. Can we get away with this? Aren't we attracting too much attention? The stares at the Café Havana were extremely inquisitive, and when we burst into the restaurant all heads pivot in our direction again. A group of ten boisterous men with two women in their midst – what's going on here? But the waiters laugh and bow and push three tables together without being asked.

"It's not a fancy restaurant, as you can see," Shawqi whispers. "We come here every week. At least, the richest among us do!" He orders a bottle of *araq*. Small dishes of appetizers appear spontaneously on the table, and by the time the grilled fish arrives everyone is slightly tipsy.

These men are clearly not used to female company. The young woman, a student of Arabic literature, is very attractive, but she's also shy. She'd like to talk about literature, about the books she's read, the stories she tries to write. But the men make suggestive comments, peer down her blouse and tell her to drink up. Shawqi keeps an eye on things and later, like a strict teacher, intervenes and takes her under his wing.

Meanwhile, the man opposite me tells me that I have mysterious eyes, complains about how noisy the restaurant is and invites me to his home in the country – the only place, he says, where we can really talk. I laugh in his face. No one talks to me like that afterwards, and for the rest of the afternoon my would-be seducer is teased repeatedly about his advances.

Our table is in the middle of the restaurant, and the people seated around us listen openly to our conversation. One man turns around in his chair and even laughs along heartily when Khairi tells a joke. In one corner, hidden behind a newspaper, is a writer who fled Iraq and has been granted political asylum here; Shawqi suspects him of being a double agent. "I don't care if he's listening," he says casually, "I have nothing to hide." Not so long ago, someone from the *mukhabarat* came in and sat down at a table by himself. Shawqi invited him to come sit with them. The man was so embarrassed he didn't know where to look; they never saw him again after that.

As the afternoon wears on I become better acquainted with the group that gathers each week around *ustaz Shawqi*. Some of them work for newspapers or government offices, others have been blacklisted, but they all seem to feel the same way about this country: constraints loom wherever they look, and none of them have succeeded in molding their own destiny. "But this weekly meeting is sacred," Shawqi says, "no one can take this away from us."

One of the men gets drunk and falls asleep, a cigarette still dangling from his lips. The setting November sun sheds a soft red light on his deeply lined face. When the others start making moves to leave, he wakes up and shuffles along with us to an old café in the *souq*, where they've decided to smoke the *nargileh*.

On the way one of the men tells me he's writing a book. Not just any book – no, this is going to be a quartet. He's already come up with a title: *The Damascus Quartet*. Do I know *The Alexandria Quartet* by Lawrence Durrell? It'll be something like that. As it turns out, he's never written a thing. When I cautiously enquire whether his project isn't a bit too ambitious, whether a more modest scheme might not have more chance of success, he looks at me in annoyance: "Why should I settle for something minor when I can dream about something big?"

At the café, Khairi sucks on his pipe glumly. He's just published a book, but that doesn't seem to make him happy. It's about the nomadic tribes which fought each other at the time of the Crusaders, and destroyed Byzantine culture in the process. He provides me with a detailed rundown of the plot, as if he's afraid the book will meet with no response, as if the only way his ideas can be passed along is by word of mouth. The book seems to be about the past, he says, but of course it's also about the present.

He sighs in distress at the name of every Arab author I mention. Amin Maalouf, Tayyib Salih, Edward Said, Anton Shammas – according to him, they all pander to Western tastes. He wishes I could read his books, they're so much more profound. Of course he spoke out when Salman Rushdie was condemned to death, but isn't even Rushdie a clown who tells the West exotic stories about his homeland? Khairi doesn't believe in a cosmopolitan civilization the way Walid does, and Walid's imagery of hybrid plants doesn't appeal to him. "When you cross a horse and a donkey, you get a mule," he says, "and, as you know, mules are sterile."

Hala once told me that years ago, when Khairi was serving in the army on the Golan Heights, he was captured by the Israelis and spent ten months in various Israeli prisons. "Why don't you write about that?" I ask.

He looks at me dolefully. "I've tried. If you only knew how often I've tried. But I can't write it down, I just can't."

A few days later, on my way downtown in a taxi, I see Khairi waiting for a bus amid a group of housewives. Apartment buildings loom up behind him, and there's a cluttered market with merchants pacing back and forth to keep warm. He tugs pensively on his pipe and plays with his prayer beads. On the ground next to him is a big burlap bag full of groceries. The image is so unlike the ponderous Khairi I met that it takes me a moment to recognize him.

Then I suddenly recall a scene from the café in the *souq*. Everyone was talking at the same time and complaining about everything under the sun. Khairi smoked his pipe and was quiet for an uncharacteristically long time. Then he said: "But the worst thing is that there's no electricity during the day." We all laughed, and Khairi laughed hardest of all. I now realize that he had probably been deadly serious at the time.

❖

The doorbell rings. Hala went down to the *mukhabarat* early this morning for a new permit to visit Ahmed. I usually don't answer the door when she's not here, but these days – you never know. The man standing at the door looks at me hesitantly and asks for *umm Asma* (the mother of Asma). I shake my head and say that Hala isn't at home, all the while studying his pale face. Dark hair, skittish glances – no, it's not Ahmed. Besides, Ahmed wouldn't stand there so uncertainly, he knows I'm here.

The man shivers in his thin gray trousers and jacket and seems about to go away, but then says something again, so softly I can barely understand him. I ask if he speaks French, English or German, but he shakes his head timidly and asks again for *umm Asma*. I believe he wants to know whether she lives here. I say yes, and ask him his name. He mumbles something unintelligible, takes a step backwards, bows slightly and walks away. He's obviously not used to walking around freely: he carefully puts one foot in front of the next, and steps aside in fright when two schoolchildren come whooping around the corner. My eyes meet those of the woman across the street, who's been watching the whole thing from her window. I pull the door shut guiltily; once again I have the feeling that I've seen something not intended for my eyes.

"*Umm Asma*, is that what he said? Then it must have been one of Ahmed's friends." Hala puts a metal pitcher of water on the gas stove, shovels in two large spoonfuls of coffee and starts stirring. "That's what they call me at the prison," she smiles, "it's a sign of respect." She came home all flushed, three other prisoners' wives in her wake. Now she paces busily back and forth, taking the special cups for visitors out of the box in the cupboard, arranging them on a tray, pouring coffee.

The visit to the *mukhabarat* turned into a massive debacle. A lot of people with relatives in the prison had been called in at the same time. As soon as they were all inside, the *mukhabarat* officers who had to write out the visitor's permits began railing at them. "We've opened the prison doors," they shouted, "but those stubborn asses refuse to leave!"

Hala suspects that these were the same officers who talked to the prisoners. "Apparently most of them have refused to sign the document – the *mukhabarat* are enraged by their obstinacy." No one has actually seen the document, but by now the grapevine has relayed its contents: the prisoners have to promise to distance themselves from the party to which they belonged, to ward off the advances of any other party that approaches them and to co-operate with the *mukhabarat* when asked.

"They think they're stronger than we are!" one of the officers yelled. "But we'll see about that. It'll be seven years before they get another chance!"

"Seven years, that's when the next elections will be held," Hala says stoically.

A woman who had brought her child along sat in her chair, weeping. "Let me see my husband," she begged, "I'll talk him into signing." A father shouted that he never wanted to visit his son again if he had actually refused to sign 'that stupid piece of paper'.

When it was Hala's turn, the officer looked at her in disgust. "Your husband is thoroughly bull-headed," he snapped. "He's been behind bars for eleven years, and he refuses to go free. And you keep visiting him! You care about him, but do you think he cares about you?"

"I do it for my daughter," Hala said weakly.

"And you think he cares about his daughter?"

"It's his decision," Hala protested, but even as she said it she wasn't so sure. Wasn't Ahmed deciding her fate as well? And Asma's? What did that document really mean? They were like hostages, they were being coerced – would a statement signed under such conditions be worth anything?

The three women in the front room are speaking in hushed tones. A fire is burning in the iron stove, and cigarette smoke hangs heavily in the room, blending with the sharp odor of coffee. Hala lights a cigarette too, and puts the chestnuts she bought on the way home on top of the stove to roast. When Sahar calls they pass the phone around and tell her about their morning in shrill, excited voices. When Hala imitates the officer who barked at her, everyone bursts out laughing. But Sahar is angry. If her husband doesn't sign the document she'll never visit him again, she blusters. Hala winks at me: "I'll believe that when I see it!"

By the time Asma comes home from school the atmosphere in the front room is so convivial that she stares around in amazement. "Are they going to let Papa go?" "No, not yet." Hala hands her a roasted chestnut. "We'll hear more about it tomorrow." For, despite all his abuse, the officer gave her a permit to visit Ahmed. But this would be the last time, he shouted threateningly; if Ahmed didn't change his mind they'd transfer him to the prison at Tadmor. "They're hoping we'll pressure our husbands into signing," Hala says, "that's why they called us in."

"I'm coming along," Asma decides, "I'll tell him to sign."

Hala takes her in her arms: "OK, you can come along. We'll try to convince him."

Hala's not as cheery when she comes home the next afternoon. She plops down on the couch without a word. It looks like she's been crying. "Would you like some coffee?" She nods. I hear her talking angrily on the phone, and when I come in with the coffee I see that she's crying again.

"What's wrong?"

"Oh, all these people, I wish they'd just leave me alone!" She points to the phone. "That was my mother-in-law. She says I should divorce Ahmed and marry someone else. She's worried that otherwise I won't have enough children to take care of me when I get old!"

Asma has nuzzled up against her. Hala runs a hand over her hair. Ahmed's parents, his brother Rashid and his wife – they all went to the prison to ask him to sign the statement. But Ahmed didn't want to listen. "You don't know what it's all about," he said. "They want us to work for them!" He had to whisper, because one of the *mukhabarat* beside him was listening in. They wanted to set them free as individuals, he said, but his party had decided to leave only as a group, and not before their leader was released as well.

Hala sighs. "I understand what he means, but still . . . When we were students we dreamed of ending up in prison: that was the firmest proof that you were on the right side. But what sense does it make now?" Ahmed and his fellow party members are hardliners, she says sadly – Stalin is their model. There's no place for a party like theirs in Syria today, but they're too stubborn to admit it. The real world wants them back, but they don't want to come down off their thrones and enter the real world; they want to keep being heroes, and they expect their wives to behave just as heroically. She laughs bitterly. "They have no idea how tame we've become!"

Banners and election posters were hanging in the prison as well. 'The prisons are the solid wall behind Hafez al-Assad', she read somewhere. "Your 'no' means nothing if the rest of the country says 'yes'," she told Ahmed. "The government is stronger than we thought, you have to be able to admit defeat."

Rashid tried to convince him too, but Ahmed only became angry. "It's not like outside," he said, "we live much closer together, we can't let each other down just like that."

When Asma said she wanted him to come home he began to cry. But fortunately he had calmed down by the time they left. Hala told him about the prisoner who rang the doorbell yesterday but didn't know what to say to me. "That guy spent years here studying French!" he laughed in amazement.

Asma has jumped up and run to the bedroom. Hala watches her go. "I'm afraid of losing her," she says. Ahmed's father was quiet at first this morning, but suddenly he said to Ahmed gruffly: "You have to get out of prison, your daughter is growing up. Before long she'll need a man around the house to keep her from going too far." *Going too far!* Hala was stunned. Would they soon start seeing Asma as someone who needed their protection?

Asma is bustling about in the bedroom. She's put the stuffed monkey she was given a few days ago in a big white bag with her dolls, so they can get used to each other. Today she's organized an introductory meeting. She's taken a blanket and spread it out on the floor, then put all her dolls on it, with the monkey in the middle. After a while she decides it's too cold in the bedroom, folds up the blanket with all the dolls in it, throws it over her shoulder like a burglar's loot and starts all over again in the front room.

"What are you going to do now?" I ask Hala.

"Nothing, we just have to wait and see." Apparently not every prisoner has to sign the same statement; Ahmed's father is going to see whether the conditions imposed on his son can be toned down.

"And in the meantime, life goes on," she says. Tomorrow she wants to go to the Damascus Film Festival, which has started at the Al-Sham Hotel. She's heard that some of the films selected by the festival committee have been rejected by the censors. The discussion concerning Arab films co-financed by the West has reached fever pitch. Someone has claimed that the Zionists are trying to infiltrate the Arab world by way of Tunisian cinema. The film-makers will hold a public debate on the subject tomorrow.

"It's all because of the peace talks, and because of this insane election fever," Hala says. "People have the feeling that, in the midst of all these 'yeses', they should say 'no' at least once."

"But they should think first before deciding what to . . ." The glint in Hala's eye makes me decide to hold my tongue.

❖

The discussion is well underway by the time I get to the conference room at the Al-Sham Hotel. The film-makers are seated at a long table, answering questions from the audience. After looking around a bit, I spot Hala. She's sitting tensely in her chair, as if she might jump up at any moment. The woman next to her raises her hand and asks for the floor. Where do I know her from? As soon as she starts talking, it dawns on me: it's

278

Fathia, the psychologist who had her swimming pool filled in after the Gulf War and put in an Oriental garden instead. Fathia, who thought things hadn't been all that bad in Eastern Europe, who claimed that the revolution there was organized by the West. She has a grim and determined look on her face, and raises her finger pedantically to emphasize her words. It's not hard to guess what she's railing against. I worm my way up to the front and buttonhole a journalist I recognize from the meeting at the Café Havana. "What are they talking about?"

He shrugs. "All a bunch of hysterics." Fathia raves on. When she's finished, the sympathizers seated around her give her a thundering ovation. Hala, who has been listening with flushed cheeks, stands up and walks over to me.

"What was Fathia saying?" I ask.

She looks at me hesitantly. "I don't think you want to know."

At the table where the film-makers are seated, Michel, a Palestinian film-maker who lives in Brussels, turns the microphone towards him. As Hala listens, a smile creeps over her face. "He sounds just like you!" she whispers.

"What do you mean?"

"He says the Arabs shouldn't always try to blame their problems on the outside world, that they should face up to their own responsibilities." Michel strikes out hard against one of the earlier speakers, who had attacked him for including a pornographic scene in his film and accused him of making movies for Europeans. All the Arabs who come to Europe want to see Western porn movies, he says – so why shouldn't he be allowed to do a nude scene?

Now he points at the TV camera aimed at him. "Where do you think that camera was made? In the West! All technology comes from there. So what are we talking about? Why do we import perfume from Paris? Why don't we have any technology of our own? Those are the questions we should be asking!"

Another film-maker takes the microphone from Michel. "That's Nouri, the Tunisian director whose movie got the whole discussion going," Hala whispers excitedly. "They say he got money from Canon, a Zionist production company."

"A local paper has claimed that I'm a Zionist," the Tunisian film-maker says calmly. "That's the tragedy of the Arab world: whenever someone moves ahead faster than the others, they accuse him of Zionism."

I hear chuckling here and there, but Hala's expression is tense and hostile. I look around. I've never witnessed a public discussion like this here before. People laugh, nudge each other, exchange knowing glances. It reminds me of the chaotic gatherings I attended at the start of the revolution in Hungary: this seems like Arab glasnost! Now the man sitting next to Fathia has taken the floor. His voice sounds perhaps even more ominous than hers.

"Put us in prison if we've done it all wrong!" Michel shouts. I look at Hala out of the corner of my eye. The audience is divided, and even though we're standing next to each other and will go home together later on, I suddenly feel that we belong to different camps. That look in her eye – I've seen it before, but never as clearly as today. There's suspicion in it, but also fear, and something that frightens me even more: xenophobia. Outside, in the world where the film-makers seem to move so easily, the great conspiracy is being plotted: the Zionists, with Western support, are out to destroy the Arabs. After the attack on Canon, the Dutch Hubert Bals Fund, from which some of the film-makers have received money, is being depicted as a Jewish organization too.

Omar, a Syrian film-maker who spends part of his time in Paris and hasn't spoken a word so far, stands up and walks to the exit. His whole bearing breathes elegance and erudition. I've met him before: we have friends in common in Paris, where he's a respected director. But Hala follows his exit with an angry stare. Omar is one of the organizers of the festival and therefore partly responsible for the row going on at the moment; she thinks he should have known that many of the films chosen for the festival were too controversial. What's more, rumor has it that he not only received money from the French government for his latest film, but that he's planning to claim a large part of the Syrian film budget as well.

I gesture to Hala that I'm going outside, and walk over to Omar, who's leaning against a balustrade with his hands in his pockets. He looks disgusted. "Even the Prophet emigrated," he says. The Prophet emigrated? He must be referring to Mohammed's flight from Mecca to Medina. The trading elite in Mecca was hostile towards him: they saw him as a threat to established tradition.

"The left wing here is so disappointing," he continues. "When you listen to them, you realize how effective this country's regime really is: it's completely destroyed their ability to think. Their ideas haven't changed for the last twenty years. The way they go on about America and Zionism – it's like talking to an official from the Ministry of the Interior!"

We lean over the balustrade, which looks out over the busy lobby where Khairi is sitting like a pacha in a leather lounge chair, surrounded by a group of friends. Omar continues, almost as if he's talking to himself. "This country can best be compared with Romania under Ceausescu," he says. "The oppression is so intense that the opposition has become completely deformed.

281

They're petrified, they have absolutely no curiosity about what's happening in the rest of the world. They don't listen to you, and they have their reply ready even before you've finished speaking. I spend half the year in France, but no one ever asks me about life there. A culture can only remain alive when it integrates its history into modern times, into different cultures. To do that, you have to be prepared to forget your own past. But here people hide behind their history; they talk about it as if it's something that took place in absolute isolation."

His words echo what Walid said back in Aleppo, as well as my own thoughts. I look at Khairi, sitting down there in the depths. With one arm slung over the back of his lounge chair, he removes the pipe from his mouth and mumbles something that makes his friends laugh loudly.

"Maybe you have to have travelled to be able to see things that way," I say.

Omar nods. "They hate us; they hate every film-maker who's made it in Europe, who's bridged the gap with the West. Anyone who dares to cut himself loose from his tribe is immediately labelled a traitor. The tribe wants everyone to sink to the bottom like a stone. They can't stand it that some pebbles float, that there are exceptions." His voice is angry, defiant. "This society pulls you down. We're all invited to wallow in the *merde*." He looks at me, silent for a moment. "To make the transition to another society, you have to be the child of your talent," he says deliberately, "and not of your country, your tribe or your political system."

There's a hum of voices behind us. The debate is over and people are pouring out of the hall. Collared by a colleague, Omar excuses himself. A bit further along, Hala is talking to a little group of people. She's wearing a pink sweater that she borrowed from Shirin, one with golden threads woven into it. It doesn't look good on her; it makes her appear rounder than she already is. As I stand there looking at her, I feel a desperate tenderness welling up. Of everyone in this room, she's the one closest to me – a precious little sister. How I'd love to show her Walid and Omar's world, how I'd love to pull her in that other direction.

I know one of the men in her group. He studied in Russia. He waves his arms angrily as he explains something; the others egg him on with little nods and noises of agreement. When I walk by he suddenly wheels on me and says maliciously: "That Omar you were talking to . . . his mother is a Jewess."

"If Omar's a Jew, then so am I," I say fiercely. The others look around in alarm, to see if anyone has heard us. I should learn to keep my big mouth shut, it occurs to me in a flash – this place is crawling with *mukhabarat*. "Please, not another quarrel you two," Hala begs, "it's bad enough as it is."

I walk down the stairs, heading for Khairi who invites me with a sweeping gesture to sit on the arm of his lounge chair. "What are you doing here?" He grins. "This is the only time of the year that I can sit in the Al-Sham Hotel without having the staff chase me away." He introduces me to his friends. He lived in Egypt when he was young – he knows some of them from back then. "This is our only chance to meet."

"I saw you a few days ago," I say, "you were waiting for the bus."

"Me?" He wrinkles his brow. "Where was that?" I tell him. "That wasn't me," he says decidedly. "It must have been someone else."

A change of subject seems wise. "Were you in on the discussion?" I point upstairs.

Khairi laughs. "Oh no, I follow the whole thing from down

here – my friends come and tell me everything that happens."

"Well?" It suddenly seems important to know what he thinks. Khairi puffs on his pipe. "Patriotism," he says through his moustache, "misguided patriotism, of course."

❖

Hala is sitting in front of the stove on her little stool, her hands folded in her lap. "What did Omar say? I bet he was angry." Should I tell her what he said? She wouldn't want to hear it any more than I'd want to hear her friends' comments. "He's very intelligent," I say stubbornly. "I'm afraid I rather agree with him."

"Omar has lost touch with the people. He wants to go too fast," she fumes. "If he thinks we're bumpkins, he should stay in France." I wish I could listen to her without getting angry, but I can't. "There was a time when we too wanted to change everything fast," she continues, "but I know now that that's impossible. The Germans once made a study of the behavior of spiders: they let a spider spin its web and then kept taking it away. Finally, the spider went crazy, it forgot how to make a web."

She clenches her hands, as though she's cold. "You can't understand what's happening to us right now, and I can't explain it to you. At least not in French. You'd have to know Arabic to understand."

Unbelievable! For the last five months we've been able to discuss everything in French, and suddenly that language no longer suffices! The term 'obscurantism' pops into my mind, and I have to struggle to push it away.

"It's because of all those 'yeses' everywhere. It's making everyone jumpy. I feel like hanging a big sign in this room with 'no!' written on it. Just for once."

"But you're saying 'no' to the wrong thing!"

"What's so wrong about it? I'm against these co-productions, because whoever pays has a say."

"What difference does it make if the French government helps pay for something? Do you want all Arab film-makers to be dependent on their own governments? As though *they* have their best interests at heart!" I truly believe that I don't understand her, or rather, I don't want to understand her. Father Léon would laugh if he heard me going on like this. "You try to deal with these people logically," he once said to me. "You shouldn't do that: you have to approach them psychologically, you have to listen to what's behind their stories. People so often yell 'no' at the top of their lungs, just before they say 'yes'." He's probably right, but something in me refuses to accept it. I've never looked at Hala from such a distance, she's always been much closer to me.

"What are you so afraid of?" I ask.

"Of losing my Arab identity."

Arab identity! I've never heard her use that expression before. "And what might that be?"

She doesn't seem to know herself. "I want to be free to choose what I want," she says hesitantly.

I've stood up; I think I could use a vodka. But it's only in the kitchen that I become really angry. After all the disappointments she's been through, how can she possibly talk about Arab identity?! I go back into the room. "What do you mean by that? Are you talking about all the misery I've watched you going through for months now? Your husband in prison, your family who never leaves you alone, no heating oil, no water, no electricity – is th' what you're so keen on preserving? Is that what you call h free to choose?"

She looks at me accusingly. "Go ahead, talk like that, but don't be surprised if someday I choose the other side."

"The other side?" But I don't have to ask what she means by that – I already know. This afternoon, when I was leaning over the balustrade with Omar, the thought had crossed my mind. "Do you mean the Muslim Brothers?" Hala nods.

It's quiet for a moment. Then I say, more softly: "If everyone who has dealings with the West is a traitor, then aren't you one too? After all, you've taken me into your home – I'm a Westerner too, aren't I?"

"You're different," she murmurs.

"You think so? I consider myself pretty much a typical European." Hala plucks at one of the golden threads in Shirin's sweater. "But now maybe you're sorry that I came," I say.

"No, no." She shakes her head frantically. "The only thing I'm sorry about is that I haven't been able to make you love this country."

"After everything I've been through? How can you expect me to love this?"

"I wanted to show you that life goes on, even though my husband's in prison . . ." She looks at me helplessly. "We're not used to discussing things in public the way we did today. The last time that happened was when I was still at school. They let all the intellectuals speak their mind, listened to what they had to say, and then the *razzias* began. Top officials were fired, the executive staff at the university was replaced and a lot of people weren't allowed to publish anymore. Maybe the same thing will happen now."

The world seems to draw in around us as she speaks. How much danger lurks here in unexpected corners, how grim the plots that play through Hala's mind. We sit across from each other, silent. "I'm sorry about what I just said," I say. "We shouldn't fight, not us."

Hala nods. "It's all because of the festival," she sighs. "We're all afraid of each other. If they would let us talk more often, things would be different."

"Maybe you'd like me to go away for a while." Hala shakes her head again. "Hasn't that occurred to you? That I should go away?"

"No."

"Be honest."

"This afternoon I thought we should stay out of each other's way for a while. But in that case I would have left you here and gone to my mother's."

I breathe a sigh of relief. "What's wrong with us? We've all become a bit hysterical."

Hala laughs. "Too much freedom," she says. The discussion this afternoon lasted five hours, and when she looks back on it she has to admit that there was something to what everyone said. "I caught a documentary too, this afternoon," she says mysteriously. "About Assad!" The film was a couple of years old, and if anyone had bothered to watch it again they would definitely have edited out part of it: at one point the narrator's voice said, "Syria establishes contacts with progressive countries", and Assad appeared on the screen in a tight embrace with Ceausescu!

Hala looks at her watch. Asma is playing with a girlfriend who lives nearby – it's time to pick her up. I'm glad to have the blue sweater Father Léon loaned me, because it's bitterly cold outside. I take Hala's arm as we walk. "Is it over? No more fighting?" She nods, and points to an election poster for Assad. "It's all his fault."

Later that evening we're sitting in front of the TV. The city is one great mass of movement. Girls Asma's age are singing: "Hafez al-Assad defends us, we've cut our hair for him, we carry arms." Men are dancing the *dabkeh*, the way they did at the Alawite wedding we saw in Lattakia. The Minister of Agriculture is riding on someone's shoulders down the street, and even the sheikhs are whirling around, clapping their hands. "It looks like we're in Africa," Hala says in a disgruntled tone.

I usually go off by myself in the evening to write, but now I hesitate. How would Hala take it? Wouldn't it look as if I were writing a report for the people back in Europe? The air has been cleared between us, but the words that were spoken still float through my mind and I wonder whether they will ever go away. It's as though I've caught a glimpse of the limits of our friendship, and after all the emotion of the last few hours that thought fills me with a dull sadness.

❖

Early the next morning the telephone rings and I hear Hala talking excitedly. It's Friday and Asma doesn't have to go to school, but a bit later I hear her clear voice as well. What could be going on? I put on my bathrobe. Asma is lying in the crook of Hala's arm, looking up at me when I come in, eyes shining with friskiness. "Has Ahmed . . .?" Hala laughs. "No, a group of Palestinians have been freed. They'll be dancing the *dabkeh* in the Palestinian camp today!"

She pulls Asma up against her. "My daughter wants to know where her father will sleep when he comes home." "Well?" "Not with us in any case, that's what she's decided." Hala musses Asma's hair. "It's not going to be easy for her. She wants her father back, but she doesn't want to surrender her position."

They spend the morning treating each other like sweethearts. Hala toasts bread and makes tea and little doll dishes of cheese, olives and *makdous*. They eat kneeling at the low coffee table, but even that isn't cozy enough for Asma. She stretches a blanket between the armchair and the table, and installs herself beneath it with her monkey, her Walkman and the leftovers from breakfast. She peers out from underneath her shelter, wary-eyed. Hala is no longer allowed to speak French with me, and when I glance at myself in Asma's mirror in the hall she yells at me angrily to go and look in my own mirror. "*Mais enfin, Asma!*" Hala protests, feigning anger. Yet those eyes gleaming from under the blanket are more familiar to me than Hala could imagine. Isn't it the very same look she's had in her eyes for the last few days? Their sheltered life is on the verge of breaking open; it's been so long since they've taken part in what's happening outside that they're running for cover.

Hala and I don't talk about what happened yesterday, but I haven't stopped thinking about our clash. There are suddenly so many things that we can't talk about. I feel uncomfortable – as though these rooms where we've felt so at ease during the last few months have become too small. Finally I go into the bedroom and start writing anyway. Hala brings me a cup of tea and looks over my shoulder. "How's it going?" She should be preparing for a class, she says, but hadn't I noticed how Asma was acting this morning? And this afternoon she has to go to the Palestinian camp to congratulate the prisoners who were freed.

"Can I go with you?"

She hesitates for a moment, then says resolutely: "No, I don't think that would be a good idea. There are bound to be a lot of *mukhabarat* there."

When the doorbell rings, Hala hastily pulls on a bathrobe over her nightgown. "That must be Ahmed!" But the visitors standing at the gate don't come in. Asma sits half hidden in her little hut, her ears pricked up to hear what's being said.

"It's begun," Hala whispers when she comes back into the room.

"What?"

"The problems with the *mukhabarat*." My heart skips a beat. So here it is! Hala searches for her papers, can't find them in her haste, turns the whole cupboard inside out. When she walks back to the gate, Asma races after her. I stand in the middle of the room, lost. Shouldn't I be hiding? But where? And then again, why? What have I done wrong?

The gate slams shut. Hala comes in waving a letter: a summons to appear before the *mukhabarat*, tomorrow. Asma jumps around her fearfully in her pink pajamas. "You're not going alone, someone has to go with you! Maybe they'll try to keep you there, just like Papa!" I look at her tenderly. She's usually shy around strangers, but how fast she reached the gate when she heard what was going on, how unconditionally she threw her little body into the fray. She showed the men that Hala was not alone, that they had her to reckon with.

"Could it have something to do with me?"

Hala shrugs. "I don't know, they didn't say." Suddenly, I remember a strange telephone call I'd taken a few days ago. A man's voice asked for Hala. When I said she wasn't home, he started speaking English. I didn't like his tone of voice, there was something clumsily arrogant about it. He wanted to know how long I had been here, what my name was. His English was terrible; I acted like I didn't understand him, and said he should call back when Hala was home. "Could that have been the *mukhabarat*?" Hala looks at me distractedly. "Who knows?"

I heap reproaches on myself. I shouldn't have gone to the Café Havana. I've been talking to everyone and flaunting my opinions about everything. Hanging over the balustrade with Omar at the Al-Sham Hotel, what was I thinking of? And then the argument with Hala – it seems like they've been waiting for this very moment to butt in. "Shouldn't I go away? Wouldn't that be better?"

"No, of course not. If we go, we go together." She stares pensively into space. "We'll move over to my mother's for a while. It's safer there." To Tété's house! Watching TV in the middle of the day, bickering, eating – and nowhere in the house for me to get away. What an infernal twist of fate: even I'm being driven into her arms by the *mukhabarat*.

Hala paces back and forth through the room, wringing her hands. Did she say something wrong at the film festival, or do they want to question her about my visit? She didn't think my coming here was a problem, she thought all those limitations were done with now that Syria wanted to show the world its democratic face. But now the doubts begin anew. "Before you know it, Ahmed will be let out of prison and I'll be thrown in."

"Why would they put you in prison?"

"Foreigners aren't supposed to know that people here live the way I do." She looks at me in despair. "Do you see what an absurd situation it is? No one is supposed to know that I exist. I'm Syria's secret."

A sense of doom comes rolling towards me like an enormous snowball. How much do they know about us? Everything we've ever done together suddenly seems reckless and dangerous. Even Baghdad, the city where we met, is a forbidden place. Hala sinks down on the stool in front of the stove and pores over t summons in her hand, as though trying to draw out the si cance of the printed words. The man who came to the gate with the *mukhabarat* agent was her landlord. He's been complaining for a long time about how little rent she pays: he needs more money, he wants to sell the house. Could he have called in the *mukhabarat*? The agent also looked familiar. Maybe he lives in the neighborhood, perhaps these two are friends who are trying to take her for a ride?

Or did one of the shopkeepers in the street report her to the *mukhabarat*? The poultryman who always stands in the doorway, his back to the cackling and the flying feathers; the barber who places his rack of towels out on the sidewalk every afternoon; the man who sells *foul* on the corner – all innocence is slowly being drained from our street. "Have you ever noticed the man with the plastic dolls?" Hala asks. "He just shows up and then disappears again. I don't think he ever sells a thing." The cigarette boy with his leather jacket, his arrogant expression, his condescending smile – could he be . . .?

"What the two of us are doing right now," Hala notes, "is exactly what I did with all my friends after Ahmed was arrested." The memory seems to soothe, not frighten her. "We mustn't panic, let's not make any rash decisions." And then, why flee to Tété? The landlord would only laugh up his sleeve. It would be like admitting our guilt. "No, we're staying here," she says, suddenly assertive. "And if they come to bother us, we'll throw stones at them, just like the Palestinians."

We won't talk to anyone about this, she decides, and we'll have to be even more careful on the phone, because they'll definitely be tapping it now. She won't go to the Palestinian camp – that can wait. By evening she's thought the whole thing through. Maybe things aren't so bad after all.

Asma is lolling about in front of the TV. I've never seen her eat as much *bizr* as she has today. She goes through her stockpile like a whirlwind, littering the floor with shells.

I fall into an uneasy sleep. In my dream our little house is no longer separated from the street by a high fence, and the gate has turned into a flimsy railing. Passers-by look in unashamedly, and there's a man at the gate asking me all kinds of questions. Is our house for sale or for rent? I want him to go away, but when I try to close the gate I discover that it won't shut.

The next morning Hala is remarkably calm: before long she will look her persecutors in the eye and know what they want. Anything is better than uncertainty. She dresses with more care than usual, does her eyes and puts on lipstick. "Men like these like to see a woman look vulnerable," she smiles.

When I hear her come home a few hours later, I run to the gate. She looks at me almost triumphantly. "What did I tell you? The landlord!" She's not absolutely certain, and he would be the last to admit it, but everything points to him as the one who got the ball rolling. The *mukhabarat* officer was very courteous. He wasn't too happy about it either, it seemed. He offered her a cup of coffee, and even a cigarette. He wanted to know whether she sub-let her house – which is against the law, especially if I paid her in foreign currency.

"What did you tell him?"

"That you're a friend of mine. And that the landlord wants his house back, which is why he reported me."

"That's all there was? Nothing about the film festival?"

"No, they didn't ask about that. But you never know what will happen next. The landlord may have more tricks in store." Her face clouds over. "You see how far things have come? We should be fighting the system, but we fight each other instead." She also tried to find out more about Ahmed, but the officer knew nothing; he said it wasn't his department.

Hala looks around the room. "We should do something here, don't you think? I've been wanting to rearrange things for a long time."

"Like what?"

She points to the cupboard with the glass doors. "Shall we move that? What do you think?" The whole enterprise doesn't make much sense to me, but Hala goes to work right away. By the time Asma comes home the cupboard has been moved and Hala is pleased as punch. "When they took Ahmed away, I rearranged everything too," she says. "It's the only thing here that's not forbidden: arranging your furniture the way that you want."

Tété calls up and complains about a light-colored wash she just did: she threw in a black sock by mistake and everything came out gray. When she added bleach, it all turned yellow. "Tell me, who has a mother like that?!" Hala laughs when she hangs up. She only hopes the *mukhabarat* were listening in; over the next couple of days they'll find out all about what her mother has cooked or is planning to cook, about Shirin's pregnancy and the arguments with Farid. "Pretty soon they'll start feeling sorry for me!"

But when darkness comes, she starts worrying again. Why was the officer so nice to her this morning? Could it be a trap? "I haven't seen the last of that landlord yet," she says grimly. Suddenly, she puts on her black cardigan and goes outside. Asma points meaningfully to the house across the street. When Hala returns, she's out of breath and obviously feeling satisfied. She gave the landlord a real tongue-lashing. "You should have seen his wife! She was shocked out of her wits!"

I'm woken in the middle of the night by people walking

around and talking loudly out in the street. The *mukhabarat* is the first thing that comes to mind, and I'm out of bed before I know it. Hala's awake too. "What's going on?" We walk out to the gate, peer outside. People run past us, heading for the other end of the street. "Fire," Hala whispers. Men are shouting, women screaming, the smell of smoke teases my nostrils. "A short circuit, nothing serious," Hala assures me. Two men who are rushing to the scene in their pajamas hear us speaking French and look at us in surprise. I instinctively duck back. But a bit later I poke my head outside again. There's no law against being curious, is there?

❖

The closer we get to election day, the more improbable the slogans in the street become. "We have chosen Assad from eternity, until eternity passes away," Hala reads aloud to me one afternoon. Prominent Damascene families have hung banners in front of their homes referring to Assad as their 'father', and even the people who design the banners have got in on the act: 'Khaled, the poster-maker of Salhieh, says "yes" to the leader'. "If a psychiatrist ever went to the trouble of analyzing these texts, he would find himself entering the Syrian subconscious," Hala says. She thinks the newly released prisoners should actually organize a *masira* of their own. Imagine that, men in thongs and shabby prison uniforms, holding hastily scrawled signs reading: 'Hafez al-Assad is the hero of all Syrian prisoners'.

"He'll get a hundred per cent of the votes," I predict.

"A hundred per cent? You mean more than a hundred per cent!"

Martial music awakens us on the morning of election day –

the greengrocer has hung two loudspeakers outside his shop. The music will blare on until late at night: 'Hafez al-Assad is the symbol of justice. Hafez forever'.

Hala is supposed to go to the university to cast her vote, but she's not going to. If she voted 'no' an investigation would be started right away, because all the ballots are checked. Someone will probably vote 'yes' on her behalf.

Two days later Assad appears on TV to thank his people for the dancing in the street, for the slaughtering of sheep, for the enormous show of support. Hala peers incredulously at the screen. "Doesn't he realize the whole thing was rigged?"

No one seems interested in the election results, but one afternoon Hala comes home with an anecdote. Assad's campaign manager called the president to congratulate him. "Only three hundred and eighty-nine people voted against you, Mr President, what more could you ask?" To which the president answered grimly: "Their names."

❖

Heating oil has become so scarce that Hala has to stand in line with jerry cans at the filling station. And now, to makes things even worse, the electricity has gone out. It's because of the elections, everyone whispers, they cost a fortune. If they don't cut back now, there won't be any electricity by the end of the winter. Asma does her homework by candlelight, Hala and I put big pots of water on the stove for the bath. One evening, as I lift the lid off a steaming kettle in the poorly lit bathroom, the smell of soup engulfs me. When I've finished washing I don't smell of soap, but of bouillon.

The rumors about the prisoners' release keep flowing in.

Now that Ahmed has failed to return before the elections, Hala has her hopes set on the approaching holidays. "If he's not home by New Year's Eve, I'm giving up," she says.

Hayat, one of the three prisoners' wives who visited us a while ago, is so nervous she can't sleep at night because of stomach cramps. Recently, she moved to Dummar, a new suburb just outside Damascus – maybe the taxi driver can't find her address and her husband is driving around her house in circles!

Some of the prisoners' homecomings are accompanied by family dramas. One prisoner who no longer loved his wife had urged her to forget him. But she continued to visit him faithfully. One night he just showed up at her door. She was so surprised that she fainted. When she came to, she was alone: her husband had walked over to his parents' house. Hala went there to congratulate them; the man was beaming, she says, but his wife looked pale and withdrawn.

That same evening we receive a visit from one of Ahmed's acquaintances who has just been freed. He's brought his sister along to act as his guide through the labyrinth that Damascus has become for him. He's skinny and balding, drinks his coffee without sugar and turns down a piece of the pie that Hala's bought. He lays one hand shyly on his stomach: he's still not used to the food on 'the outside'. He refers to her as '*umm Asma*' and 'missus', which irritates me after a while – as though Hala doesn't exist on her own, only as the extension of someone else. Is there anything he can do for her, he asks, is there anything she needs? As though he's not the needy one! He hardly talks about prison, and even though he speaks a bit of English and the questions burn on my lips, I don't dare ask. After half an hour he stands up and smiles apologetically: he must be going. "I want to live," he says. "I want to see everything, all at the same time."

His words surprise me – they don't fit his tired appearance, his frugal movements.

When he has left, Hala resignedly picks up the plates. "That's how they all are when they come back," she says, "dreamy and fragile."

"You didn't seem all that enthusiastic."

"What do you expect? It was a courtesy call. He was doing it for Ahmed." She sits down, the plates in her lap, and sighs. "Can't you tell? I'm completely back in the rut. I can't get out of it." In a few days she has to go to the wedding of a Palestinian acquaintance who's been released from prison. "If you want to, we can go together."

"Wouldn't I attract too much attention?"

"No, he's been out for six months already." She laughs. "The *mukhabarat* have other things on their minds at the moment!"

I remember my pathetic winter wardrobe. "What do people wear at a party like that?"

"Nothing special. There will be a lot of old revolutionaries there, a lot of people who say 'no'." She turns up her nose. "There may even be a few who don't wash themselves!"

On the evening of the party, Asma takes a schoolbook with her; she says she knows it's going to be boring. The taxi takes us to a working-class neighborhood on the other side of town, and stops at a run-down little hall. Long ago someone painted a happy bridal couple on the facade. Inside we run into Sahar and Aisha. We hug each other. "Any news?" "Nothing yet," Sahar says sadly.

The hall is packed with people talking excitedly, but suddenly everyone falls silent. They all turn around and stare at the doorway, where the bride and groom have appeared. She's wearing a long white dress, he has on a stiff-looking blue suit.

When they begin their march down the aisle, the guests burst into thunderous applause. Hala has tears in her eyes. "*Ce sont des moments volés de la tristesse,*" she says.

The bride and groom seat themselves on the gilded chairs on the podium. When everyone has wished them luck, the groom gets up, extends his right arm to an old woman in traditional dress sitting in the front row, takes her hand and leads her onto the dance floor. He's not quite sure how to dance with her, and she seems uncomfortable in his arms as well. She takes his head in her hands, pulls it to her, kisses him on the forehead and begins to cry. He carefully pushes her away, laughs to the audience and tries to go on dancing, but the woman is now weeping so uncontrollably that he leads her back to her chair, embarrassed. "Is that his mother?" Hala nods.

But a bit later all emotion is drowned out by the band they've hired. Hala's friends look at each other and cover their ears as one Egyptian hit after the other sets the room throbbing. "How did they come up with this?" I shout. Hala turns up one corner of her mouth in uncertainty. That's also part of the insecurity of ex-prisoners, she tells me later: the bride-groom has been gone for so long that he doesn't know how to organize a wedding; he probably let his family make the arrangements.

After that evening I start to understand why Hala fears Ahmed's homecoming. It won't be the way she wants it to be at all; she'll be snatched up and carried away by a whirlwind of events. No one will ask her opinion, she'll just have to yield to family tradition. His parents plan to butcher a camel and a few sheep, which means there'll be a huge party; Hala's house is too small for that. So they'll get Ahmed to come to their house, and get him to bring Hala and Asma along. They'll spend days doing nothing but accepting the congratulations of hundreds of vague acquaintances.

We've heard nothing more from Hala's landlord, and the seemingly impossible happens: our life resumes its normal rhythm. The heating-oil vendor has showed up again and filled the reservoir to the brim, causing Hala to exclaim: "Now we can swim in oil!" One afternoon I even go to another gathering at the Café Havana, where rumors are rampant. Someone has heard on the radio that a large group of prisoners have been freed. The announcer stumbled over his words when he came to the number of people involved, because the government has never officially admitted that there *are* any political prisoners in Syria. One of the journalists at the table shrugs indifferently. "Three thousand, is that all? And what about the other twelve million?"

I phone Hala, but she's not home. "Then her husband will be coming home to a locked door," Shawqi says. Acting on impulse, I pull on my coat and take a taxi home. Asma's school is already out – could they have gone to Tété's? Tété sounds excited. "That's right, they were just here. I think they've gone to the prison to pick up Ahmed." As soon as I hang up, the phone rings. It's Sahar. "Is Ahmed home already?" A little later, Hala calls up and asks me the same thing. "No, I thought you were . . ."

"Stay where you are," she says, "I'm on my way."

She and Asma stumble in half an hour later, giggly and out of breath, loaded down with shopping bags. When Asma came home from school and heard the news on the radio, there was no stopping her: she was determined to pick up her father. Tété's neighbor offered to drive them to the prison. Hala had expected the gates to be wide open and the square in front of the prison to be packed with buses, but it was strangely quiet. When they asked the watchman what was going on, he said that the prison was empty, that all the prisoners had left.

"Look what I bought." Hala pulls a big pan out of the cupboard. She's going to make mutton shanks, just like she did the day Ahmed was arrested. "Maybe now he'll finally come along and eat them." They set to work in the kitchen. Asma cuts up the heart, kidneys and liver like she's been doing it all her life; Hala keeps running to the phone. People she hasn't spoken to for ten years suddenly call up, from all over the country. Three busloads of prisoners have arrived in the north-eastern town of Qamishle; at Hama, thousands of people are lining both sides of the road into town. Tété calls up to say that she'll come to Hala's house on bare feet when Ahmed arrives. "Barefoot in the taxi is more like it!" Hala snorts. When Ahmed's mother calls to ask if Asma is still at home, Hala is alarmed for a moment; does this mean that Ahmed has been released? Is he on his way over here to take Asma away from her?

By the end of the afternoon she has gathered an assortment of loose ends which she breathlessly tries to tie together. Before they left, the prisoners were divided into two groups: those who had shoes, and those wearing thongs. Everyone in the second group was allowed to pick out a pair of rope-soled sandals, and then they were each given a hundred-pound note. At midnight they were brought to the center of town in buses. A lot of Muslim Brothers were freed, and even supporters of the Iraqi Ba'ath Party, but the silence surrounding Ahmed's party remains unbroken.

The kitchen has been cleaned up and the whole house smells of mutton shanks. Then the doorbell rings. Asma jumps up and races to answer it. She comes back disappointed: it was a little boy from down the street whose mother sent him to ask whether Ahmed had arrived. Hala sits on her stool in the front room, before the iron stove, her hands lying idle in her lap. For the umpteenth time that day I hear her sigh: "*La hawla illa billah* – may God help me." I try to talk to her, but I can't get through. She looks past me with a vacant stare. Now what, I ask myself, what are we going to do now? Hala stands up. "Are you coming, Asma? Let's go and buy a Christmas tree."

Angel's hair, glass balls, tin birds, colored lights – the two of them are at it for hours. Later that evening, when the newsreader reports the release of two thousand, eight hundred and sixty four prisoners, the air is charged with expectation. Ahmed's mother calls, this time in tears: her husband says they'll kill Ahmed for refusing to sign.

Before I go to bed I hang my clothes carefully over the back of my chair. If a bus drops Ahmed off in the center of town tonight, he could be here ten minutes later. But Ahmed does not arrive, not that night and not in the days that follow. It's Asma's Christmas break, and she spends most of her time in the niche she's made under the tree, where she's gradually moving all her belongings. She lies there, curled up on a blanket with her dolls around her, talking to herself while she stares at the lights. Sometimes she grabs the phone and carries on long, drawn-out conversations with Rami, lying on her back, jiggling the Christmas tree ornaments with her feet. She tells him that her mother is going to rent an auditorium when her father comes home.

Inspired by the presence of the tree in the room, I go to the Christian neighborhood and buy a special Christmas cake at the bakery that belongs to Louise's brother. Asma is in seventh heaven: the icing has little plastic men on it, and mushrooms on thin stalks. The cake has to be kept out in the courtyard, she decides, where it will stay fresh. We invite Louise over, and she brings her boyfriend along. Asma rattles away to Louise and looks at the boyfriend out of the corner of her eye. "Is his name really Karim?" she asks as soon as they've left. I nod. "Is he a Muslim?" I nod again. She says nothing more after that – that's all she wanted to know.

❖

Asma is sitting on the edge of my bed. Has she woken me up? That's never happened before. She's talking to mc in a voice so sweet it makes my heart melt, but I can't understand what she's trying to tell me. "It's cold," I say, pulling the blankets aside. She crawls in next to me without objecting. I'm almost afraid to move, I don't want to do anything that will chase her away. But she's thrown her arm around me and goes on talking nonstop. After a while I figure out what she's saying. It's snowing, she just saw it on TV. Not in Damascus, but in the mountain villages close by. She racks her brain in search of French words: she wants to make a *garçon* of snow with *boutons* down the front. She points to the telephone next to my bed: maybe I could call Louise – she has a car, hasn't she? She could drive us there.

"What's this I hear?" Hala pushes the door open and looks down on us laughingly. "This isn't the time to call Louise," she admonishes. "I'm sure she has other things on her mind."

Asma is sitting straight up in bed now. "All the other kids get to play in the snow, but not me!" She glares angrily at her mother. "Why don't we have a car?"

"All the other kids don't have a father who's a political prisoner." For the first time in days I detect something like pride in Hala's voice. She pulls Asma to her and rocks her in her arms. "Remember what we're going to do tonight? You haven't forgotten that, have you?"

❖

There are no lights along the road to Dummar. The bottles of wine at my feet have fallen over, but I'm afraid that if I reach over to set them upright the warm dish of food might slide off my lap. Hulu is also holding a dish; I can see the foil glistening in the dark. Asma sits in front. She's spent the whole day pouting in front of the TV, watching children make snowmen and zip down hills on sleds, but this evening she's reconciled to life once more. Clenched in her hands is the packet of sparklers she'll light at midnight.

This is New Year's Eve, the way they've always celebrated it. Sahar and Aisha will be there, and so will all the others. Hayat, the hostess, still gets nervous cramps in her stomach, even though it's clear by now that her husband won't be coming home. Tonight they'll eat, drink and dance. If the electricity's working, the children will watch TV while the women sit on the floor and talk about their husbands in prison. Hala peers sadly out the window. She had hoped to get out of it at least this once.

"Let's go to Aleppo then," I'd suggested a few days earlier. A suite at the Baron Hotel, an evening with Walid and his friends – I could picture the whole thing. But when Tété heard about it she became hysterical. She didn't have long to live, she cried, and now – on her very last New Year's Eve – Hala wanted to go to Aleppo! "Blackmail," I said angrily, but I saw that Hala had already sounded her retreat. "What if Ahmed comes home?" she said. No, this was the wrong time to go to Aleppo.

She hasn't spoken a word since we got in the taxi. Could she be thinking about Firas? She's seen him again this week. If the women waiting for us knew, they'd never forgive her. But she needs him now more than ever.

"Is something wrong?" I ask hesitantly.

"It's starting again," she says.

"What's starting?"

"Waiting for Ahmed. It'll be years before he gets another chance." She breathes a weary sigh. "I know about the period that comes after this, I've been through it all before. Last time it took me a year to get over my disappointment. I don't want this anymore, I don't believe in it anymore."

Now that my eyes have grown accustomed to the dark I see that we are driving through a landscape of bare and jagged rock. "Do you know the story about the woman and the *mudjadara*?" Hala launches in without waiting for my reply. A woman ran away from home because she was sick of making *mudjadara* – a rice and lentil dish – for her husband. She went out onto the road, where she was picked up by a gallant gentleman who suggested going to the beach for a romantic stroll, after which they might . . . The woman leaned back in the car seat, pleasantly surprised. "But first," the man said, "I want to find a place where they serve *mudjadara* . . ."

Hala laughs, a mirthless laugh that startles me. "It's not all that bad," I protest softly. "There are other things . . ."

"Such as? I said I wasn't going to visit Ahmed anymore if he didn't sign. I said I'd file for divorce, but do you think I ever will? And even if I did, what difference would it make?" She's turned around to face me. "If this were a novel, don't you think this would be the moment when something dramatic would happen to the main characters, something which would draw all the threads of the narrative together? They'd die, or their lives would take some drastic turn. But here, everything just stays the same."

It's cold in the taxi. I warm my hands against the dish on my lap and notice that Hala does the same. "I always feel so sorry for the women in Egyptian movies," she says. "The ones where the parents make them marry a man, even though they're desperately in love with someone else. I'm always hoping they'll go after the man of their dreams, but in the long run they all do what their parents want them to do. I'm afraid that's how things will turn out for me too – like in an Egyptian movie."

She stares out the window again. The tops of the rocks are covered here and there with a fine layer of snow. In the distance, the lights of Dummar appear. Hala peers at them defiantly. "Everyone's going to spend the night at Hayat's," she says, "but not us, no way! Not even if I have to walk home with all my dishes under my arm."

LONELY PLANET JOURNEYS

JOURNEYS is a unique collection of travellers' tales – published by the company that understands travel better than anyone else.

It is a series for anyone who has ever experienced – or dreamed of – the magical moment when they encountered a strange culture or saw a place for the first time. They are tales to read while you're planning a trip, while you're on the road or while you're in an armchair, in front of a fire.

JOURNEYS books will catch the spirit of a place, illuminate a culture, recount a crazy adventure, or introduce a fascinating way of life. They will always entertain, and always enrich the experience of travel.

ISLANDS IN THE CLOUDS
Travels in the Highlands of New Guinea
Isabella Tree

This is the fascinating account of a journey to the remote and beautiful Highlands of Papua New Guinea and Irian Jaya: one of the most extraordinary and dangerous regions on the planet. The author travels with a PNG Highlander who introduces her to his intriguing and complex world, which is changing rapidly as it collides with twentieth-century technology and the island's developing social and political systems. *Islands in the Clouds* is a thoughtful, moving book, full of insights into a region that is rarely noticed by the rest of the world.

SEAN & DAVID'S LONG DRIVE
Sean Condon

Sean and David are young townies who have rarely strayed beyond city limits. One day, for no good reason, they set out to discover their homeland, and what follows is a wildly entertaining adventure that covers half of Australia. Highlights include the weekly Hair Wax Report and a Croc-Spotting with Stew adventure.

Sean Condon has written a hilarious, offbeat road book that mixes sharp insights with deadpan humour and outright lies.

LOST JAPAN
Alex Kerr

Lost Japan draws on the author's personal experiences of Japan over thirty years. Alex Kerr takes his readers on a backstage tour, exploring different facets of his involvement with the country: friendships with Kabuki actors, buying and selling art, studying calligraphy, exploring rarely visited temples and shrines...

The Japanese edition of this book was awarded the 1994 Shincho Gakugei Literature Prize for the best work of non-fiction: the first time a foreigner has won this prestigious award.

RELATED TITLES
FROM LONELY PLANET

Jordan & Syria – a travel survival kit

Explore the ruins of rare civilisations, ride a camel across the Wadi Rum desert or snorkel some of the finest coral reefs in the world in the Gulf of Aqaba. This practical guide offers travellers the opportunity to get off the beaten track and experience traditional Arab hospitality.

Middle East on a shoestring

All the travel advice and essential information for travel in Afghanistan, Bahrain, Egypt, Iran, Iraq, Israel, Jordan, Kuwait, Lebanon, Oman, Qatar, Saudi Arabia, Syria, Turkey, United Arab Emirates and Yemen.

Arabic (Egyptian) phrasebook

This phrasebook is full of essential words and phrases that cover almost every situation. The inclusion of Arabic script makes this book useful for travellers visiting other Arabic-speaking countries.

Also available:

Arab Gulf States, Egypt & the Sudan, Iran, Israel, Trekking in Turkey, Turkey, Yemen, Turkish phrasebook.

Available late 1996:

Jordan, Syria & Lebanon travel atlas

PLANET TALK
Lonely Planet's FREE quarterly newsletter

Every issue of PLANET TALK is packed with
up-to-date travel news and advice including:

- a letter from Lonely Planet founders Tony
  and Maureen Wheeler
- travel diary from a Lonely Planet author
  – find out what it's really like out on the road
- feature article on an important and topical
  travel issue
- a selection of recent letters from our readers
- the latest travel news from all over the world
- details on Lonely Planet's new and
  forthcoming releases

To join our mailing list contact any Lonely Planet office.

LONELY PLANET PUBLICATIONS

Australia: PO Box 617, Hawthorn 3122, Victoria
tel: (03) 9819 1877 fax: (03) 9819 6459
e-mail: talk2us@lonelyplanet.com.au

USA: Embarcadero West, 155 Filbert St, Suite 251,
Oakland, CA 94607
tel: (510) 893 8555 TOLL FREE: 800 275-8555
fax: (510) 893 8563   e-mail: info@lonelyplanet.com

UK: 10 Barley Mow Passage, Chiswick, London W4 4PH
tel: (0181) 742 3161 fax: (0181) 742 2772
e-mail: 100413.3551@compuserve.com

France: 71 bis rue du Cardinal Lemoine, 75005 Paris
tel: 1 44 32 06 20 fax: 1 46 34 72 55
e-mail: 100560.415@compuserve.com

World Wide Web: Lonely Planet is now accesible via the World
Wide Web. For travel information and an up-to-date catalogue, you
can find us at http://www.lonelyplanet.com/

THE LONELY PLANET STORY

Lonely Planet published its first book in 1973 in response to the numerous 'How did you do it?' questions Maureen and Tony Wheeler were asked after driving, bussing, hitching, sailing and railing their way from England to Australia.

Written at a kitchen table and hand collated, trimmed and stapled, *Across Asia on the Cheap* became an instant local bestseller, inspiring thoughts of another book.

Eighteen months in South-East Asia resulted in their second guide, *South-East Asia on a shoestring*, which they put together in a backstreet Chinese hotel in Singapore in 1975. The 'yellow bible' as it quickly became known to backpackers around the world, soon became *the* guide to the region. It has sold well over half a million copies and is now in its 8th edition, still retaining its familiar yellow cover.

Today there are over 180 titles, including travel guides, walking guides, language kits & phrasebooks, travel atlases and travel literature. The company is one of the largest travel publluhon in the world. Although Lonely Planet initially specialised in guides to Asia, we now cover most regions of the world, including the Pacific, North America, South America, Africa, the Middle East and Europe.

The emphasis continues to be on travel for independent travellers. Tony and Maureen still travel for several months of each year and play an active part in the writing, updating and quality control of Lonely Planet's guides.

They have been joined by over 50 authors and 155 staff at our offices in Melbourne (Australia), Oakland (USA), London (UK) and Paris (France). Travellers themselves also make a valuable contribution to the guides through the feedback we receive in thousands of letters each year.

The people at Lonely Planet strongly believe that travellers can make a positive contribution to the countries they visit, both through their appreciation of the countries' culture, wildlife and natural features, and through the money they spend. In addition, the company makes a direct contribution to the countries and regions it covers. Since 1986 a percentage of the income from each book has been donated to ventures such as famine relief in Africa; aid projects in India; agricultural projects in Central America; Greenpeace's efforts to halt French nuclear testing in the Pacific; and Amnesty International.

Lonely Planet's basic travel philosophy is summed up in Tony Wheeler's comment, 'Don't worry about whether your trip will work out. Just go!'